The Rise and Fall of 'The Model Republic.'

E

FALL

LIC.

THE

RISE AND FALL

OF

'THE MODEL REPUBLIC.

LONDON
PRINTED BY SPOTTISWOODE AND CO
NEW-STREET SQUARE

THE

RISE AND FALL

OF

'THE MODEL REPUBLIC.'

BY

JAMES WILLIAMS,

LATE AMERICAN MINISTER TO TURKEY:

AUTHOR OF

'THE SOUTH VINDICATED.'

LONDON:

RICHARD BENTLEY, NEW BURLINGTON STREET,

PUBLISHER IN ORDINARY TO HER MAJESTY.

1863.

TO THE

FRIENDS OF RATIONAL LIBERTY

AND TO THE

ADVERSARIES OF DESPOTIC GOVERNMENT,

WHETHER ADMINISTERED

UNDER THE RULE OF A SINGLE TYRANT

OR

OF A MULTITUDE,

THIS VOLUME IS DEDICATED

BY

THE AUTHOR

PREFACE.

WHATEVER divergence of opinion may be found to exist between the author and the reader of the following pages, there will doubtless be an entire agreement in regard to the pertinence of the title by which the late Government of the United States of America is designated. If it had been described as the 'American Union,' the question might suggest itself to the well-informed reader—'What Union?' Because, in the country which forms the subject of this volume, three Federal Unions had followed each other, and two of them had been extinguished before the third was dissolved by the secession of the Confederate States.

To have employed the term 'United States' would equally have required an explanation, for they are not now what they were during the period concerning which I have written, although there was *a* United States still in being at the date of our last advices from Washington.

But when we say the 'MODEL REPUBLIC,' none can mistake its signification. All the world will agree, that the words describe one, and but one.

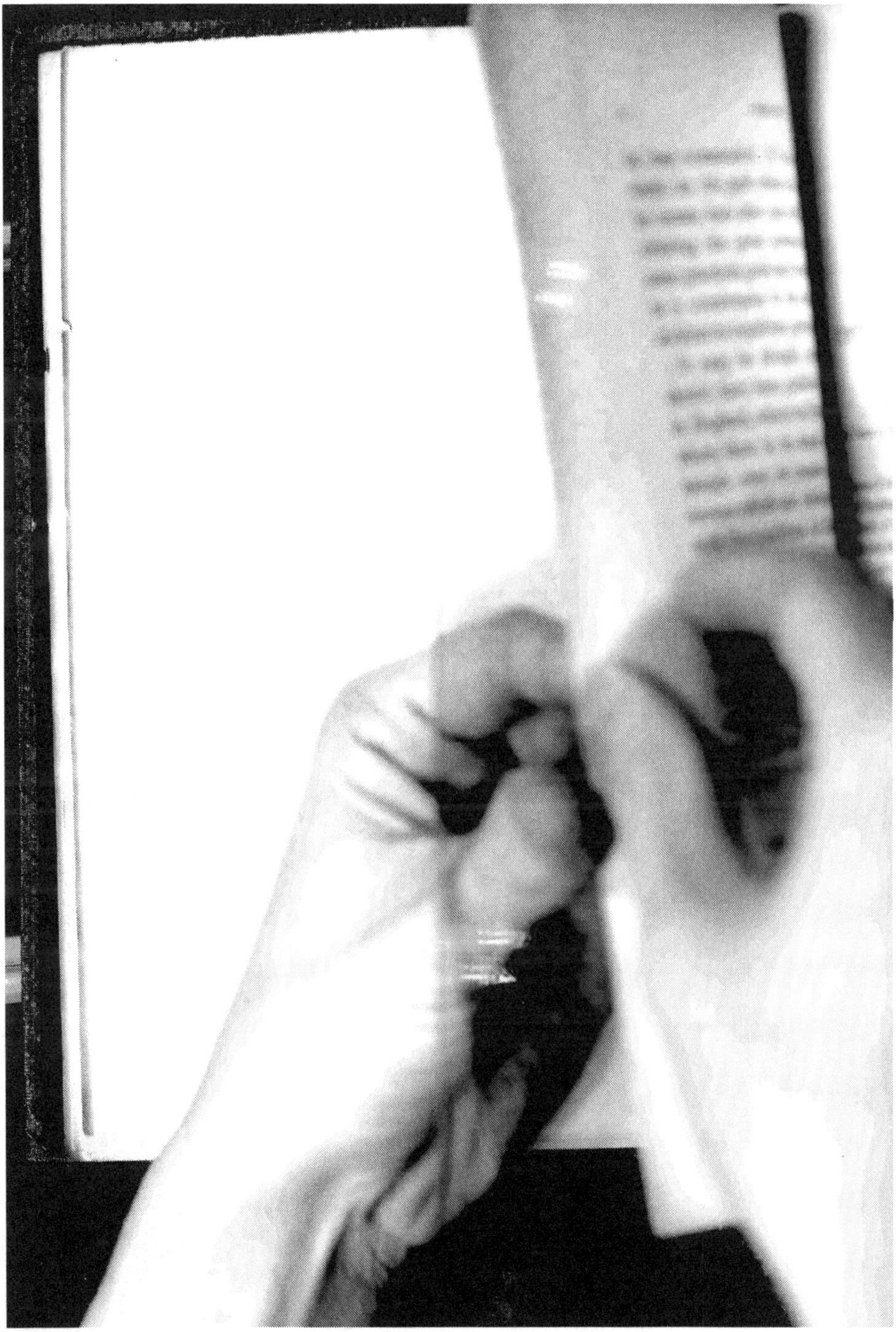

PREFACE.
WHATEVER divergence
to exist between the
the following pages, there
agreement in regard to the
which the late Government
America is designated. If it
the 'American Union,' the
itself
ot prove
—Com-
itutions
America
e Value
l by the
94
rcises of
her it be

Confederacy, that has ever existed, and that they obviate the necessity of further explanation.

It is not always that an adjective prefix, or a phrase employed to designate the quality of a party, or a State, or a system, is conceded by common consent to be a truthful exponent of the thing described.

American factions or parties are rarely permitted to wear unchallenged the names by which they designate themselves. Their adversaries employ other words to describe the same thing—such as Barn-burners, Silver-greys, Loco-focos, or Copperheads—when they refer to the Democratic party; or, on the other hand, Woolly-heads, Negro-worshippers or Exterminators, by way of retort upon the Republicans. Nevertheless, these nicknames, which, however bewildering to strangers, are well understood in the localities where they are employed, are all meant to imply a reproach, and are therefore not admitted by universal consent to be legitimate appellatives.

In the present case we encounter no such difficulty. When the proselyte of the *vox populi vox Dei* school of politicians desires to illustrate the practical advantages of his theory of government over all others, and at the same time to achieve a climax, he exclaims with an air of undoubting triumph, 'Behold the Model Republic!' and almost as though they were the returning echo of his own words comes back the response from his adversary, 'Aye! Behold the Model Republic!'

Whether the one regards it as a model of perfection and the other a model of deformity—an example to be imitated, or an example to be avoided—does not matter. They are agreed that 'it is a representation'—a something 'in imitation of nature'—a standard by which Democratic institutions 'are to be measured.'

Congratulating himself, then, as its author does in having adopted a name by which to designate the Government concerning which he has written that cannot fail to be satisfactory to all parties, he fears that from this point of agreement there will be a divergence between the opinions he expresses and those which are entertained by the Radicals of every political school, whether of monarchical or democratic tendencies. He has said too much, perhaps, to expect forgiveness from the one, and not enough to secure the approbation of the other. He trusts, however, that he may fall back for support and countenance upon that larger and more practical class which, like truth, is found to exist between two extremes.

The author would have been wilfully blind not to discover the seat of the disease which has afflicted the late Confederation, and dishonest, if he wrote at all, not to expose it. To have suggested a remedy too mild to be efficacious, or so violent that it would have been peremptorily rejected by the patient, would have been alike unavailing in the achievement of any desirable end.

In his treatment of the subject the author has addressed himself only to the facts. Where these condemn he has condemned; where these commend he has commended. If he has failed to clothe truth in the garb which will produce conviction, he trusts that abler pens will be employed in elucidating the great problem, and that eventually some practical good may be evoked, which may serve as a counterpoise to the admitted evils which are incident to republican government.

It may be thought, perhaps, that this volume should have been published in America rather than in England, where real liberty is enjoyed by all, and where there is no single element of power strong enough even to menace its overthrow. Yet, for reasons which are obvious to those who are familiar with the condition of affairs in America, this would have been impossible.

The author nevertheless hopes that the subject, if not attractive to the great mass of European readers, will not be without interest to a few; and that these, in estimating the merits of the volume as a whole, will give credit for the fidelity which has been observed in his statement of the facts of American history to which he has made allusion.

LONDON, *Oct.* 30, 1863.

CONTENTS.

he has [illegible] [illegible] has failed to clothe truth in the [illegible] [illegible] will produce conviction, he trusts that [illegible] [illegible] will be employed in elucidating the [illegible] [illegible] that [illegible] [illegible] some point [illegible] [illegible] overlooked, which may serve as a [illegible] [illegible] [illegible] [illegible] which are [illegible] [illegible] [illegible]

It may [illegible] [illegible] [illegible] that this volume should have [illegible] [illegible] in America rather than in England, where [illegible] liberty is enjoyed by all, and where there [illegible] [illegible] [illegible] power strong enough [illegible] [illegible] [illegible] [illegible]. Yet, for [illegible] [illegible] [illegible] [illegible] those who are familiar with the [illegible] [illegible] [illegible] America, this would have been [illegible]

He [illegible] [illegible] [illegible] hopes that the subject, if not attractive [illegible] [illegible] [illegible] European readers, will not be [illegible] [illegible] [illegible] and that these, in estimating [illegible] [illegible] [illegible] as a whole, will give [illegible] [illegible] [illegible] which has been observed [illegible] [illegible] [illegible] [illegible] American history [illegible] [illegible] [illegible] [illegible]

[illegible]

CONTENTS.

RISE AND FALL

OF

"THE MODEL REPUBLIC."

CHAPTER I.

REAL AND ASSIGNED CAUSES OF THE DISSOLUTION OF THE FEDERAL UNION.

THE American Union as it existed in the days of Washington is no more and will never be again.

It is not surprising when a great Government is in process of dissolution, and is disappearing from the family of nations amongst which it had occupied a conspicuous place, that men should behold the spectacle, even from afar, with an interest deepened and intensified in proportion to the magnitude of the political edifice which is falling into ruins.

The gigantic structure of the Federal Union has been broken in twain, and as mankind gaze into the yawning gulf which widens and deepens with each convulsive movement of the dissevered fragments, they wonder and seek to divine the cause and to fathom the future of the catastrophe.

There are those now living who assisted in placing

the first foundation stone—who aided in the construction of its massive walls—who watched its progress until the last tile was adjusted upon its roof—and who are now in their old age gazing upon its ruins. Not the ruins of the great principles upon which the structure was reared—not the ruins even of the dissevered fragments—for though they may never again be re-united, each one, and it may be others constructed out of the abundant and sound material, may yet attain to a greatness surpassing that of the edifice from whose *débris* they sprang. But the overthrow of the Federacy, as a unit of power—the wreck of that Government which proclaimed by its motto '*E pluribus Unum*' the nature of its powers, the source of its authority, and the limit of its duration, has been fully and irremediably accomplished.

It was a magnificent structure, erected under the guidance of patriotic and wise counsels; and even as men now contemplate its fallen condition, the philosophical mind is more impressed with respect and admiration for its founders, than when in the fullness and completeness of its proportions it towered amongst us, the pride of every American, and the wonder of mankind.

It may be likened unto a great ship, which the architects and machinists had constructed after a new model and upon an untried principle, whose mission it was to sail in hitherto unexplored seas. Ridiculed by those who could discover no merit in anything new, and in the estimation of whom even vices become sanctified by age into virtues—feared by many who believed that such an innovation upon established principles might exercise a dangerous influence upon the subjects of other Governments, and thus involve them in the ruin which they predicted would ensue when the vessel would be cast among the breakers — opposed by the universal practice of mankind, and in contempt of previous failures where the same principles had been partially applied, the constructors boldly, though perhaps with some misgivings, launched their new ship upon the stormy ocean, and sent her forth upon the mission for which she had been created. And right gallantly did she buffet the winds and the waves, and to the multitude she seemed to grow stronger as she grew older. Her friends were buoyant with hope, and her enemies became less sanguine of witnessing her speedy destruction, while her successful voyages made a deep impression upon those who had hitherto been sceptical in regard to her powers of endurance. There were occasions when the more thoughtful of those by whom she was directed feared that a tempest might arise which would overtax her capacity for resistance; but anon she passed on into smooth waters and confidence was again restored : and her friends believed that she could safely ride through any storm; and her adversaries scarce dared to hope that she would ever encounter an overwhelming disaster. But notwithstanding all she was wrecked in the midst of what appeared to be her most prosperous voyage. Not because the model was imperfect, or the machinery too complicated to be kept successfully in motion—not from any defect in the principle upon which she had been constructed—but for the reason that a single simple detail, a solitary wheel was misplaced, which by constant friction with another part finally wore them both away. She did not perish because she fell among the breakers while the pilot slept, nor from any external violence; but because her crew—who might have seen her defective element, and who, if they had so willed, could have substituted another which would have made it secure against every internal shock—failed to see, or if seeing refused to provide the only remedy. The ship dashed madly on and perished. It is in the convulsions of her dissolution, even more than in the greatness of her brief career, that the world has discovered the magnitude of her power.

No spectacle in the past has been exhibited to mankind which has absorbed more deeply the attention of the civilised world than that which is now being exhibited upon the American continent. Though the theatre of action is so remote from the great European centre of civilisation, the interest excited by the terrible struggle between the divided parts of the great Confederacy is scarcely less general than would be produced by a similar catastrophe to some long established European Power.

In reference to the causes which have culminated in this conflict the minds of men have been variously affected. Some have regarded the event with satisfaction, believing it to be a deathblow to the system of government upon which the States composing the Confederacy were founded; while others, for the very same reason, are overwhelmed with mortification, grief, and dismay. Both are essentially wrong in the premises from which they derive their conclusions, while both may be right in believing or fear-ing that a long night of gloom may succeed to the bright sunlight of liberty which the establishment of the American Republics diffused throughout the world.

Whatever may be the immediate results following the terrible conflict which the dismemberment of the Union has so unnecessarily produced, the lapse of time and an intelligent contemplation of the real causes by which it was accomplished will show that the origin of these results had nothing whatever to do with the fundamental principles of government upon which the Confederacy rested.

It is difficult, I might almost say impossible, for a stranger who has not been himself an eye-witness to the operations of the American Constitution, or rather the Federal compact, to comprehend fully and be able to trace to their true sources all the currents and counter currents which, increasing in volume and in the rapidity of their movements with the lapse of time, have at length engulphed the Union. In considering a result already achieved, observers, even the least interested personally in the event, generally decide upon its causes according to their own peculiar prejudices or partialities, without following the thread of events by which it was achieved, and thus arriving at a truthful solution. It is unfortunately true that moral and political philosophers, who have exercised a controlling influence over the public sentiment of mankind, have generally sought to adapt events to their theories, rather than to correct their theories by events. They set out by assuming the correctness of certain general principles, to which they adhere under the most diverse circumstances. They treat a political question in the same manner that a mathematician would demonstrate a geometrical problem, without considering the material difference that in proving the truth of the latter the absurdity of any other result is at the same time established, while the former can only be shown to be true under a given state of circumstances. Mere theorists soon degenerate into partisans, and partisans rarely state the cause of their adversaries with fairness.

The events which are transpiring in America, and the causes by which they were produced, deserve to be considered from a higher platform than that which is occupied by the mere partisan. The interests of mankind are too deeply involved in a truthful solution of the great problem which has been at issue in the New World during three quarters of a century to accept the conclusions of mere partisans in regard to the causes which have led to the catastrophe. Sovereigns and their subjects, Conservatives and Liberals, may learn invaluable lessons from the experience of America, by comprehending clearly the truth; but it cannot in the end subserve any worthy object to give to the events we are considering an interpretation which would lead to false conclusions. There is much in the career of the late Confederation which, if properly understood and wisely and frankly acted upon, ought at least to shorten the distance which divides the sincere adherents of the two great leading systems of government. If both would sink the partisan, and in good faith accept the lesson which is now unfolded by the bloody drama which is being enacted by the American Republics, the terrible conflict would not have been altogether in vain. The history of the Government of the late United States proves much in support of and against the doctrines of both, and it is deeply interesting to decide aright upon which side the weight of testimony inclines.

In the 'SOUTH VINDICATED' I set forth, in advance of the actual catastrophe, the material active visible causes which soon thereafter terminated, as it was manifest would be the result, in the disruption of the Federal Union. I think that I stated them fairly. I do not believe that I did injustice to the North, nor that I did more than justice to the South. But, being a Southerner, it may be that my strong convictions were in some degree influenced by my very natural desire to serve the cause of my own country. In attempting in that work to vindicate my countrymen against the cruel aspersions of their enemies, I did but utter the feelings and sentiments and opinions of the Southern people, though I had no authority to speak for them than such as I derived from my right of citizenship, a common interest, and a common danger.

In discussing now the moral causes which led to and finally produced the rupture of the Union, I can have no personal, or party, or sectional interest to subserve, which is not shared alike by the citizens of both the North and the South. Whether or not my conclusions may be just, they cannot exercise any influence in deciding upon the question of might, which is now the only one at issue. Argument has been abandoned—the sword has been tendered by the North and accepted by the South as the arbiter, and by the sword alone may the material questions at issue be solved. However this issue may be settled, it cannot lead us to a correct appreciation of the causes which produced the conflict. What were those causes which have been attended with such stupendous results?

The adversaries of democratical forms of government believe that the catastrophe to the Union originated in a radical defect or error in the fundamental principle upon which the Government was founded. These do not duly consider that all the various forms of government which have been devised and adopted have been subject to convulsions and revolutions, similar in kind and character to that which is now progressing in America. Such a solution might be accepted if conflicts of a like nature had not signalised the history of the world; but we may not justly apply a test to the Republic which would have to be exceptional, or which, if applied to other forms of government, would equally condemn them all. If, however, the fact of the war might lead the mind to such a conclusion, the events which have signalised the conflict—the immense power and skill which have been displayed by both sections of the former Union—the indomitable energy and zeal with which each pursues its object (the one for conquest, the other for independence) might well dispel the delusion that a Government which could display such qualities and develope such enormous resources did not possess many of the attributes which make nations durable and powerful.

The fundamental error of those who draw the conclusion indicated, from the disruption of the

Union, consists in the fact that they regard the dissolution of the Federal compact as involving the principle of Republican government. The Federal Union was, in fact, but the creature of the States composing it. The Constitution, as justly interpreted by Lord Brougham and other distinguished commentators, was a mere treaty of alliance, offensive and defensive. The States who were the parties to this league were and remained sovereign. That they were so is proved by the fact that they delegated certain defined sovereign powers, which they could not have conferred if they had not been sovereign. The real government of the country, in regard to its internal affairs, rested always with the States. The constitutions of all these embodied the principles of Republican government, and this fact caused the framers of the Federal Constitution to insert a clause guaranteeing to every State a Republican form of government. If this had been omitted, nothing remained which would have precluded a monarchy from becoming a member of the Federal Union. It would, therefore, be an error to suppose that the rupture of this league had anything to do with the Republican basis upon which the Governments of the States were founded.

Others find a ready solution by attributing it to that prevailing disposition of the stronger to subdue the weaker, when unrestrained by countervailing influences. This may be admitted to be true in one sense, though false in another, since this active cause was itself in a great measure an effect proceeding from another and a more powerful cause.

There are others still who find no difficulty in

arriving at the conclusion that the Institution of African Slavery which existed in a number of the States was the prime source of all the evils which have befallen the country. This, too, may be said to be partly true and partly false. It is true just in the sense that the purse of the unfortunate traveller is the immediate cause of his being robbed upon the highway. But if he had not been possessed of a purse, his watch, or his horse, or his cloak, would have been quite sufficient to stimulate the highwayman to the employment of his dagger or his pistol. Slavery may be said, more properly, to have been a pretext rather than the cause; but if the Institution of Slavery had never existed, other pretexts would have been employed to subserve a like purpose.

There are others still who believe that the disaster which has befallen the Union had its origin in the fact that the powers delegated by the States to the Federal Government in the compact of union were too great; while the adversaries of these are quite sure that precisely the reverse is true. Even these adverse propositions may be partially true, and yet both are false. If the Government had been less strong, it would probably have given less cause to the States of the South to distrust its intentions. If it had been stronger, or if the rights of the States and their reservation of sovereignty had been less clearly defined, those who were aggrieved by the tyrannical application of its powers might have been deterred from attempting their own deliverance. After allowing due weight to the arguments upon both sides, and carefully considering the facts, we are constrained to conclude that even though the general Government had been shorn of some of its powers—or, if upon the other hand, its authority had been more despotic—the revolution could not thereby have been averted.

The judgment of mankind may, to a certain degree, justly decide that some of the causes referred to exercised a powerful influence in producing the disruption of the Union. Yet these were but effects of a previously existing cause. The former were active, immediate causes, visible to the eye, palpable to the sense; but they were only results of, or owed their developement to, a passive remote cause. There were physical living causes which were, however, only brought into mischievous action through the instrumentality of a latent moral cause, which slowly, silently, but not less surely, accomplished its mission. This great source of evil—this cancer upon the body politic, which diffused its poison throughout the whole sytem—was the *Presidential election.*

The fact was no secret to thoughtful citizens. Intelligent politicians knew that the presidential contests were undermining the foundation of the Government, and that sooner or later the destruction of the Federal Union would ensue. They could not if they would have concealed this knowledge from themselves, and yet none dared publicly to proclaim it. None had the boldness to suggest the only remedy Amid all the various plans of compromise which were suggested—with a view to avert for the time being the impending calamity, which commenced to develope itself upon the success of the North as a section in the presidential contest of 1860—it is fair to presume that not one of the intelligent movers thereof believed that the adoption of any proposed scheme would do more at most than postpone for a season the denouement of a foregone conclusion. There would have resulted at best but a truce of longer or shorter duration, because the same primary cause of disaster would have remained in full force, and sooner or later the Confederacy would have been obliged to succumb to that ever present, active, unaltered, irresistible first cause.

It may be asked why did not some self-sacrificing patriot or statesman of the dominant section fearlessly define the nature of the evil, and point out to the people the only remedy? To this interrogatory it may be answered that the patriots and statesmen of the North, and to a lamentable degree of the South also, had long before been obliged to yield themselves as vanquished, under the irresistible influence of that very cause, by the mere demagogues and place-seekers who had been their rivals for the smiles of their Sovereign—the people. Were the recipients of royal or popular favours ever known to subject themselves voluntarily to the frowns of their sovereign by suggesting unpalatable reforms, or by intimating that their master was not a proper or a safe custodian of power? As an apology for the courtier it may be admitted that such exhibitions of patriotism generally terminate in the discomfiture or disgrace of those who have the courage thus to speak. Few monarchs are willing to relinquish the pageantry, much less the substance of power, except under the pressure of an apparently overruling necessity. Courtiers and demagogues mutually laugh at and upbraid each other for their servility to their respective sovereigns. Each 'would scorn to crook the pregnant hinges of the knee' to the master of the other; yet in the very act of deprecating servility towards any other description of potentate than the one to which they each respectively proffer their devotion, they administer the most exquisite flattery. Both are doubtless sincere when they pronounce all other dispensers of honours and patronage and smiles to be less worthy of adulation, or of the unswerving loyalty and self-sacrificing devotion of loving subjects, than the particular one which they have the honour and the happiness to serve. Republicans are as wary about uttering unpalatable truths to their sovereign as other courtiers; and hence, from the moment when the cloud, no bigger than a man's hand, first made its appearance upon the horizon of the 'Great Republic'—hour by hour, and day by day, and year by year, thickening and darkening, and expanding, until the whole heavens were shrouded in gloom, up to the very instant of time when the storm burst forth in all its terrible fury, spreading desolation and death throughout the land—men witnessed it all—foresaw the result—knew there was one and but one place of shelter; and yet of all those whose lust of place and power had precipitated the catastrophe, not one was found who possessed the moral courage to say to the people—

'The independence of the individual States in all that concerns their internal relations being essential under our system of checks and balances to the preservation of liberty; and the election of presidents by a majority of the people of the Union being incompatible

with the sovereignty and equality of the separate members, besides being a perpetual fountain of bitter personal, political, and national animosities among the people: a perseverance in such a mode of designating the chief officer of the State can only end in the total estrangement of the different sections and the subversion of the Government. Let us, therefore, consolidate and perpetuate the blessings of that freedom which we may possess by not abusing its privileges. Let us remove the temptation by relinquishing the power to destroy liberty. Let us surrender the empty honour of making and unmaking our four-year-kings, that we may be spared the heart-burnings, the jealousies, the convulsions, the enmities, the irremediable dangers which follow, as the night the day, the struggle of conflicting interests in the settlement of an uncertain succession to the supreme power of the State. Let us take warning from the mutterings of that storm which is evidently approaching, and learn wisdom from that Past whose history has been written in characters of blood, and from whose dark pages we are taught that the epoch of greatest danger to Governments, and of disaster to the people, has been at the period of transition between the vacation of the kingly office, by the extinction of one line of monarchs and the permanent installation of another.'

In declaring that presidential elections were the primary cause of the overthrow of the Government, I am uttering a truth which has been rarely, if ever, spoken by American politicians who occupied a position or enjoyed a personal popularity which might have given force and effect to their opinions or advice. Yet I repeat, that while intelligent citizens may have closed their eyes, and refused to read or interpret the hand-writing upon the wall, the conviction of the fact was indelibly inpressed upon their minds. The hectic flush which mantles the cheek of the consumptive patient during the last struggle of the vital principle of life, to maintain itself against the slow but sure approach of death, is not more palpable to the sense of sympathising friends who watch by his dying bedside than, to the minds of thoughtful Americans, was that flood of evils springing from this source, which growing broader and deeper and darker, with the lapse of time, moved onward in its certain unvarying course to the gulf of dissolution.

However this may be, the great Confederacy of Free States, which was developed into such vast proportions before even those who assisted at its creation had all passed away—which still numbered upon its pension lists many who had fought in the war which called it into being as a nation—which startled mankind by the exhibition of a gigantic internal power which has never been surpassed by any other nation, has indeed passed away for ever. There are few disinterested spectators of the events which have followed its dissolution who can believe, or hope, or fear, that its dissevered elements can ever again be re-united into a harmonious whole, either by the physical power of the one or by the voluntary assent of the other. A new nation has sprung forth from the ruins which has already been baptised in fire and blood, between which and its former confederates there is a broad, deep, impassable gulf.

filled with the bodies of its slaughtered citizens. It can scarcely be believed that any tardy measure of redress, however comprehensive, would be accepted as an atonement for the horrors through which it had been forced to pass; or that any feeling or sentiment of fraternal regard for the North, as a nation, can ever again animate the bosoms of the Southern people.

How far the action of foreign nations may modify the natural course of events it is impossible to foretell. The Governments of the civilised world may, to a certain extent, be regarded in the aggregate as a confederacy, bound together by certain laws tacitly recognised, which regulate their intercourse with each other, and define their respective rights and obligations. It could scarcely be possible, under the circumstances existing, for a single nation to maintain itself in that perpetual isolation which would be the consequence of a persistent refusal on the part of others to recognise its existence. If, therefore, the other Governments of the civilised world will not consent to treat with the Confederate States in any other capacity than as dependencies of a Government composed of their former confederates, until the assent of the latter is first accorded, it may not now be decided what influence it may exercise upon the future of the dismembered parts of the late Union. Left, however, to the operation of natural causes, uninfluenced by any repelling external influence, whether passive or active, the reconstruction of the Union, if not impossible, is altogether improbable.

CHAPTER II.

THE FACT OF THE RUPTURE OF THE UNION DOES NOT PROVE THE INEFFICIENCY OF REPUBLICAN GOVERNMENT — COMPARISON OF THE RESULTS OF DEMOCRATIC INSTITUTIONS IN THE UNITED STATES AND OTHER PORTIONS OF AMERICA — MEXICO: AS SHE IS AND AS SHE MAY BE.

SO far as it might affect the fortunes of the fallen Union, a decision in regard to the causes which produced its overthrow would be of no avail, yet a correct comprehension thereof cannot fail to be profitable to all who may have an interest in discovering the faults, as well as the advantages, resulting from the system of government upon which the Confederation was established.

I have said that the presidential election was the source of these evils. It was, as it were, a Pandora's box, which attracted and collected within itself the various elements of ill, only to expand, develope, and then scatter them broadcast throughout the land. It may not be said absolutely to have created the poisons; but it intensified them, increased their virulence, and administered them to the victims. It will not be denied that there existed other elements of destruction which would, at a later period, have developed themselves without the aid or stimulant of presidential elections. There were other causes constantly in operation which would, in all probability, have enforced the division of the country into smaller and more homogeneous States; but these would have equally existed under any conceivable form of government, and might have been developed to their legitimate results according to natural and invariable laws, more potent in their efficacy in accomplishing their mission than any statutory enactments which could have been devised for the prevention of such a consummation. The presidential election prematurely developed these causes, and hastened the final catastrophe. It was the opportunity and the temptation, inviting instead of repelling them; cultivating instead of destroying them; and luring them on to crush out the life of the nation at the very moment when it appeared to be growing stronger and stronger. It hastened the dissolution, instead of allowing the confederacy to live on its allotted time, and then to pass away under the immutable natural laws which would have determined the limit of its duration.

Many of the wisest politicians and statesmen of Europe believe that if the Government had been a monarchy the catastrophe would not have occurred. I think it may be easily established that this *was not necessary* to the attainment of the end, even if a resort thereto had been practicable; but its application under the circumstances was not only not essential, but impossible.

It has been a misfortune to mankind that a large proportion of those whose genius or intellectual endowments have enabled them to impress their ideas upon others have permitted themselves to be the slaves of theories which they have traced out to seemingly legitimate conclusions, without giving due consideration to the many causes, moving in opposite courses, which in the practical affairs of real life give a totally different direction to the ever-shifting current of events. They note the developement of certain principles or measures, under a certain existing state of circumstances, and within certain fixed boundaries; and having witnessed their successful developement within that limited sphere, they conclude that all mankind would be gainers by being subjected to the same laws. Thus the theoretical monarchist would impose his favourite form of government upon the whole human family, while the radical democrat would abolish all distinctions of rank, and capacity, and race, and complexion, and bring all men, in theory at least, to the same social and political level. Each may be right, considered in reference alone to the isolated communities and within the limited circle from a study of which they have respectively imbibed the inspiration of their thoughts; but both will be found seriously at fault when they attempt to generalise mankind, and apply to all the same fixed laws. The British Government may be admirably adapted to the British people. It may be admitted that it is scarcely possible to conceive any other system which could have achieved such great results. It is quite probable that any sudden and violent change, either in the direction of a monarchical or democratic despotism, would result in disaster, and perhaps the final subversion of a power which during many centuries has exercised a controlling influence over the destinies of mankind. Notwithstanding, however, the admitted adaptation of British political institutions to the requirements of the British people, it may scarcely be believed that they could be put into successful operation, or if in operation that like results would ensue, if applied even upon the nearest neighbouring territory. They would be still more out of place in countries more remote, where the tastes, habits, and traditions of the people were formed under totally different auspices, and under the operation of opposite causes.

The people composing a nation may be imperceptibly led to change their habits of thought by education and by long training, yet a reverence for a particular form of government, or for the principles upon which a government is founded, are not the growth of a day, but of generations and ages. Radical changes in the constitution, or even in the pageants of a state, cannot be effected to the advantage of its subjects by a *coup d'état*, or a sudden revolution, unless the tastes and habits and minds of those to be effected thereby have been educated to the transformation by a long process of preparation. The mass of mankind are slow to adopt, and slower to revere, a new order of things suddenly and without due preparation brought into operation. The great changes which have been made in certain Governments of Europe, when the present is contrasted with some epoch in the past, have been accomplished silently and by such a slow and gradual process that no period can be assigned as the date of their commencement or their consummation.

If we consider and apply these same natural laws

to the late Federal Union, it will be discovered that the successful establishment of a monarchy would have been, under the circumstances existing at the period of the formation of the Government, so nearly impossible as to have rendered it in every respect in which it might have been viewed wholly undesirable.

The discovery of the American continent opened a new era in the history and habits, as well as in the government of mankind. Emigrants from the Old World who flocked to its shores acted under the influence of the same general causes. They entered upon their new life having in view the same general objects. They did not go as kings and nobles and serfs, though all classes contributed to swell the population of the New World. A great continent was before them, abounding in all the elements of wealth, wholly unoccupied, save by roving savages who disappeared before the advancing tide of civilisation. In a contest with the wilderness and the wild Indian rank and title were of no avail. The strong arm, the resolute will, the superior sagacity, the greater capacity for physical endurance, constituted the qualities of mind and body which could alone secure preeminence. With an almost illimitable expanse of territory, of which each occupant might appropriate to his own use all that he could reclaim from the savages, and subdue by the arts and for the uses of civilised man, it was to be expected that he would soon forget or disregard the habits of thought as well as action which prevailed amongst the overcrowded populations of the Old World from whence he had withdrawn himself, and to which he never expected to return. In process of time, kings born to the inheritance of crowns were for him a historical incident of the past, and for his descendants a tradition of another hemisphere handed down to them from their ancestors. The fact that monarchs still lived was only made palpable to his senses by their exactions through their agents and representatives; for he never beheld them with his own eyes, and was never captivated by the pageantry with which royalty is surrounded. When these isolated individuals grew into communities, and from communities into states, they organised democratical forms of government, under the operation of the natural laws which will govern the people of Great Britain when they assist at the coronation of a successor to the Queen. We may reasonably conclude that it would have been even more impracticable to have established a monarchy in the United States than to suddenly transform a long established European monarchy into a republic.

The territory embraced within the limits of the United States had been divided, up to the moment when its history as an independent confederation may be regarded as having commenced, into a number of provinces of unequal extent and population, which were totally distinct from each other in regard to the administration of the laws by which they were respectively governed. These provinces, on entering upon the struggle for independence, very naturally joined themselves together in a league for mutual defence, but in doing so they carefully reserved their individual rights of sovereignty over all their internal affairs. They had been living under the operation of the British Constitution, divested of its kings and its hereditary nobles. Hence their governments had been in fact republics, though tributary to a monarchy. When, therefore, the authority of Great Britain was withdrawn, all that was monarchical disappeared, and the thirteen provinces thereby became independent republics, united for certain defined purposes under a single head, deriving its authority from themselves. They were republics, but they did not become so by revolution: for in the very act of separation from the foreign power to which they had been tributary they were left in that condition. The monarchical element under which they had previously existed was not, and never had been, a feature in their own political institutions. Those who organised the governments may not therefore be properly said to have instituted the republican form, for it existed before, in letter and spirit. To have created a monarchy would have involved a revolution in the established order, and would moreover have been in discord with the prevailing sentiments and established usages of the people. They wisely chose to create governments in harmony with the principles, tastes, and habits of those for whom they were instituted. Hence the transition from the condition of colonial dependence was unaccompanied by any palpable change in the relation of the citizens towards each other, or the State.

It is not my purpose to bring in question the relative abstract merits of different forms of government, but only to insist that, in the application of the general principles of political science, we find that a certain form may be proved to be best under a given state of circumstances and when applied to a particular community; but under other circumstances, and applied to a different community, it may be that it would be the very worst. In general terms, it may be said that the form of government is best which secures for its subjects the greatest amount of happiness. The source from whence the powers of a government should emanate depends upon the capacity, and habits and tastes: even the traditions and prejudices of the governed. It must be conceded that, in view of all the circumstances, the form adopted by the people of the British provinces in America, upon the establishment of their independence, was for them the one best calculated to promote the legitimate objects for which governments are instituted amongst men. Yet it does not follow that in the arrangement of its details they may not have committed a fatal error, or that in practice it approached any nearer to the attainment of the legitimate ends of government than others constructed upon a different basis. So far as regards the real liberty of the subject, we may learn by the history of the United States since the year 1860, if the lesson had never been taught before, that there may exist as ruthless a despotism under the forms of democratic or republican freedom as could be developed under the absolute rule of a single despot.

But it would be a grave error to conclude that the disruption of the Union, or the war which it has engendered, or even the gross violations of the principles of liberty which have marked the career of the United States Government, under its present rulers, have demonstrated the insufficiency of republican institutions, properly organised, to accomplish within the limits of the late Union all the purposes for which governments are established. If such exceptional tests are to be regarded as conclusive against the republican principle, in a thousand fold stronger degree, because in a thousand instances similar results having signalised the career of monarchies, they also must be condemned.

The partisan of other forms of government may prove, by a reference to the events now transpiring in America, that democracies, like monarchies, are subject to disintegration, to war—civil war, if he chooses to give such an improper designation to the conflict between the North and the South—that they may be diverted from their legitimate course by the exercise of a despotic power, which for the time being banishes every vestige of individual freedom from the land: he may prove that man's nature, his impulses, his actions, are governed or directed by the same natural laws, under the operation of the one as the other; but he can establish nothing more. There may, or may not exist, substantial and conclusive reasons why the monarchical form of government is the best; but the proof is not furnished by *the fact* of the disruption, nor by *the events* of the war.

While, however, it may be maintained that the republican form, guarded by a wise system of checks and balances, would be best adapted to the wants and interests and sympathies of the people composing the late Union, and that no other would have been likely to develope from the same materials such great results, it cannot be denied that in almost every other part of the American continent the experiment of democratical institutions has ended in complete and hopeless failure. Whether we cast our eyes over the little republics of South America, engaged in their ceaseless occupation of warring upon each other, or themselves; or to Central America, where the degeneracy of the European race has been attended by physical as well as mental imbecility, and where the wandering tribes of aborigines are beginning to assert their supremacy over the soil; or to the lovely plains and valleys and mountains of Mexico—a land abounding in all the natural elements of greatness—a prolific soil, a salubrious climate, and withal a brave people, characterised by many high traits of character—throughout the whole we discover, though in different degrees, the evidences of intrinsically bad governments, badly administered. Neither can there be discovered anything in their past history or their present condition which might give rise to even a glimmering hope that the future would not be under like auspices, but a repetition of that which has already transpired.

Mexicans may well hail the establishment of different political institutions, founded upon a properly organised monarchy, as the turning point in their destiny—the full stop in their downward career, the harbinger of a great future for the nation. It would be a grave error to suppose that the Mexican people have degenerated in the ratio of the decay of the political fabric by which they were governed. On the contrary, there still exists among a large portion of the population all the elements of character which distinguish the

European race from whence they sprang. There is a class of Mexicans, by no means small, who would do honour to any country. Their usefulness has been destroyed by the crushing incubus of a badly administered Government ; but upon the instant that a stable Government is established, they will at once show themselves to be fully competent for the task of regenerating the country.

It is certainly true that a large proportion of the humbler classes have been thoroughly demoralised by the part they have been required to act in the ceaseless civil broils in which they have been engaged by ambitious or factious leaders. It is also true that the blood of the ancient Spaniard has been much adulterated by admixture with the inferior races which inhabited their territory.

We may account for a very large measure of the superior energy of the European races in the United States over those of Mexico, by giving due weight to the fact, that in the former they always maintained a social and political superiority, not only over the aborigines but over the multitudes of Africans who had been transported as slaves to their territory. The pride of race, which in the one forbade an amalgamation, had no existence in the other, among the great body of the people. The degeneracy of the latter was the inevitable consequence.

No truth has been more clearly established by the test of experience than that Europeans, when brought into contact with the aboriginal or transplanted races upon the American continent, on terms of social and political equality, generally retrograde to the level of their associates; while the latter rarely ascend higher in the scale of civilisation than by the adoption and practice of its vices.*

But this evil will doubtless to a great extent be mitigated by the influx of European emigrants, who will flock to Mexico as to a land of promise, when

* A practical illustration of this fact was furnished a few years ago at the meeting of a 'Ladies' Association for the Civilisation and Christianisation of the North American Indians,' which took place in Washington. A distinguished officer in the Indian wars upon the then frontier, Col ——, of Tennessee, had in early life become enamoured of a beautiful Indian girl, whom he soon after married, somewhat to the annoyance of his friends. The domestic life he led was not, according to his own account, of the happiest character Although he continued to feel for her a strong attachment there was but little accord between them He was a man possessed of excellent understanding and a brilliant wit, which made him always a welcome companion for his friends, though unhappily his habits in regard to sobriety precluded him from the attainment of that station, and influence to which he might otherwise have aspired He happened to be in Washington when the meeting referred to was called, and the fact being known that he had passed the greater part of his life among the Indians he was invited by the ladies to be present upon the occasion of their celebration In the course of the evening the presidentess of the meeting called attention to the fact that the distinguished Col. ——, of Tennessee was present, and expressed the hope that he would favour the meeting with his views in regard to the best and speediest means by which the Indians might be taught the truths of Christianity and the arts of civilisation

In response to the invitation the Colonel arose, and said that a circumstance which had occurred to him in early life had directed his mind in the same channel, and had engaged all his energies in the accomplishment of the philanthropic purpose which animated the society in the formation of their association. He was familiar from constant association with the difficulties which might attend any general scheme for leading the Indians into the paths of civilisation, so he determined to accomplish the task if possible upon a smaller scale. He set to work with great diligence, and during twenty-five weary years he had laboured incessantly to lead a single one into the path of civilisation He commenced this labour of love when he was in the prime of early manhood 'My hair,' he continued, 'is now whitened by age—my earthly career, in the ordinary course of nature, will soon be ended—and now I am obliged to admit to you, ladies, that the result of my life-labour has been that, so far from civilising this one savage, she has made a savage of me! I shall be most happy if you can turn my experience to profitable account.'

order and peace are restored by the establishment of other political institutions. Every philanthropist should rejoice in the prospect which is now held out for the establishment of a great and prosperous empire in that rich and beautiful country; for if no external causes should intervene to impede its progress, it is not to be doubted that there are those now born who will live to see Mexico take her position as one of the first-class Powers, not only of the American continent, but of the civilised world. While the consummation of such a result could not work injury to any other nation, the whole civilised world have an interest in its realisation. Beside the advantages to Europe which would ensue in consequence of Mexico's increased productions and enlarged capacity to consume the manufactures of other countries, the establishment of a stable Government would be a boon to the over-crowded populations of the Old World, for whom Mexico has been during many years as though it had never been discovered.

There is not on the globe a country more diversified in its productions, or more prolific under proper cultivation than Mexico. In the yield of coffee it may be made equal to Brazil; in sugar and tobacco to the island of Cuba; in cotton it approximates more nearly than any other country to the planting States of the Confederacy; in Indian corn and wheat to the States of the West. Its mines of silver and gold and iron and copper are rich and inexhaustible, and in the variety of its delicious fruits it is unsurpassed by any other tropical country inhabited by civilised men. The climate is as various as the soil in production, and under the benign influence of a stable government there would be no part of the continent which would present stronger inducements to the emigrant in search of a home in the New World.*

In considering the past and present condition of this unhappy country, while it cannot be denied that it has been produced by a developement of vices which may be said to be incident to the republican system of government when applied to a people to whose wants they are not adapted, the diametrically opposite condition of the States composing the late Federal Union confirms me in the opinion that no other form of government could have been better suited to the circumstances of the people of the United States than that which they adopted, and under the operation of which they rose so rapidly from weakness to power.

In short, if we may decide in reference to practical results, and not according to the requirements of theories, it would appear that in the late United States it is only necessary to amend or correct errors of mere detail, without abandoning the fundamental principle upon which the political institutions rested; while in Mexico the only hope of regeneration consists in wiping out the past, and laying the foundations of future prosperity by the adoption of a monarchical Government.

* This reference to the condition of Mexico, and the probability of a proximate change in the form of government in that long distracted country, was suggested by the late interposition of the Emperor of the French to save Mexico from that state of hopeless anarchy to which she has been so long tending. There were few disinterested spectators who did not desire to witness the complete success of this truly philanthropic

enterprise Even jealousy itself yielded to the imperious necessity of the actual circumstances; and commendation was bestowed upon this great movement in quarters which had previously regarded with distrust anything calculated to add to the prestige or to increase the power or renown of the great and sagacious ruler of the French nation.

The nomination of the Archduke Ferdinand Maximilian of Austria, brother to the present emperor, and a descendant of the former sovereigns who exercised dominion over Mexico when it was a province of Spain, is a most auspicious *finale* to the intervention of the French, and we may reasonably hope and expect that it is the harbinger of brighter days for Mexico

The selection of this distinguished prince was most fortunate Not only will he carry with him, should he finally accept the crown of Mexico, the prestige of a scion of one of the most renowned of the royal families of Europe, which still rules over one of the greatest empires of the world, but even more important than this, his intellectual qualities, his great personal worth, his thorough appreciation of the true principles of constitutional Government, all designate him as the prince above all others who is most likely to succeed in accomplishing the great work which he has been called upon to perform.

During forty years the energies of the Mexican people have been crushed out by the despotic factions which in the name of Democratic Liberty have constantly exercised the most odious tyranny. A great people has sunk into lethargy—property has depreciated in value—all the incentives to enterprise and the acquisition of wealth have been suppressed—in consequence of the uncertain tenure by which property was held The nation bowed to a despotism which they had not the power to shake off But a people who were once great, and who would be so again under the operation of a good government—a soil once rich and prolific, and which would once more yield abundantly under the stimulants of peace and security—all await only the reconstructing hand of the enlightened prince, whose high destiny, let us hope, is with these ample materials to build up a great, a prosperous, and a happy empire.

CHAPTER III.

THE FRAMERS OF THE AMERICAN CONSTITUTION WERE OPPOSED TO THE ELECTION OF THE PRESIDENT BY A POPULAR VOTE—PROCEEDINGS OF THE CONSTITUTIONAL CONVENTION IN REFERENCE TO THE BEST MEANS OF CHOOSING THE CHIEF EXECUTIVE OF THE GOVERNMENT.

AMERICANS profess and doubtless really entertain a deep veneration and profound respect for the opinions of their forefathers who established the American Union. These feelings are entertained in common with the friends of republican government in Europe. With the lapse of time many of the incidents which gave a particular direction to their acts have passed from the public mind, and with them the special and exceptional reasons which often decided them to do that which abstractly considered their better judgment condemned. This may be said to be true in regard to the plan which was adopted for providing a chief executive head for the Government. It was a subject of long and anxious discussion, and in the Convention which formed the Constitution there was, in regard to details especially, much diversity of opinion. By consulting the meagre records of the debates which have been preserved, we discover that the plan finally agreed upon was not in accordance with the wishes or the judgment of even a respectable minority of that distinguished body of statesmen. They were driven to its adoption by the force of circumstances which they could not control; but the act may be almost said to have been done under protest.

When we consider the times and the general state of popular opinion throughout the civilised world at the moment when this Convention assembled to frame a Constitution for a people without a king or a hereditary aristocracy, or a tradition which could serve as a rallying point for those whose judgment might lead them to oppose the prevailing radicalism, which in Europe sought to transfer to the people the despotic powers which had been hitherto exercised by their rulers, our wonder is that a frame of government so conservative as that of the Constitution of the United States could have been the result of their deliberations. It was at a period when the strong passions evoked by the French Revolution had dethroned reason—when the struggle which had been inaugurated by the people to overthrow tyrants had degenerated into a war against all who placed themselves in opposition to the despotism of mere numbers—and when the desire for liberty which had stimulated the masses to rise in rebellion against their oppressors had been merged and lost in the still stronger passion of hatred.

The American Constitution was a great concession on the part of the radical adherents of the then French school, as well as of those whose opinions inclined towards a more conservative Government than that which was finally adopted. I propose to quote briefly the opinions of leading members of the

Convention upon the important question which arose in regard to the best means of supplying the office of chief executive head, in order to show that the prevailing sentiment was not only adverse to the system which was finally accepted as a settlement, but that in practice it failed utterly to accomplish their intentions.

Alexander Hamilton, of New York, in a plan of a constitution submitted by him privately to Mr. Madison, and which in substance he subsequently brought before the Convention, proposed that the President should be selected by electors chosen by the citizens having an estate of inheritance, or for three lives in land, or a clear personal estate of the value of one thousand Spanish milled dollars, who should hold his place during good behaviour, removable only on conviction upon impeachment for some crime or misdemeanor. He likewise proposed that the senators also should hold their places during life, subject only to removal by impeachment. These propositions, however, were never submitted to a vote of the Convention. The actual state of public opinion precluded the hope of their ratification, even if it had been the part of wisdom to have adopted them.

The remarks of Mr. Hamilton in support of his views, delivered in Convention, June 18, 1787, are worthy of special attention. He was in favour of a monarchy, and he had the boldness to avow it in the face of an overwhelming popular sentiment which imperiously demanded republican institutions. He was in favour of the abrogation of the State Governments, which in truth would have been essential to the successful operation of the Government he suggested. But with all there is a clear admission that the States were not liable to coercion by the general Government, as it was in consequence of that very feature of independence and sovereignty on the part of the various members that he was opposed in the first place to the plan of a constitution which was adopted. A few extracts from the speech in question will serve to illustrate the view of a trusted friend of Washington, who was also one of the most prominent politicians of the day, and who represented the opinions of a large and respectable class of citizens. Differing from him as I do widely in his estimate of the efficacy of the remedy he proposed—more widely still in regard to the influence of the State Governments, which I consider to have been the great bulwarks of liberty in the American system, yet there are many points in which his views are worthy of consideration and respect:—

Mr. Hamilton said (I quote from Madison's reports) he had been hitherto silent on the business before the Convention, partly from respect to others whose superior abilities, age, and experience, rendered him unwilling to bring forward ideas dissimilar to theirs. The crisis, however, which now marked our affairs was too serious to permit any scruples whatever to prevail over the duty imposed upon every man to contribute his efforts for the public safety and happiness. . . . The great and essential principles necessary for the support of government, are—1st. An active and constant interest in supporting it. This principle does not exist in the States in favour of the Federal Government. They have evidently in a high degree the *esprit de corps*. They constantly pursue internal interests adverse to those of the whole. . . . It may be remarked, too, that the citizens have not that anxiety to prevent a dissolution of the general Government as of the particular Governments. A dissolution of the latter would be fatal, of the former would still leave the purposes of government attainable to a considerable degree The sovereignty of the

State Government is immediately before the eyes of the people; its protection is immediately enjoyed by them; from its hand distributive justice, and all those acts which familiarise and endear a government to a people, are dispensed to them. . . How can military force be exerted (by the general Government) on the States collectively? *It is impossible—it amounts to a war between the parties.* Foreign powers will not be idle spectators—they will interpose. The confusion will increase, and a dissolution of the Union will ensue. *Influence*—he did not mean corruption, but a dispensation of those honours and emoluments which produce an attachment to the Government—almost all the weight of these is on the side of the States, and must continue so long as the States continue to exist.* All the passions then, we see, of avarice, ambition, interest, which govern most individuals and all public bodies, fall into the current of the States, and do not flow into the stream of the general Government. The former, therefore, will generally be an overmatch for the general Government, and render any confederacy in its very nature precarious. Theory is in this case fully confirmed by experience. The Amphictyonic Council had, it would seem, ample powers for general purposes; it had, in particular, the power of fining and using force against delinquent members. What was the consequence? Their decrees were mere signals of war. The German Confederacy affords another lesson; the authority of Charlemagne seemed to be as great as could be necessary. The great feudal chiefs, however, exercising their local sovereignties, soon felt the spirit and found the means of encroachments, which reduced the imperial authority to a nominal sovereignty. The Swiss Cantons have scarce any union at all, and have been more than once at war with one another. How, then, are all these evils to be avoided? Only by such a complete sovereignty in the general Government as will turn all the strong principles and passions before mentioned on its side. . . . The general power, whatever be its form, if it preserves itself, must swallow up the State powers—otherwise it will be swallowed

* A few years experience demonstrated the fallacy of this assumption. The facts were precisely the reverse. The patronage of the Federal Executive grew to be greater perhaps than that of any monarch upon earth, whilst offices under the State Governments were scarcely sought for by ambitious men, except as accessory aids to reach employment under the general Government.

up by them. Two sovereignties cannot co-exist within the same limits. If the State Governments were extinguished, he was persuaded that great economy might be obtained by substituting a general Government. *He did not mean, however, to shock the public opinion by proposing such a measure* . . . He was almost led to despair that a republican government could be established over so great an extent. *He was sensible at the same time that it would be unwise to propose one of any other form.* In his private opinion he had no scruple in declaring, supported as he was by the opinion of so many of the wise and good, that the British Government was the best in the world, and he doubted much whether anything short of it would do in America The members most tenacious of republicanism, he observed, were as loud as any in declaiming against the vices of democracy. This progress of the public mind led him to anticipate the time when others as well as himself would join in the praise bestowed by M Neckar on the British Constitution, namely, that it is the only Government in the world which unites public strength with individual security. In every community where industry is encouraged there will be a division of it into the few and the many. Hence separate interests will arise. Give all the power to the many, they will oppress the few—give all the power to the few, and they will oppress the many. Both, therefore, ought to have the power that each may defend itself against the other. To the proper adjustment of this the British owe the excellence of their Constitution. Their House of Lords is a most noble institution. Having nothing to hope for by exchange, and a sufficient interest by means of their property in being faithful to the national interest, they form a permanent barrier against every pernicious innovation, whether attempted on the part of the Crown or of the Commons. No temporary senate will have firmness enough to answer the purpose. Gentlemen differ in opinion concerning the necessary checks from the different estimates they form of the human passions. They suppose seven years a sufficient period to give the senate an adequate firmness, from not duly considering the amazing violence and turbulence of the democratic spirit. When a great object of government is pursued which seizes the popular passions, they spread like wild-fire and become irresistible. As to the executive, it seemed to be admitted that no good one could be established on republican principles. Was not this giving up the merits of the question; for can there be a good government without a good executive? The English model was the only good one on this subject. The hereditary interest of the king was so interwoven with that of the nation, and his personal emolument so great, that he was placed above the danger of being corrupted abroad; and was, at the same time, both sufficiently independent and sufficiently controlled to answer the purpose of the institution at home. One of the weak sides of republics was their being liable to corruption and to foreign influence.* What is the inference from all these observations? That we ought to go as far in order to attain stability and permanency as republican principles will admit. Let one branch of the legislature hold their places for life, or at least during good behaviour. Let the executive also be for life. On the plan of appointing him for seven years he would be ambitious, with the means of making creatures, and as the object of his ambition would be to prolong his power, it is probable that in case of war he would avail himself of the emergency to evade or refuse a degradation from his place. An executive for life has not this motive for forfeiting his fidelity, and would therefore be a safer depositary of power.

I repeat that, however just may have been the views of this distinguished statesman in regard to the difficulties of the position in which the country found itself, yet his scheme was entirely impracticable. Theory as well as practice are opposed to an elective monarchy where the duration of the term is

* This eulogy upon the British Government by a member of the Republican Convention, however justly bestowed in regard to its more important features, is certainly historically inaccurate in the avowal that 'the monarch is placed above the danger of being corrupted from abroad.' The reverse has been true in more than one instance. The prediction that the Government of the United States would be liable from its nature to be corrupted by foreign influence has proved to be an erroneous assumption. That foreign taste, habits, arts, interests and persuasions, may have and did exercise a powerful influence in widening the breach between the North and the South is doubtless true. But this was far from being the result of any corrupt influence brought to bear upon the Government itself. Whatever may have been the faults and errors of Presidents or other officials of the Government of the United States, we have no reason to believe that any corrupt foreign influence has ever been exercised in a single instance over any one of them, whatever may have been his station.

for life. Germany, Rome, and notably Poland, have proven that this mode of choosing an executive head for a government is of all others the most pernicious. Mr. Hamilton admits that a monarchy under the then existing circumstances would have been impossible, although he believed it to have been eminently desirable; and yet he rather illogically opposes the seven-year term as too long, because he feared that it might result in the permanent establishment of the President upon the throne of the Republic. It will be observed, however, that the prevailing fears of the framers of the Constitution were, that the President would become corrupted by the possession of power, and that he would endeavour to secure himself permanently in the position to which, by virtue of the Constitution, he could lay claim to but a brief tenure. There were few who seemed to apprehend that the means by which the executive power was established would corrupt the great body of those who assumed to act in the name of the people, rather than the individual who might be chosen to fill that station. Fewer still credited the probability that, in process of time, obscurity and insignificance would be a surer passport to the presidency than the highest qualities of statesmanship. Many feared that the President might perpetuate his power by the employment of the appliances of office, yet none of the wise men who framed the Constitution had any apprehension that, before the lapse of half a century, the reelection of an executive chief after one term of service would be rendered impossible by the determined opposition of previously disappointed or expectant office-seekers.

Of all the various modes which were proposed in the Convention to provide for the appointment of the chief executive officer, it is worthy of observation that none were received with such universal marks of disapprobation as those which proposed that he should be chosen by a direct vote of the people. The committee to whom the subject was first referred reported in favour of the following:—

A national executive shall be instituted to consist of a single person, to be chosen by the National Legislature, for the term of seven years, with power to carry into execution the national laws, to appoint to offices in cases not otherwise provided for, and to be ineligible a second term.

This proposition was debated during many days. In the report (by Mr. Madison) we find:—

Mr. Gouverneur Morris, of Pennsylvania, was pointedly against his being so chosen. He would be the mere creature of the Legislature. He ought to be elected by the people at large—by the freeholders of the country. That difficulties would attend the mode he admitted. If the people should elect, they would never fail to prefer some man of distinguished character or services. Some man, if he might so speak, of continental reputation. If the Legislature elect, it will be the work of intrigue, of cabal, and of faction. Real merit would rarely be the title to appointment He moved to strike out 'National Legislature,' and insert 'citizens of the United States.'

Mr. Sherman, of Connecticut, thought the sense of the nation would be better expressed by the Legislature than by the people at large The latter will never be sufficiently informed of character.

Mr. Pinckney, of South Carolina, did not expect this question would again have been brought forward—an election by the people being liable to the most obvious and striking objections. They will be led by a few active and designing men. *The most populous States, by combining in favour of the same individual, will be able to carry their points.*

Mr. Morris.—It is said that in case of an election by the

people the populous States will combine and elect whom they please. Just the reverse would be true. The people of such States cannot combine. [The event fully justified at a later period the truth of Mr. Pinckney's prophetic warning.]

Col. Mason, of Virginia, conceived that it would be as unnatural to refer the choice of a proper character for chief magistrate to the people as it would to refer a trial of colours to a blind man. The extent of the country renders it impossible that the people can have the requisite capacity to judge of the respective pretensions of the candidates. [On the motion to make the President elective by the people every State voted 'No,' except Pennsylvania. This unanimity of opposition on the part of the entire Convention to the submission of the choice of President to a popular vote is conclusive proof that they did not foresee that such would be the practice under the system which they finally adopted].

The clause 'for the term of seven years' being taken up—

Mr Broome was for a shorter term.

Dr. McClung moved to strike out 'seven years,' and insert 'during good behaviour.'

Mr. Gouverneur Morris seconded the motion. He expressed great pleasure in hearing it. This was the way to get a good government. He was indifferent how the executive should be chosen, provided he held his place by that tenure.

Mr. Broome highly approved the motion. It obviated all his difficulties.

Mr. Sherman considered such a tenure as by no means safe or admissible. As the executive magistrate is now [by a vote just taken] rendered re-eligible, he will be on good behaviour as far as will be necessary. *If he behaves well, he will be continued*; if otherwise, he will be displaced on a succeeding election. [How entirely this expectation was disappointed has been shown by subsequent events]

Mr. Madison was not apprehensive of being thought to favour any step towards monarchy. The real object with him was to prevent its introduction. Experience had proved a tendency in our Government to throw all power into the legislative vortex. The executives of the State are in general little more than cyphers The Legislatures were *omnipotent*. If no effectual check be devised for restraining the instability and encroachments of the latter, a revolution of some kind or other would be inevitable.

Mr Gouverneur Morris was as little a friend to monarchy as any man. He concurred in the opinion that the way to keep out monarchical government was to establish such a republican government as would make the people happy, and prevent a desire for change.

Dr. McClung was not so much afraid of the shadow of monarchy as to be unwilling to approach it; nor so wedded to republican government as not to be sensible of the tyrannies that had been and may be exercised under that form. He desired that the executive should hold his office 'during good behaviour.'

On the question for inserting 'good behaviour' in place of 'seven years,' New Jersey, Pennsylvania, Delaware, and Virginia, four, voted 'Aye.' Massachusetts, Connecticut, Maryland, North Carolina, Georgia, and South Carolina, six, voted 'No.'

After long discussion it was decided that the election of a President should neither be made by the general Congress nor by the people. It will be necessary to my purpose to make only a brief reference to the various means suggested to attain the end proposed:—

Mr. Gerry, of Massachusetts, urged the expediency of the appointment of the executive by *electors to be chosen by the State executors* (that is, the governors of the several States). The people of the States would, he said, by this means choose the first branch of Congress, the Legislatures of the States the second branch, and the governors of the States the national executive. This he thought would form a strong attachment in the States to the national system. The popular mode of electing the chief magistrate would be the worst of all If he should be so elected, and should do his duty, he would be turned out for it.

Mr. Ellsworth, of Connecticut, moved that the President should be chosen by electors appointed by the Legislatures of the several States.

Mr. Williamson, of North Carolina, had no great confidence in electors to be chosen for the special purpose. They would not be the most respectable citizens, but persons not occupied in the high offices of the Government. He was for a long term. If the elections are too frequent, the best men will not undertake the service, and those of an inferior character would be liable to be corrupted.

Mr. Wilson, of Pennsylvania, moved, 'That the executive be chosen by electors *to be taken by lot* from the National Legislature, who shall proceed immediately to the choice of the executive, and shall not separate until it be made.

Another great point of difference was in regard to the unity of the executive head:—

Mr. Randolph, of Virginia, strenuously opposed an union in the executive ministry. He regarded it as the fœtus of monarchy He had, he said, no motive to be governed by the example of the British Government as our prototype He did not mean, however, to throw censure upon that excellent fabric. If we were in a situation to copy it, he did not know that he should be opposed to it; but the fixed genius of the people of America required a different form of government. He could not see why the great requisites for the executive department could not be found in three men as well as in one man

Mr Wilson, of Pennsylvania, said that unity in the executive, instead of being the fœtus of monarchy, would be the best safe guard against tyranny. He repeated that he was not governed by the British model, which was inapplicable to the condition of this country—the extent of which was so great, and the manners so republican, that nothing but a great confederated republic would do for it.

Mr. Dickinson, of Delaware, said: In the British Government the weight of the executive arises from the attachment which the Crown draws to itself, and not merely from the force of its prerogatives. In place of these attachments we must look out for something else. One source of stability is the double branch of the Legislature. The division of the country into distinct States formed the other principal source of stability. This division ought, therefore, to be maintained. This was the ground of his consolation when contemplating the probable future fate of his country. Without this, and in case of a consolidation of the States into one great republic, we might read its fate in the history of smaller ones. If ancient republics have been found to flourish for a moment only, and then vanish for ever, it only proves that they were badly constituted, and that we ought to seek for every remedy for their diseases. One of these remedies he conceived to be *the accidental lucky division of this country into distinct States*. A limited monarchy he conceived to be *one* of the best governments in the world: it was not certain that the same blessings were derivable from any other form. It was certain that equal blessings had never yet been derived from any of the republican forms. A limited monarchy, however, was in America out of the question. The spirit of the times, the state of our affairs, forbid the experiment if it were desirable. Was it possible, moreover, in the nature of things to introduce it, if even these obstacles were less insurmountable? A house of nobles was essential to such a government: could they be created by a breath or by a stroke of the pen? No! they were the growth of ages, and could only exist under a complication of circumstances, none of which exist in this country; but though a form of government, the most perfect in itself, be unattainable, we must not despair.

The venerable Dr. Franklin moved that what related to the compensation of the *executive* be postponed, in order to substitute—'whose necessary expenses shall be defrayed, but who shall receive no salary, stipend, fee, or reward whatsoever for their services':—

Sir (said he), there are two passions which have a powerful influence on the affairs of men. These are ambition and avarice—the love of power and the love of money. Place before the eyes of men a post of honour, that shall be at the same time a place of *profit*, and many will move heaven and earth to obtain it. The vast number of such places it is that renders the British Government so tempestuous. The struggles for them are the true source of all those factions which are perpetually dividing that nation, distracting its councils, hurrying it sometimes into fruitless and mischievous wars, and often compelling a submission to dishonourable terms of peace. And of what kind are the men who will strive for this profitable preeminence through all the bustle of cabal, the heat of contention, the infinite mutual abuse of parties tearing to pieces the best of characters? It will not be the wise and moderate, the lovers of peace and good order, the men fittest for the trust. It will be the bold and the violent—the men of strong passions and indefatigable activity in their selfish pursuits. These will thrust themselves into your Government and be your rulers; and they, too, will be mistaken in the reputed happiness of their situation: for their vanquished competitors, of the same spirit and from the same motives, will be perpetually endeavouring to distress their administration, thwart their measures, and render them odious to the people

The proposition of the venerable sage was treated, says Mr. Madison, with great respect, but rather out of consideration for the author of it than from any apparent conviction of its expediency or practicability. Though it may be said that he mistook the remedy for the evil to which he referred, yet experience has shown that he had a prophetic perception of the disease which would finally destroy the fabric of the Union.

The manner of choosing the President, as finally prescribed by the Convention, and modified by a subsequent amendment, was as follows:—

ARTICLE II. SECTION 1. The executive power shall be vested in a President of the United States of America He shall hold his office for four years. . . .

2. Each State shall appoint, in such manner as the Legislature thereof may direct, a number of electors equal to the whole number of senators and representatives to which the State may be entitled in Congress. The third clause provides for the manner in which the votes of the electors in the different States shall be transmitted to the President of the Senate, and also for the manner of choosing a President. If a majority of the electors should not vote for one person, in that event, 'from the persons having the highest number, not exceeding three, on the list of those voted for as President, the House of Representatives shall choose immediately by ballot the President; but, in choosing the President, the vote shall be taken by States—the representatives from each State having one vote.'

From the foregoing extracts from the proceedings of the Convention we deduce the fact that the clause just recited was acquiesced in as a settlement of a difficult point, rather than approved as an original proposition. It ended a most perplexing source of dissonance in the opinions of the members, but it does not seem to have been in accordance with the first preference of any. Still they believed it to be more conservative than in practice it turned out to be. They doubtless thought that it would protect the sovereignity of the individual States, and in furtherance of this purpose they gave to the States the privilege of making known their preference in regard to the presidency in such manner as they might themselves direct. They did not even advise the States to submit the decision to the popular vote. Still, in practice, the choice of the President was after the lapse of a few years submitted to a direct vote of the people in every State of the Union. except South Carolina. This State never did depart, in practice, from the spirit of the Constitution, but continued to the last to confide the choice of presidential electors to the Legislature. Consequently South Carolina was exempt from those periodical popular excitements which so often disturbed the tranquillity of the other States. For this cause, more than perhaps for any other, she was hated by the radicals of the North, and bitterly reproached for her persistence in such an 'aristocratic mode of electing the President;' but the great body of the citizens seemed too happy in their exemption from the evils which such excitements produced in the other States to have any desire to change their system.

It would appear, moreover, that the authors of the Constitution had a clear perception of the danger of convulsing the nation every four years by a popular contest for the important office of chief magistrate. They endeavoured, by the agency of an electoral college, to provide a remedy which might at least break the force of its influence upon the popular mind, and I may add the public morals. But for the evidence which has been left upon record, that they entertained little doubt in regard to the efficacy of the provision, we could scarcely credit the fact that so wise a body of statesmen could have been so thoroughly deceived in regard to the result. But it is certain that even those who had the least confidence in the system of popular elections did not perceive that the Electoral College would become a nullity.

Alexander Hamilton himself, if not satisfied with the result, supported it after its adoption with all his influence. In advocating afterwards the merits of the Constitution, while urging its adoption and ratification by the States, he wrote (see 'Federalist'):—

> It was desirable that the sense of the people should operate in the choice of the person to whom so important a trust as the presidency was to be confided. This end will be answered by committing the right of making it, not to any preestablished body, *but to men chosen by the people for the special purpose*, and at the particular juncture. It was equally desirable that the immediate election should be made by men most capable of analysing the qualities adapted to the station, and acting under circumstances favourable to deliberation, and to a judicious combination of all the reasons and inducements that were proper to govern the choice. A small number of persons selected by their fellow-citizens from the general mass will be most likely to possess the information and discernment requisite to so complicated an investigation. It was also peculiarly desirable to afford as little opportunity as possible to tumult and disorder, but the precautions which have been so happily concerted in the system under consideration promise an effectual security against this mischief. The choice of *several* to form an intermediate body of electors will be much less apt to

convulse the community with any extraordinary or violent movements than the choice of *one*, who was himself to be the final object of the public wishes. . . Without corrupting the body of the people, the immediate agents in the election will at least enter upon the task far from any sinister views. Their transient existence and their detached situation afford a satisfactory prospect of their continuing so to the conclusion of it. This process of election affords a moral certainty that the office of president will seldom fall to the lot of any man who is not in an eminent degree endowed with the requisite qualification. It will not be too strong to say that there will be a constant probability of seeing the station filled by characters prominent for ability and virtue.

Without multiplying evidences of the opinions of 'the republican fathers,' touching the general subject we have been considering, it is clear that if the American people take their example as a guide, or if they really entertain that veneration and respect for their wisdom which they profess, they will speedily abandon a system of electing their presidents in a manner so opposed in practice to the unanimous judgment of the framers of the Constitution. They believed that they had provided a remedy against the evils of popular commotions by the interposition of the College of Electors. Yet, notwithstanding their sanguine hopes and expectations, experience soon demonstrated that this was the fatal error of their great work. Even though its provisions had been carried out in good faith, if the plain intent and meaning had not been set at nought, it still involved in practice a clear violation of the fundamental principle of equal state sovereignty, which was the corner stone of the Constitution; and the preservation of which was essential not only to the perpetuation of the Union, but to the security of liberty. Nevertheless, the provision in regard to the electors was, as already stated, in effect a dead letter. The forms were complied with, but its spirit was utterly perverted; presidential electors were chosen by the people in due form of law, but they were not permitted to assume the functions of a deliberative body. They did not sit in judgment and decide upon the relative merits of the different aspirants for the presidency. They elected the presidents, but simply as agents appointed to register the edicts of the people. They were mere clerks who were called upon to do a certain thing, under specific instructions from their employers. The people, or more properly the managing party politicians, put up a candidate for the presidency, and then electors were chosen who were pledged, in advance of their appointment, to vote only for the individual previously selected by the nominating party convention. This vocation required the exercise of no judgment, no deliberation nor discretion, but simply fidelity in doing the particular thing in the particular manner pointed out by their employers. In truth, the announcement of the result of the contest for electors was the announcement of the name of the successful candidate for the presidency, although the form, or rather the farce, of a subsequent election by the Electoral College was a necessary antecedent to the entrance of the new chief upon the discharge of his official functions.

Thus the election of a President was, in fact, accomplished sometimes by a majority, sometimes by a plurality, of the people of the States, but always in undisguised contempt of the plain spirit and intent of the Constitution—a dangerous and demoralising practice, which soon familiarised the public mind with the contemplation of still more fatal inroads, both upon the letter and spirit of the fundamental requirements of the compact of the Union. Thus, too, was created a fatal antagonism and a perpetual conflict between the theory and the practice of the Government. Thus the sovereignty of the States, the great conservative palladium of constitutional liberty, was, in effect, merged into that of the people of the States as a unit; and the check of the one upon the other, which pervaded every other provision of the Federal compact, was practically annulled. Thus did the American people pursue the fatal policy of cheating the Constitution, and cheating the States composing the Confederacy, until finally, as in the instance of Mr. Lincoln's election, they cheated themselves by placing a President in power, in direct violation of their own will as expressed at the ballot-box.

But greater even than the material injuries inflicted was the moral influence of these elections upon the popular mind. A majority, without reference to qualifications or integrity, or honesty, was endowed with the prerogative of conferring supreme power. The people were taught to accept the expression of the will of the majority as the will of Omnipotence. The voice of the people, thus announced, was the will of God. Constitutional limitations were considered as unwise and unjust restrictions upon the prevailing popular sentiment, and politicians and place-seekers more or less boldly or covertly announced the doctrine that the will of the people, as expressed by a majority, or even scruples of conscience in regard to certain constitutional obligations, justified a violation of the oaths of office which the elected official was required to take on entering upon the discharge of his duties.

The demoralising influence of the system became more and more apparent as we receded from the days of Washington and the men of the Revolution. It is true that the violence and rancour of party spirit displayed itself at a very early period; but each party had its adherents in every State. They were not bounded by geographical lines, but by political principles, by measures of public policy, or by personal predilections.

There was exhibited in these party contests much bitterness, often coarseness, but rarely the reckless frivolity which attended the later struggles between individuals and parties. If they wrangled about the possession of power, they at least brought forward their greatest men to lead them.

As time passed away, however, the presidential contests degenerated more and more upon every recurring election into mere scrambles of office-seekers and run-mad extremists and radicals in religion and politics. The nation became divided, as it were, into hostile camps, acting upon the principle that 'all is fair in war which wins,' and each led by chiefs who stimulated their followers to desperate efforts, by the unblushing announcement that 'to the victors belong the spoils.' The people were, in effect, taught by their accepted leaders that the only legitimate object to be attained by the election of a President was to open the way to office for his adherents, and to enable them to lay hands upon the public treasure. Under such circumstances, it soon became impossible to elect a President for a second term, because the 'outs,' who were looking forward eagerly to the enjoyment of places and spoils, were numbered by hundreds of thousands, while the 'ins' could only be counted by thousands.

The result of an election did not possess, however, the merit of representing the will of a majority of the people; for, as the Constitution had been cheated by the abrogation of the duties appertaining to the Electoral College, so in turn were the people cheated by the party politicians and place-seekers, who usurped the prerogative of naming the candidates of their own selection. The people were virtually obliged to accept, and adopt, and elect, those only who were appointed to be candidates by irresponsible, irregularly-constituted 'conventions,' composed for the greater part of the most selfish, the most corrupt, and the least trustworthy citizens. These assumed to themselves this duty, or privilege, without being subjected to any legal restraints, and, we may fairly conclude, in a majority of cases for the sole purpose of compassing their own private purposes.

It is only necessary to consider somewhat in detail the progressive steps which finally conducted the obscure or the distinguished citizen, whichever it was thought would for the moment best answer the ends of the party, to the high position of chief executive officer of the Republic, to satisfy the intelligent mind that sooner or later the Government would be obliged to succumb under the pressure of such a great and frequently-recurring evil.

CHAPTER IV.

PARTY CONVENTIONS — THEIR ORIGIN — THEIR AGENCY IN MAKING THE PRESIDENT—THEIR USES, AND THEIR ABUSES

IT is more easy to comprehend the good or evil of a system of government by noting the stages of its actual development in practice, than by abstract reasoning founded upon general principles. The latter sometimes leads to correct conclusions; the former, always. It is a sage axiom, often employed by American politicians, that 'Power is always stealing from the many to the few.' Certainly the truth of the aphorism has never been more fully verified than in the late Federal Union, if we regard the monosyllable 'few' as a relative term employed in contradistinction to the multitudes who, in theory, were the custodians of the powers of the Government. No nation of the world, having the semblance of a constitution, was ever so completely subjected to the despotic rule of the few as the late United States of America. Unhappily, it may be added, that, as a rule, though they always professed to govern in the name of the people, there was no element in the character of those who thus usurped the powers of the many which commended them to the full confidence or regard of any other citizens than those composing the faction to which they belonged.

Foremost amongst the appliances which were set in motion to achieve this purpose were the party conventions. They were unknown to the Constitution; yet by these caucuses the Government of the United States was kept in motion. They were, of a truth, a power behind the Throne, greater than the Throne. They had more influence in managing the affairs of Government than the Congress, whose policy they dictated, or even the people, in whose name and in obedience to whose prerogative of sovereignty they professed to act. They were greater than the President, for they made him, and, before confiding into his hands the reins of government, they dictated the policy of his administration, and obtained his solemn promise to carry out the programme to the very letter.* They were a great but an unavoidable evil growing out of the system for which there was no antidote. They usurped all power, and, though they were known to be usurpers, there was no practicable resource against submission to their authority. They constituted an irresponsible despotism, for whose crimes no punishment could be inflicted; but the alternative of repudiating their acts was anarchy. All the world bowed to their dictation, because to rebel was to lag behind in a

* A forcible illustration of the despotic influence exercised by party conventions over the President may be found in the published Messages of Mr. Lincoln, when he was confronted with the reality of secession and the alternative of war. When urged to pursue a policy of peaceful conciliation, he always replied, in effect, 'I cannot depart from the plain letter and spirit of "the Chicago Platform." I am bound by a solemn pledge to carry out its doctrines, and I would be a dishonoured man were I to violate its requirements. Come what may, the Chicago Platform must be the rule of my actions.'

powerless minority, while those who submitted marched on to victory. In the very nature of things, it was impossible to dispense with them; and yet, to yield up cherished partialities or honest convictions at their command was one of the least of the evils connected with the system.

They were a consequence, flowing naturally and unavoidably from the system of electing Presidents by the popular voice, over such a great number of States of diversified interests, pursuits, and tastes. By no other means could the strength of a party contesting for the presidency be concentrated. There was a natural tendency among the people to divide into two parties. There were sometimes third parties; but the great mass of men prefer to be the real contestants for political power. Hence we find from the beginning of the Government two great parties. One of these parties, in order to settle the rival claims of different aspirants, calls a convention of its friends, to decide which one shall receive the support of the party. If they divide their votes amongst a number of their adherents they will suffer defeat. Rather than submit to this, the people prefer to submit to the dictation of a convention, which is informally invested with the power to decide upon the merits and availability of the respective claimants. One party having nominated a single candidate, and agreed to give him an undivided support, what must their adversaries do? Give up the contest, by supporting each one his own particular favourite? There would be no necessity for going to the polls under such circumstances. Defeat would be inevitable. There is no help for it.

They, too, must call a 'convention.' The delegates meet, and there decide upon the man who is to be—who must be—chosen by the people as the President. We may denounce conventions as incompatible with 'our birthright of sovereignty.' We may prove that by such a system the ruler of a great nation is, in effect, chosen by an irregularly-constituted caucus, called together without the authority or the restraint of law; but no man in the United States may ever hope to cast his vote for the successful contestant unless such candidate has passed the ordeal of a 'National Convention.'

It was a long time before the people would submit quietly to such an infringement upon what they were at the same time taught to believe were their prerogatives. They always had a vague perception of the truth that it virtually took the election of President out of their hands; and a suspicion, amounting almost to conviction, pervaded the better informed, that they had not surrendered their high privilege into trustworthy hands. They grumbled, rebelled in fact—caused two elections to be thrown into the House of Representatives—became disgusted with that mode of solving the difficulty, and, being obliged to choose between two bad systems, at last adopted the Convention as the least of two very enormous evils. It is difficult to discover in what manner they could have done better, although it would not be easy to tell how they could have done worse. It was a cruel mockery, under such circumstances, to tell the people (meaning the great body of citizens) that they were the real sovereigns of the Republic; and it is still more incomprehensible that they should have credited so transparent a fallacy, and have clung with such tenacity to a system which not only made them mere puppets, but which virtually conferred all power upon the very class who, of all other citizens, were least to be trusted.

Let us now glance at the process by which the Convention was brought into being.

At least two years before the period of an election, the party leaders begin to shuffle the political cards for a new deal. The opposition to the ruling party is joined by the disappointed politicians and office-seekers, who have made up their minds to go over to the enemy; and the incumbents of stations, high and low, beginning to feel uneasy and insecure, in view of the brief and feeble tenure by which they hold their places, are also on the alert. The contest for a year longer is kept up by secret caucuses, management, and intrigue. At this early period none of the factions dare openly to announce the names of their favourites. If they should be so rash, whatever might be their merits as men or as politicians, long before the day of nomination arrived their characters would have been so picked to pieces, and their real or assumed weak points so thoroughly exposed by their adversaries, that they would be sure to be rejected by their partisans as 'unavailable candidates.'

It may be here stated that, in the later days of the Confederation, the actual occupant of the presidential office, long before that epoch of the 'canvass' of which I now speak, would have rendered himself so odious to his own party, by his 'very injudicious and improper appointments to office,' that his name would be rarely spoken of as an aspirant to be his own successor, except by those who wished to ridicule his pretensions. In the early days of the Republic, a President was almost always chosen for a second time. In fact, all the Presidents, except the two Adamses, up to 1837, served two terms. But it was at last decided to be of evil influence, and exceedingly inconvenient to outside expectants, to retain Presidents in office for so very long a period, and it was never done from that date.

At the stage of the proceedings referred to there are two important points for the attainment of which the leaders of the numerous factions embraced within the great parties labour night and day. They are most difficult of accomplishment, as may well be imagined, for they involve at the same time the disclosure and the concealment of the name of the candidate they propose to bring before the Convention.

First, by private correspondence, and by the employment of such other appliances as may serve to aid them in their plans, they seek to secure the co-operation of prominent local politicians throughout the various States; and secondly, to keep back the name of their favourite from the great body of the people. The last is important, for reasons already stated, and the first from considerations which will readily suggest themselves, when we consider the process by which the 'National Nominating Convention' is brought into being.

About six months before the stated period of election, some irregularly—sometimes self-constituted bodies—such, for example, as the 'Central Committees' in the several States—announce through the newspapers that upon a certain day, and at a place named—generally the State Capitol—there will be held a State Convention of the representatives of the people, for the purpose of nominating delegates to the National Convention, which is to assemble two or four months thereafter, 'to discharge the high and responsible duty of nominating a candidate to be supported (by the party calling the convention) at the approaching presidential election.'

The next step follows soon upon the heels of this. The local newspapers of the various electoral districts call upon the people to assemble at some central town, in order to comply with the requisition of the central committee. The appointed day arrives. A few of the initiated leaders, together with a smaller number of really earnest patriots, interspersed with stragglers attracted by curiosity, assemble in the public hall. The number present is quite small. The people are not sufficiently excited at this early period to quit their avocations in order to join in this seemingly unimportant service. Those who are present, however, organise the meeting by the appointment of a president, a vice-president, and a secretary. After a short pause, some gentleman rises, and, having delivered 'a few eloquent and appropriate remarks,' proposes that Messrs. A. B., C. D., and others, be appointed to represent the people of that district in the State Convention. The proposition is seconded and carried *nem. con.*, and the meeting is adjourned *sine die*. Thus ends the 'primary convention,' and here closes the agency of the people in the selection of a candidate for the presidency. Henceforth, they have no other duty or privilege than to do as they may be commanded. With thirty millions of people from whom to choose their ruler—as they say—behold the 'sovereigns of America,' not only virtually denied a voice in the matter, but obliged to adopt and register their votes for the one man who may be suggested to them by others!

At the appointed time, the delegates thus chosen assemble at the respective State Capitols. At this stage the plots and counterplots begin to manifest themselves more palpably to outsiders. After the organisation is completed, numerous discourses are pronounced, in which the speakers declare that their adversaries are hurrying the country on the road to ruin, and proclaim that there is but one means left open to avoid such a catastrophe; that is, of course, to place their party in power. At length delegates are chosen to represent the State in the 'grand National Convention' of the party. It is perhaps needless to add that the 'wire-workers' employ great activity in securing the appointment of such persons as will support the man of their choice for the Presidency. Thus ends the 'State Convention.'

At last the great day arrives for fighting the battle for the candidacy in the National Convention, preliminary to the final struggle before the people. Delegates from all the States assemble, and, if they represent the stronger party, the result of their deliberations will decide who is to be the President, although they will shift the responsibility upon the shoulders of the people, who can alone give legal effect to their proceedings. Vast crowds of anxious citizens follow in their wake, to mingle as outsiders and lobby members in the exciting contest. Then comes the tug of factions. The names of statesmen and distinguished citizens are sometimes presented by earnest and sincere patriots; but the very prominence to which they have attained by means of their superior abilities constitutes an almost insuperable barrier to their success. These are, for the most part, summarily rejected, upon the ground that they have had a public career, and hence it might be troublesome satisfactorily to explain or define some of their acts. There may be also another reason for the indisposition to adopt them as candidates. Such men are rarely willing to bargain away the offices and the spoils, even to secure the countenance and support of the multitudinous place-seekers. There is sound philosophy, however, in the opposition of the partisans to the selection of a citizen who has already been for a long period of time before the public. His history is already known; and however brilliant may have been his past political career, however important a part he may have enacted, there are of course some weak or assailable points in his character. The greater his pretensions and fame, the more likelihood there is that the contest before the people will be made to turn upon the personal merits of the candidate rather than upon the party or sectional issues prepared and set forth by the professional politicians. His party, instead of being the assailants, are kept constantly upon the defensive. This position has been found to be even more untenable in politics than in war; and hence in modern times the rule has been, with rarely-occurring exceptions, to consider great qualities and a long public service as a bar to the presidency. The fact has been a source of deep regret and mortification; but, like the conventions themselves, it was deemed an unavoidable evil, growing spontaneously out of the system. This may be said to a certain extent to have been the policy of all parties, but, for the reason that the radicalism existing in the United States was, on account of certain local or special causes, more characteristic of the Northern than of the Southern States, I will assume that the Convention whose proceedings we are now considering is the representative of the Northern sectional party.

The political drama progresses. The various cliques establish 'club-rooms,' in which, during the recesses of the Convention, they assemble to discuss the probabilities growing out of 'the situation.' Here propositions for compromise are made, bargains are proposed, agreements are entered into, and the principle upon which diverging interests may be adjusted and harmonised are laid down, and accepted or rejected according as the terms offered coincide with the relative strength and importance of the factions. Again the Convention assembles, and the balloting is recommenced. The excitement grows apace; and as the uncertain contest progresses, the interest increases to an absorbing passion. All is noise, bustle, confusion. Anxiety is depicted upon every countenance, and an accession of strength to a candidate from among the wavering or the indifferent, or the development of an agreement entered into at the 'club-room,' by which a large accession of strength is added to the supporters of a particular candidate, is received with loud cheers of approbation upon the one side, and murmurs and hisses upon the other.

By means of the telegraphic wires, the varying fortunes of the day are flashed to every town and city throughout the country. The excitement within the hall of the Convention itself is now scarcely greater than that which pervades every class and occupation of the people. Every avenue of approach to the telegraph offices is crowded to suffocation with eager citizens, who shout back the news to those who are unable to get within reach of the bulletin board. The whole American people are now aroused; and no subjects of a royal line of kings in danger of becoming extinct ever listened with more eagerness for the first gun which announces the birth of a hoped-for prince than they to the voice of that caucus to which they have transferred the right of appointing their chief ruler.

And well may the people feel a degree of excitement in awaiting the momentous announcement. At all times it has been a deeply interesting event, but now a hundred fold more absorbing, because, in all human probability, he who will be then appointed to be the future President will become the commander-in-chief of an army whose mission it will be to lay waste the homes of millions of those who are now awaiting the announcement of his name, and to spill the life's blood of many tens of thousands of the noblest citizens of the Republic. The people whose liberties are thus menaced on both sides of the dividing line, and before whom the place-hunters of the Convention bow down and worship with the self-abasement and apparent devotion of Eastern courtiers, can only look on from without! For less than a mess of pottage they have given up their boasted birthright!

It would be profitless to record in detail all the incidents which fill up the interval between the opening and the close of the deliberations of the caucus. They may be readily imagined by considering the materials of which the body is composed, and the grave interests which are involved in the final result of their deliberations. At an earlier or a later period, depending upon the obstinacy with which the friends of the different candidates adhere to their favourites, some one receives the requisite majority of votes A resolution is then offered, and adopted by a majority, declaring that the fortunate individual is 'unanimously accepted and nominated as the candidate' of their party for the office of the presidency; and the nominee may from that instant consider himself to be the heir apparent to the throne of the Great Republic. Three times three noisy huzzas welcome the advent of the incipient sovereign.

'Who the devil is he, anyhow?' asks an intelligent and anxious lobby member, in whispered though excited accents, of his nearest neighbour.

'Oh! Do n't you know him?' responds the questioned individual, with a beaming and satisfied expression of countenance. 'He is justly regarded as one of the most promising and prominent men in his neighbourhood!'

'But how are his antecedents? Are they of the right kind? Are they of a character to satisfy the "sovereigns"?'

'Splendid! Magnificent! Glorious! They could n't

possibly be better,' responds the well-informed gentleman.

'Yes, yes; there is no doubt of that: but what are they?'

'*He has n't any*! The Convention could not possibly have hit upon a more available standard-bearer for our great and glorious party!'

'Capital! capital! Thank Heaven,' murmurs the now satisfied enquirer. 'We 'll be able to put him through to the White House despite the machinations of our wicked spoils-seeking adversaries; and the country will be saved,' he adds, with an earnestly patriotic intonation, accompanied by a moistening of the eyes, and a convulsive grasp of his neighbour's hand.

These evidences of patriotic weakness are soon, however, displaced by a movement which indicates that something important is about to be said or done, and in common with the vast crowd of spectators he turns his eyes and his thoughts upon the floor of the Convention.

The shouts, the cheers, the buzz, and the murmurs which followed the important announcement have subsided. All eyes are turned in the direction of a gentleman, a bosom friend and companion of the nominee, who rises to thank the Convention in the name of his absent friend and fellow-citizen for the 'distinguished and unsolicited honour which had been by their action bestowed upon one of the purest patriots and most eminent statesman of this or any other age.' A highly wrought and elaborately prepared eulogy is pronounced by the orator, in which he traces the history of the future President from the cradle to the present day. Not the least interesting among the characteristic incidents of his life are those concerning his early years, when he was distinguished above all the stalwart youths of his native country as 'an unrivalled "rail-splitter!"'

'In fact,' continues the orator, warming with his subject; 'only a little more than a year ago, our candidate—What did I say? Our next President (loud cheers)—he, who in the Providence of Heaven and by the fiat of the American people will be shortly called to fill the most exalted station ever occupied by man upon the green surface of God's footstool (tumultuous and long continued applause), having been informed that a poor widow residing in his neighbourhood had met with the heavy misfortune of having had her fence burned to the ground, shouldered his axe, and marching straight into the forest, set to work, and scarcely paused to take a long breath until he had actually split two hundred rails, which he forthwith caused to be conveyed to the afflicted lady (immense sensation). I will not attempt,' he continues, 'to describe the joy and gratitude which penetrated the bosom of that bereaved and almost heart-broken lady, when the generous and noble action was made known to her. But the monarch who vainly seeks beneath his golden canopy a feverish rest, to fit him for the joyless pageantry of the morrow, might well envy the peaceful slumbers and the happy dreams which we may suppose welcomed our future President to his humble couch upon the night of that most memorable day.'

After a pause of sufficient duration to allow

order to be restored, the audience having given vent to their feelings upon the conclusion of the foregoing narrative by long continued and spontaneous bursts of applause, the orator continues in something like the following strain:—'My fellow-countrymen, what a glorious spectacle is presented to mankind this day by this august Convention of the delegates of the real people, the bone and sinew of our magnificent Republic. What a sensation will it create among the monarchs and their courtiers, as well as among the down-trodden millions of the Old World, when they receive the momentous intelligence that he who will soon be the greatest and the loftiest of all earthly rulers has been selected from amongst the sturdy hard-fisted wood-choppers of the back woods of the Far West! (great applause). But, my friends,' he continues, in a more subdued tone, 'we should look more in pity, than in anger or exultation, upon the rest of the unhappy human family who, ground down under the iron heel of ruthless despotisms, may scarcely dare to hope for the dawning of that auspicious day when they, too, may have the honour of being ruled over by a statesman springing directly from the very humblest ranks of the people. But in the midst of our exultation it may not be unprofitable for us to cast our eyes back over the history of our own country during the dark period of the last few years, and survey the frightful abyss which through the misrule of the corrupt faction which has so long governed this great country yawned before us!

'Yes, my countrymen, we have passed through a long and heart-rending season of gloom, in the midst of which the stoutest hearts commenced to throb with painful apprehension, and many were ready to exclaim, "The Republic is lost." Even yesterday I confess that my own heart almost sank within me, when I remembered that the aristocratic slave oligarchy of the South still shared with us the management and control of this great and glorious land of the free and home of the brave. Now, how all is changed—peace, prosperity, happiness, and freedom for all, loom up before us, as one of the first results of the glorious work we have this day accomplished. This is the day of doom for the aristocrats. The nation speaks in thunder tones and says, "The encroachments of the slave power will no longer be endured." And though the battle may be fierce, as sure as election-day dawns, victory will perch upon our standard; while the high bird of liberty will scream through the air, bearing in its beak our glorious motto—*free soil, free homes, free speech, a free press, and free men!*'

'Wind up with free niggers,' shouts a jocose individual, in a voice loud enough to be heard above the din of approval which greeted the closing flight of the speaker. The suggestion is received with a round of laughter, in which the greater part of the audience as well as the members join.

'Do n't do any such stupid thing,' responds another in the same strain; 'coloured individuals have no votes in my State; and besides, the Northern sovereigns can swallow any other nauseous dose with fewer contortions of visage than free niggers.'

'You are quite right,' exclaims a third; 'say down with the slave-ocracy as much as you please;

but don't say up with the nigger, if you expect to get any white men's votes in my neighbourhood.'

The eulogy is finished, and other speakers have addressed the Convention in a somewhat similar strain; but the labours of that important body do not terminate with the nomination of a candidate. It is necessary that he and they should go before the country upon a 'platform.' The putting together of the 'planks' in such manner as will satisfy all the factions is a most difficult, delicate, and dangerous duty, and requires the exercise of the most consummate skill. It is an axiom of the old party-leaders that one may speak what he pleases, because what he says may be explained or denied; but he must beware of what he writes, for it remains a perpetual and unchangeable record against him. The Convention whose proceedings we are considering represents the 'outs,' and consequently their work is rendered more easy. They may find fault with all that has been done, or omitted to be done, in the past administration of the affairs of the Government. On other subjects, however, they are obliged to express themselves in such vague and ambiguous terms as will bear one interpretation where the measure is popular and another where it is unpopular. Upon the vexed question of the tariff upon foreign merchandise (the Convention being composed in part of Northern manufacturers and Western wheat-growers) they declare that the party entertains precisely the same views that it has hitherto announced. They are in favour of such a tariff of duties as will 'protect all the great interests of the country at large.'

Upon the eternal negro question they are not

restrained by any considerations of policy from the employment of the coarsest language of invective against the people of the South; for they do not expect or desire a single vote in a Slave State. This subject is the chief burthen of their platform. Maledictions and imprecations may be uttered without stint against the 'slave-ocracy,' for they do not thereby give offence to any one of their friends. They may indulge in the wildest flights of rhetorical denunciation, so that no word is whispered about elevating the free negroes of the Free States to a higher social and political status than they at present occupy. Their party supporters are even urged to give all needful encouragement to slave-stealers, and to make liberal contributions to the managers of the underground railroad. They may speak of welcoming the 'panting slave' under their hospitable roofs, always provided the occupant thereof is not denied the privilege of kicking him out of the house and beyond their State borders when he ceases to be a slave and becomes a 'free nigger.'

The platform generally winds up with a brief summary, couched in vague generalities, which closes the labours of the Convention. They announce that, if they are successful in obtaining the control of the Government, they will favour the adoption of a 'judicious tariff, a sound well-regulated currency, the dispensation of equal and uniform justice, economy in administering the affairs of the Government; and finally, that "whether successful or defeated," they will always cherish a lively sentiment of regard and sympathy for the people generally; but more especially for the hard-fisted yeomen, who till the soil or delve in the mines, and who they pronounce to be of all others the least fallible in their judgment, and hence the most competent to govern the State.'

One may smile while listening to the exaggerated language of adulation and flattery addressed to the multitude; and yet it is but the developement of a principle of man's nature. The American demagogue is governed by the same feelings or instincts, and adopts precisely the same means for the attainment of his purposes, as the devotee of royalty under other forms of government. He has a great favour to ask of his most gracious sovereign, which none but that sovereign can confer. He has fixed his heart upon the attainment of his object. His future prospects in life and his happiness depend upon his success. He prostrates himself before the only power which may dispense the favour he asks. Nor would it perhaps be altogether just to say that either the demagogue or the courtier is insincere in his professions of love, respect, and devotion to his sovereign; for there is a halo around the brow of him who holds supreme power, which to the eye of one whose life or prosperity depends upon his smiles, softens the most repulsive aspect—smoothes the wrinkles of age—makes a halting gait seem the perfection of grace—discovers in the dullest commonplace utterances the most brilliant sparks of genius and wit—and in all his acts and words the unerring marks of an enlightened statesmanship. Such are the relative positions of the dispensers and the would-be recipients of bounties the world over; and whether the sovereign be a single despot or a multitude, while the courtier and the demagogue may contest with each other the point of merit between their respective masters, neither can justly taunt the other for the exhibition of a subserviency which is alike common to both.

CHAPTER V.

COMPONENT PARTS OF A NORTHERN PRESIDENTIAL CONVENTION: PURITANS, ATHEISTS, SOCIALISTS, ABOLITIONISTS, ETC.

BEFORE adjourning *sine die* the Convention which has just completed its labours it may not be uninstructive to glance at the different elements of which it is composed. It is indeed a motley crowd, differing as widely in their occupations and pursuits in life, as in the objects for the attainment of which they have congregated. There is one point, and only one, upon which they all agree; and each is willing for the time being to forget all other differences, that by their united efforts they may prosecute to a successful end that one common object. They agree in the belief that the overthrow of the Southern States as an element of political power would promote their respective plans or interests. It may readily be conjectured that a majority of them look to this result only as a means by which they may obtain possession of the coveted places which are within the gift of the President. It would be a matter of extreme indifference to those whether they were upon a pro-slavery or an anti-slavery platform. All they want is to be on the highway which leads to power. The national party to which they are opposed is neither the one nor the other. The Free

States have the greatest number of votes, and hence the class of politicians to which I refer are 'anti-slavery.' The platform is constructed, therefore, in such manner as will be most popular in the North.

But it must not be supposed that there are not a number of delegates who are governed by other considerations than those named. There are earnest men there who do not seek any purely personal advantage. Slaves of a particular idea or an abstraction—their fanaticism stimulated and kept at fever heat by the often recurring presidential elections—they avail themselves of this means to secure political influence by making themselves a part of a great party. It serves at least to bring themselves, and often their ideas, into general notice.

Poverty, it is said, makes strange bed-fellows; but not less strange and incongruous are the associations which are created through the instrumentality of a Convention for the nomination of a President. There is scarcely a political, moral, or social theory of the radical school which is not represented by its advocates. Each is willing to concede everything which may be demanded by the others, provided it does not conflict with his own particular hobby. They do not come to this Convention to discuss the merits of their theories, but merely to combine as many as can agree upon a single point. The part enacted by the office-seeker, and the partisan politicians who care not a tittle as to what the platform contains, so it will have the effect of placing their party in power, we have already considered. We may also include within the number of these the 'Protectionists'—those who advocate high duties upon the imports of foreign merchandise, for the avowed purpose of 'protecting American industry against the pauper labour of Europe.' But all these may be appeased, at least for the moment. Give the one the place he seeks, and the other the protection he demands, and they would be quite content to see the slaves of the South doubled in number by fresh importations from Africa. Give them what they ask, and they have no inclination to trespass upon the rights or even the prejudices of others. The great difficulties have been that the offices are too few in number to satisfy all the claimants; and the creation of a high tariff only stimulates them to hope that, by perseverance, they may obtain a higher.

But, as I have said, there are others more honest—as the word goes, and therefore more intractable—more earnest, and therefore more formidable—more impracticable, and therefore more dangerous. Each is the advocate of a system founded upon a single sentiment. He has traced it all out according to mathematical rules. He has thought of it, dreamed of it, and brooded over it, until it has absorbed his whole soul. It constitutes his very existence. It is his God. Admit that he is right, and he may love you. Deny or oppose him, and he will hate you.

Behold the descendant of the Puritan! Two hundred years have wrought many changes in the moral, political, and social world. Kings have become plebeians, and plebeians kings. Empires have passed away, and others have been created. Old systems have been superseded by new ones, and whether or not the world has grown better and wiser its whole aspect has been altered. But the Puritan of the type we are now considering has remained unchanged in the harsh features of his nature, however much he may have been obliged to yield to the force of public opinion in the outward manifestations of his ruling passion. He is no more a regicide, because in the land where his lot is cast there are no more kings to kill. He no longer drowns or burns witches, for his ancestors exterminated them long ago. He no longer buys and sells savages in order to 'bring them to a knowledge of the true and living faith,' for the last Indian of all the tribes which peopled the wilderness has perished before the unrelenting despotism which was enforced against them by his forefathers. He no longer hangs other Christians, nor inflicts upon them the more lenient chastisement of stripes and banishment, for non-conformity to his peculiar doctrines; but he would exterminate the Southerners with fire and sword, because they are not willing to submit to his dictation in the management of their domestic affairs. He would enslave, or if need be, slay twenty millions of freemen in order to confer upon four millions of Africans what he calls freedom; but he would re-enslave these again if they transgressed one jot or tittle of the moral law as expounded by himself.

He whom we are now considering is not only a parson—an 'expounder of God's word,' and a teacher of morals, but he is a politician. He does not preach to-day in the pulpit against the sins denounced by Christ and his apostles, and deliver a stump speech to-morrow upon the party politics of the day; but in either place and in all places he blends the duties of the two together. His sermon is always a political harangue, interlarded with phrases originating in the rum-shop — his political harangue a sermon abounding in scriptural quotations. He may only be properly described by the appellation of 'political parson.'

You search in vain over the lines of his strongly marked countenance, and gaze into his cold calm eye, to find some trace of human sympathy or of human weakness. His features are never relaxed into a smile, except when he contemplates the consummation of some event which would make others weep. He feels no sentiment of compassion for the slave, but he hates the master with all the ferocity of his nature. His brow grows darker when he is told that the African slave is happy and contented with his lot; but his soul is filled with a joy unspeakable as he listens to the recital of the bloody deeds of a John Brown; and he straightway falls upon his knees and gives thanks to God that 'he has vouchsafed to his servant this great boon.' You may respect him for the strong points in his character; but you would never seek to be his boon companion. He may excite an emotion of fear, but never a sentiment of love. Whether engaged in stealing slaves from the coast of Africa, or assassinating the white men to whom he sold them, for the sin of being slave-holders, he always professes to be 'doing his duty as a servant of the Lord.' When the work of the day is finished he sings a psalm, reads a chapter in the Bible, says a prayer, and retires to the enjoyment of tranquil slumbers.

He is the master spirit, not only of New England, but of the entire North. He is hated, but he is obeyed. He has but few followers out of the ranks of the strong (or weak) minded women, and no friends; but his iron will controls the multitude. He is often hissed, sometimes pelted from the lecture-hall, even by a Boston mob, yet they go to the polls and vote as he dictates. A public meeting of the citizens of Pennsylvania resolves that the North is not and will not be ruled over by the fanatical priest-politicians of New England; yet in the very agony of the effort to shake off the incubus of their influence their dominion is recognised and acknowledged. Professing to be guided in all things by the Word of God, he announces from the pulpit that a far better and more effectual moral agency than the Bible is the bullet or the dagger. Such is the man who sits calm and unmoved amid the crowd of excited office-seekers about him. He despises the selfish time-serving politicians by whom he is surrounded, but he accepts them as instruments necessary to the accomplishment of his purpose. Their thoughts are directed to the inauguration day, and the brighter days which will follow, during which their eyes will be blessed with a sight of that golden treasure which has so long eluded their grasp; or when they will fall heirs to those honours and distinctions which the possession of office and power always confer. His thoughts rest not for an instant upon these vain objects, but penetrate into that dark future which he hopes lies but a little way beyond. His soul revels in the anticipation of the glorious consummation which is to crown all his labours. When in the contemplation of the bloody butcheries and desolated homes of those whom it would seem in mere mockery he denominates his fellow-countrymen, he may lie down upon his bed and say, 'Oh, Lord, thy servant having finished his appointed work is now ready to die!' He looks forward to that epoch 'when the black man, with torch, and bayonet, and dagger, will make desolate the hearthstone, and leave in ashes the dwelling of the white man. When the conflagration of the homes of the Southern masters will be to the down-trodden the beacon light of liberty and regeneration. And,' he adds, in softened tone, and with upturned eye, 'though I may not laugh at their calamity, and mock when their fear cometh, yet I will hail the event as the dawning of a political millennium.'*

Sitting in close proximity to the New England Puritan may be seen another character no less earnest, no less fanatical, no less honest, and no less anxious to bring the South under subjection to his particular theory. He speaks with a strong foreign accent; but he is an American citizen. Despising the institutions of his native land, where men are born kings and nobles and plebeians, just five years and a day ago he placed his foot for the first time upon American soil in search of that social 'equality and fraternity' which had been the dream of his discontented life. He discovers that white men and black men occupy a different social rank, and that they are endowed with unequal political privileges.

* The expressions here quoted are derived from the speeches of Abolition orators The reader will find the substance of the above in the published speeches of Joshua R Giddings, a 'political parson,' who was during many years a member of Congress from Ohio He is now one of Mr. Lincoln's consuls in Canada.

He is disappointed, but the presidential election holds out to him the hope of regenerating and perfecting the Republic, so that in practice as in theory all men may be made equal. Though now assisting in making a President, he hopes in the end to abolish the presidency, because it assimilates to the kingly office of the Old World. He would also abolish the Senate, because he would simplify the Government in order that there might be no impediment to the prompt enforcement of the people's will.* But it is not alone upon the continent of America, or within the narrow boundaries of the great Republic, that he proposes to limit the developement of his idea. He desires to witness the establishment of a democratic power so great that it may be wielded for the regeneration of the whole world, but more especially for the overthrow of the Government of his fatherland. It is one of his most cherished doctrines that the mission of the Republic is to 'intervene in favour of all peoples who are struggling to be free.' It is not alone moral, but physical aid which he claims from the Republic for what he denominates the 'oppressed peoples and nationalities.' In short, the purpose nearest his heart is to employ the great Republic as an instrument for the regeneration of mankind, and the destruction of all government which is not founded upon the absolute power of the majority. But that majority must, nevertheless, be guided according to his theory. He has witnessed the hypocrisy and wickedness of priests and parsons, and he avenges himself against them by denying the truth

* See *Platform of the 'Free Germans,'* 'South Vindicated,' p. 75.

of the religion which they teach. He considers God a hobgoblin invented to frighten the timid, and he hates the Bible, because it does not teach what he denominates the creed of nature. He does not know the slave-holder, for he has never seen him; but he dislikes him because he believes that being a master he must be an aristocrat. He does not hate him, nor does he love the slave; but he would reduce the one to a level with the other, in conformity with the inexorable requirements of his theory. He contemns the Puritan with all his heart; he detests his cant, and denies the truth of his religion; but he consents to unite with him in supporting the same candidate for the presidency, because he believes that in the end it will be his doctrines that will acquire the ascendancy.

Nevertheless, it is not here, in the 'great council of the nation,' that he would proclaim outright his atheistical sentiments. Even his socialistic principles must be couched under the form of vague generalities; for were he in sober earnestness to claim an equality of political and social rights for the negroes of the North, he would not long be allowed to occupy the speaker's stand. In this Convention, as I have before said, the great point is to avoid the saying or doing anything that might be personally offensive to any of the various cliques or 'isms' into which society in the Free States is divided. That which may be done or said which is calculated to stimulate the passions, and especially the hatred of the people against the South, is welcome, because they do not expect to obtain a solitary vote south of the geographical line upon which their party is based. It is upon other fields and in other conventions, more local and special in their character, where the atheist and the socialist and the political parson give full and free expression to their sentiments.

The two characters which we thus find side by side in the Convention are the representatives of the two most powerful moral ingredients of which the Northern sectional party—now called the 'Republican' party—is compounded. To one unfamiliar with the influence and operation of an election of a new king for a great empire every four years such an association might seem unnatural and inexplicable. Even those who have watched most closely the progress of events in America cannot fail to be somewhat startled at such a conjunction when they are brought face to face with the seeming anomaly. The Puritan and the Atheist! The appointed and recognised teacher of God's Holy Word, and the scoffer at all things which the Christian holds most sacred, are sitting together in the same political body, harmonising their differences upon such minor points with a view to the accomplishment of a common purpose. The first proposes to deal out death to the slave-holder in this world, while he consigns him to the horrors of eternal punishment in the next—in obedience, he says, to the precepts and commands which he finds written in the Inspired Book. The other rejects and repudiates the Bible as an exposition of the Divine will, because he discovers in it the recognition and toleration of a principle that man may buy and sell his fellow-men, and hold them as a possession for ever. The former admits that to the natural eye and to the common sense this reading of the Scripture may seem to be the true one. But he thinks that during the period which was chosen by the Almighty in which to make known his commands to men it would have been imprudent to have communicated clearly his will in this particular, as it would have been in direct conflict with the prejudices and habits of God's chosen people, and might have driven them back to the worship of idols. The atheist responds, that if the Almighty Ruler of the world had made a revelation to man, He would have communicated His will without any fear of the consequences; and that He would not have left mankind in ignorance of the law for so many thousands of years—only to be enlightened at last, he might add, through the instrumentality of their passions or their personal interests, rather than their sober judgment. It is not my province here to settle the point in controversy: I leave that to their respective friends and followers.

This, however, is not the only point of difference. The one boasts of his descent from the 'Pilgrim Fathers,' who long years ago, from the heights around Plymouth Rock, looked abroad upon a vast wilderness of forest, which, hitherto undisturbed by the footsteps of civilised man, they could claim and occupy for themselves and their posterity for ever. The other did but yesterday, as it were, place his foot for the first time upon the shores of the New World. But in their characters the dissimilarities are not less striking than in the antecedents of their genealogy and history. The one is cold, calculating, and repulsive; the other is often generous, always genial. The one acts under the promptings of the darker passions and instincts of the soul; the other is directed, in part at least, by an exaggerated sentiment of love for all mankind. The one would always command; the other would sometimes persuade. The one would prefer to accomplish his purposes by harsh and cruel means; the other, who is ready to employ the same weapons, if occasion demands it, would not object to win his adversary by an appeal to reason. The one claims the right to enforce his laws upon the American continent, for the reason, amongst others, that his ancestors peopled the wilderness, and afterwards wrested it from the political dominion of a foreign potentate; the other rests his claim to be heard upon the broad principle that the law of nature has decreed a like interest for all mankind in the earth and its fruits; and that no man, or community, or state, may justly lay claim to any part thereof as his or their own exclusive property. The one would govern as a member of an isolated body, acting by Divine authority, as the peculiar exponent of the will of God; the other, as an atom in the family of man, regarded as a unit—as a child of the same first parent, who, though for a season despoiled of his rightful inheritance, has come not only to possess himself of that which has been unjustly withheld, but to enforce the recognition of the rights of other members of the human family, who do not know or have not the power to assert or to maintain their own claims. In fine, the one is the Marat in priestly robes; and the other the Anacharsis Clutz of the Republic.

There are other representatives of distinct ideas who do not usually play their parts upon so large a theatre. Individually they exercise but small influence except in isolated communities; but collectively their power is formidable.

See that thin-visaged nervous individual, sitting in a corner, from whence his eye wanders curiously, but with a gratified expression, over the scene before him. His plain drab coat, home-spun pantaloons, and yellow silk pocket-handkerchief give a quaint aspect to his general appearance, and attract towards him many a furtive glance, amidst the occasional pauses or during the dull harangues of some of his fellow members. It is not wonderful that he should become somewhat excited when he beholds that sea of human heads, which crowd to the point of suffocation every spot from whence may be heard and witnessed the proceedings of that body which has assembled from every part of the country; and who within a few brief hours will announce to the world the name of the next President of the United States of America. I say it is not strange that he should be excited by the scene, and that the big drops of perspiration should gather upon his forehead, for he has but just withdrawn himself for a brief space from the depths of a solitude where, during weary months, he had, in common with a number of other followers of the same idea, withdrawn from the gaze of the world. He is a member of a community of socialists, or 'Fourierites,' as they are sometimes denominated. It may be that one month before it had been his regular turn to serve as boot-black for his companions, the next week to be cook's assistant, and the week following to discharge the more arduous and delicate functions of chef de cuisine. It is possible that during the seven days which preceded his departure for the fulfillment of the service in which we now find him engaged he may have been permitted to play the part of gentleman for the society—to sit in the library and read the papers. He would be thus enabled to make some preparation for the performance of his duties as a delegate to the 'Grand National Council of the North.' He must make the most of this season of 'enjoyment,' for notwithstanding all his protestations of a desire to withdraw from the world and its pomps, it is easy to discover that he is for the moment the happiest man in the whole assemblage. Next week, by the laws of his community, it may be that his turn will have arrived to serve as man or rather maid of all work.

The 'idea' of the class of which this man is a representative is not altogether new in America, although older in Europe. According to the theory which has been developed from it, mankind ought to be divided into small distinct communities, living together and cultivating in common the same grounds, and sharing alike in the proceeds of their joint labour. To suppress even the germ of an aristocracy, they require each member by turns to perform all the menial offices of the association. Nothing is more natural than that they should sympathise with any movement having for its object the eradication of the social distinctions between the different races in the South. Strange as it may seem this idea has fixed itself in the minds and hearts of many men of intelligence in the North, and while repeated failures have opened the eyes of some, there are others who still adhere to it with all a father's fondness for his unworthy offspring.*

It would not be proper to overlook another remarkable individual of the motley assemblage, who is also both an actor and a spectator. He likewise is the representative of an 'idea,' the signification of which is properly explained by its title of '*Free Love.*' They mean precisely what these words import. They propose that the two sexes should only 'be united by the spontaneous action of their own free will,' and that, when united, 'they should be permitted to separate and form other similar connections if the old relation offered fewer attractions than the new one which suggests itself as a substitute.'

Let us not, even in thought, do injustice to the motives which prompt the adherents of this idea to break through the conventional trammels, called the marriage ties, which society and religion have enforced upon mankind. However misguided, like all the other fanatics with whom he is now acting, he is no doubt sincere, and—I was going to say honest, with a reservation and explanation—but instead, I will say unselfish. He who sits before us as the representative of 'free loveism' is an old man whose locks have been whitened by the frosts of three-score years and ten. He is bowed down by the infirmities of age, and his voice is tremulous when he speaks. He left a wife at home—an enthusiast like himself in the same cause—with whom he has lived in happy contentedness from early manhood. He has a kind

* The *New York Tribune*, edited by Horace Greeley, now the chief organ of the Republican party, has been the reputed organ of this peculiar phase of socialism.

benevolent aspect; but his eye is wandering and is a little brighter than men's are who do not brood much upon a single thought.

Peculiar circumstances have no doubt directed his mind to the consequences of ill-assorted matrimonial alliances. He has witnessed the unhappiness and misery which often result from the marriage relation, and he has set himself earnestly to work to correct or to eradicate the evil. He thinks that he has discovered the means, and all that remains for him to do is to induce mankind to adopt the scheme which he has devised. By a very natural community of ideas he finds himself a member of a Convention which has assembled for the purpose of dealing a death-blow to what he conceives to be the most formidable remnant of feudalism which yet lingers in the laws and customs of a number of the States of the American Confederacy.

It would seem invidious were I to close this reference to the incongruous atoms which compose the harmonious whole of a Northern nominating convention, were I to omit a brief notice of one who represents an idea which has shaken the foundations of Northern society to its very centre. He is a stout, robust gentleman, whose hair, sprinkled with occasional patches of grey, indicates that although he has passed the meridian of life, he is still in the full vigour of manhood. He speaks in a bold, resolute tone, except when the subject under consideration refers to that better half of creation most generally denominated by college youths and bachelors the 'gentler sex.' Upon such an occasion there is perceptible a slight tremulousness of voice and a lowering of the eye, and an abatement in the vehemence of his manner, which might tempt the close observer to believe that at home he was a hen-pecked husband. In fact, at the very moment of time when the Convention we are considering is occupied with its labours, there is another assemblage, in another city and in another State, whose members are derived chiefly from that growing class not inaptly denominated 'strong-minded women.'

The wife of our delegate is one of the leading members and orators. Her nether limbs are dressed in trousers of ample dimensions, and her scanty skirts scarce reach below her knees. It may be seen at a glance that she is not a ballet-dancer by the absence of the crinoline, if not by her unprofessional gait and rather Amazonian dimensions. She wears a rakish-looking head covering, resembling rather a gentleman's hat than a lady's bonnet, it being compounded of the two in somewhat unequal proportions. The coquettish style in which it is adjusted to its place is in striking contrast with the massive strongly-defined features of her by-no-means feminine countenance.

When she rises to address her audience her manner is not at all diffident, though by no means immodest. She speaks boldly and earnestly, and vehemently of the rights which are withheld from woman by the odious tyrant man, and of the wrongs which she is made to endure. Amongst the latter is the despotism which the husband is permitted by the laws to exercise over his wife; and amongst the former are the legal prohibitions against her voting in elections, or filling the post of foreign ambassadress, or a seat in

Congress, or even the office of Chief Magistrate of the Republic. She is always ready at repartee if any rude representative of the sterner sex should have the temerity to interrupt her by an impertinent question or remark; and though nothing could cause a blush to mantle her cheek, she leaves no impression upon the mind which would lead to the conclusion that she could by any possibility be anything else than an exemplary woman and wife. She is the type of a large and intelligent class of her countrywomen, distinguished as much for the cultivation of their minds as for the boldness and vigour of their assaults upon the most strongly-cherished principles, opinions, and customs of civilised nations.

But however potent her influence within a certain sphere, in shaking the foundations upon which society has been built, she is not yet permitted to sit as a delegate in a national presidential caucus. Hence we find her husband duly installed as the representative and advocate of 'woman's rights.' It is as easy to discover in his case, as in that of his colleagues to whom I have before referred, the sentiment common to all which has drawn him into that great vortex, entitled a national Convention for the nomination of a candidate for the presidency.

The assembly whose proceedings and whose members we have been considering has closed its labours never again to be resumed under like auspices. Forming only a section of that great Confederacy, they usurped the right to dictate laws and customs and even manners to the whole. They took their measures well, so far as they involved a triumph at the ballot-box over those whom they seemed resolved to destroy. It was not in the power of human reason to protect society against such an avalanche of cupidity, and madness, and folly, and fanaticism, uniting within itself so many opposing ingredients, but which adjourned all other differences, and combined and harmonised themselves into one compact mass for the accomplishment of a single purpose.

In the very act, and at the very instant of gaining all, they have lost all, and a similar body of men, acting as the representatives of the same constituency, and having in view the accomplishment of the same objects, will assemble no more for ever. To those against whom their fury was directed there remained but a single resource. Entreaties, prayers, self-abasement, would have availed them nothing. As had been already often demonstrated, concessions would have been followed by increased demands, and present submission by more degrading humiliations. The South fell back within her own territory, and said to those who had been her colleagues, 'You will not agree that we shall live with you upon terms of political equality: let us then part in peace. You will not consent that we shall dwell together as brethren of the same political family: let us therefore separate as friends. The great continent we occupy is wide enough for us both, and millions more: leave us in the peaceful possession of that which we and our fathers before us have occupied, and which we may justly claim as our own, and we will be content.' The response of the North to this fair demand has been witnessed in the conflagrations which have marked the march of her invading armies, and in the enactment of those bloody scenes which have made every Southern home a house of mourning. The North and the South have made for themselves a new history, which, though embraced within a brief period, will demand a larger space to detail its incidents than would the entire annals of the American continent from the period of its discovery to the commencement of the great struggle. Whatever may be the decision of impartial posterity in regard to the merits of the conflict, the glory of the one will be the eternal shame of the other; and we may not doubt that the record of their deeds will form a perpetual barrier to the re-establishment of any political union.

I have enumerated only the more prominent of the many subdivisions of parties into which Northern society is divided, all of which mingle actively and earnestly in the employment of president-making. During a long period of time they were to a certain extent in opposition to each other, and the one, acting as a counterpoise to the other, delayed for a season the disasters which their combined action has at length brought upon the country. But it may be readily conjectured that if there had never been a presidential election such a concentration would never have been brought about, because, even if possible, it would have been without an object and without a result. In an evil hour the sagacious place-seekers discovered that by the concentration of a larger against a smaller section this object could be achieved. Hence all these different elements were cultivated, and their influence was enlarged with the enlargement of the sphere in which they were called to operate. The zeal of each was augmented in a degree commensurate with the importance of the uses to which it might be applied. Zeal was developed into fanaticism, and fanaticism into a blind hatred against all who opposed any resistance to its dogmatical demands. Even virtues were exaggerated into vices, and vices were cherished and nurtured into crimes. There resulted an unhealthy enlargement, a kind of moral *pâte de foie gras*, for the growth of which the presidential election furnished the unnatural aliment. It left no moment of repose to those who were once drawn within its ever circling current; and that current grew broader and swifter, until it drew everyone within its vortex. Disappointment to day did but serve to stimulate the desire for a more fortunate issue on the morrow; and the grave of one cherished hope was but the cradle of another which sprang into existence at the moment when the first disappeared.

However much we may lament the sad uses to which these enthusiasts applied their energies—however much we may loathe and abhor the conclusions to which their 'ideas' and their theories were developed, who can say that but for the influence of presidential elections they might not have been worthily employed in the interests of humanity? Who can say that instead of deluging the country in blood, they might not noiselessly and in a legitimate way have accomplished much which, in the estimation of real philanthropy, would have assigned to them a high rank among the benefactors of their country.

CHAPTER VI.

PROGRESS OF THE CANVASS AFTER THE CONVENTIONS HAVE MADE THEIR NOMINATIONS—ESTIMATE OF THE VALUE AND EXTENT OF THE SOVEREIGNTY EXERCISED BY THE PEOPLE.

THE two national conventions representing the two contesting parties having assembled nominated their respective candidates for the presidency and vice-presidency, and adjourned. The two chosen 'standard bearers' are fully before the country, and then for the first time the people are called upon by the circumlocution of 'electors' to exercise 'the high and noble prerogative of choosing their own ruler,' by deciding which one of two citizens, whose names have been thrust upon them by two irresponsible caucusses, shall be their monarch for the next four years succeeding the expiration of the term of the then incumbent! This 'glorious privilege of sovereignty, won by the valour and transmitted by the patriotism and statesmanship' of their ancestors, at last resolves itself into the unrestricted privilege of exercising a right of choice between two citizens only, of whose qualifications they perhaps know nothing—for whom, in many instances, they have no personal sympathy—who have not perhaps a solitary claim to their gratitude, or their respect, or their confidence, beyond that which may be set up with equal propriety by half a million of their fellow-countrymen; and whose chief passport from the cottage of the rail-splitter to the palace of the President, was the obscurity and insignificance which had previously concealed their acts from general public scrutiny!

And it is for the privilege of enjoying this empty honour—this miserable pageant—this childish bauble—this tinsel livery of sovereignty—this base counterfeit of real power—that the country is now deluged in blood: that vast armies of fiercely fanatical and mercenary soldiers, headed in many instances by worse than savage chieftains, are now desolating with torch and sword the fairest region of that once happy land; and that liberty itself lies prostrate and bleeding, crushed to earth beneath the iron despotism which the people themselves had erected and consecrated as the embodiment of all that was excellent in government, and deified as a direct emanation from the very fountain and source of human liberty!

One scarcely knows whether to be most surprised at the absurdity of denominating the part played by the people as an act of real sovereignty, or at the infatuation which accepted and vaunted it as a reality. The stump orator, perhaps one of the leading wire-workers of the late Convention, preludes his eulogy upon the candidate of his party by a brief reference to the unhappy condition of the rest of the entire human family who, having the misfortune to be compelled by inexorable fate to dwell beyond the boundaries of the happy Republic, have no right to participate in the glorious privilege of choosing the sovereign who is to rule over them! 'While all the other nations of the world are limited in the selection of their monarchs to *one candidate*,' he facetiously remarks, 'to you my fellow-citizens is reserved the right to select from the great body of the nation the President who is to rule over you! Glorious privilege of a free people!'

He addresses a listening and a believing audience in the main, and yet there is not a word of real substantial truth in what he says. For when the 'privilege' is fairly stated—when it is divested of all superfluous adornment, and sifted of the superabundant chaff, how very light is the little grain of seed that is left. Other nations have only one candidate from whom to choose their sovereigns, while the citizens of the great Republic have TWO! Yes, *two*; but they had no more real influence in the selection of these two than the subjects of the Emperor Alexander will have in the choice of a successor to the throne of Russia. And where was the power behind the people which imposed this limitation upon their sovereignty? It was a caucus of irresponsible citizens, most generally under the guidance of men who intended, after the people had performed the part assigned to them, by placing their candidate upon the presidential throne, to take him all to themselves, and through his agency and connivance rig themselves out in the trappings of office and riot on the plunder of the people's treasure. But what is the character of the two gentlemen between whom the choice must be made? If we are to give equal credit to the representations of both parties during the excitement of the contest, never in all time were two more graceless scamps permitted to go at large, at least without being submitted to the surveillance of the police? If we are more charitable, and believe only the half of what we hear and read, we tremble for the fate of the nation which every four years is subjected to a hazard of at least one chance in two to be ruled over by one of the most insignificant and incompetent, if not one of the very worst men of the thirty millions of people who inhabit the Republic. But if we are disposed to be censorious, and refuse absolutely to believe what is said upon either side, we will probably be much nearer the truth; but it impresses upon the mind a sad record of the degrading influences of presidential elections upon the public manners, if not the public morals.

If I and my fellow-countrymen in sober reality might exercise the right to which, by the letter of law, we seem to be entitled, at least after a manner, we might bear with equanimity even an occasional failure to exercise it aright. It would be some consolation to know that if our President was not as we would like to have him, he was at least our own. We might, as the loyal subjects of a line of sovereigns, regret their occasional short-comings and be loyal still. But to be cheated and hoodwinked—to be told that the citizen who demands our suffrages is the man of our choice, when we ought to know that the only part of the performance assigned to us is to register ourselves as his faithful subjects, and place upon his shoulders the robes of sovereignty—to be told that that king who sits upon the throne of the Republic is one of our own beloved line of monarchs, when we know that he is a bastard, a foundling, who has by schemes and tricks of selfish partisans been placed there in despite of our prerogative—to be told all these things by those who have cheated us is bad enough; but then to have them told to us in such a flattering way, and with such a deferential manner, and with so much seeming reverence for our authority, that we absolutely lock and bar the door of our senses, and believe it all is almost beyond endurance. Let us, however, take courage and consolation by contemplating the sufferings of those who have the misfortune to dwell in countries where they have only *one* candidate to choose from when they make their king? The citizens of the great Republic had *two*!

I said in the outset that the two National Conventions had met, made their nominations, adjourned, and that their candidates were fairly before the people. I was, strictly speaking, in error when I made the last announcement. I omitted to refer to the intermediary part played by the electors in the drama about to open. In truth, this provision of the Constitution, although it has always been complied with to the letter, has been, as I have said before, so utterly disregarded and perverted in practice, that for the moment I had forgotten that we were not permitted to place the name of our candidate upon the tickets which we deposited in the ballot-box. It is only necessary, however, to say that, either after or before the Conventions have made their nominations, each party, by means of another series of *State* Conventions, nominate the number of electors to which they are by virtue of the number of their inhabitants respectively entitled. They are, however, pledged at the time of their appointment to vote, if elected, for the candidate of the party who had been or was to be nominated by the General Convention. Thus the constitutional electors—that body of sages whom our forefathers intended should meet together, ponder deeply, judge wisely, and then select a President from the whole body of statesmen throughout the country—have descended in practice to serve as the mere automatons of the people. Just as the people are the mere registrars of the edicts of the Conventions, and the Conventions but too often the mere exponents of the will of the intriguants and office-seekers, who may be regarded as the real king-makers of the Republic, through the complicated machinery we have thus briefly examined.

Although I was, therefore, in error when I said that the candidates were fairly before the people, it was rather in theory than fact; for the transparency of the electors may be scarcely said to obstruct the vision of the people, who can see with perfect clearness the future President beyond them. The consideration accorded to the electors as such may be measured by the very insignificant and subordinate part they are given to act. It does not, of course, matter who or what they are; and they are never thought of in any other light than as mere messengers, whose duty is limited to the bearing of a sealed letter to head quarters, with an account of the result of the battle, as indicated by the count of the ballot-box.

With this explanation, I will say again that the candidates are fairly before the people, and the party press and party orators are engaged in the double work of building up and pulling down characters. And the giddy height to which they can elevate their own candidate, and the profound depths to which they can consign that one whom they oppose, is only a little less remarkable than the credulity which closes its eyes to all probabilities, and accepts with a trust that knows no wavering, whatever may be written or spoken—which exalts their own, or lowers the candidate of their adversaries. The marvellous celerity with which they can metamorphose an ordinary wood-chopper into an unrivalled statesman; or a military gentleman of the most modest pretensions and capabilities into a hero, to whose name the monosyllable great would but feebly express the magnitude of his military genius, is only paralleled by the transitory impression thus created upon the public mind. If the reputation which presidential candidates acquire among their friends for the possession of all the great and glorious qualities which a man of the most profound natural capacity may, by dint of enormous mental and physical labour acquire, had only been a little more enduring than the brief space occupied in its acquirement, it might have been worth the pain of suffering many hard knocks from the other side. But unfortunately, or fortunately, it departs as it comes in a tornado. If he be unsuccessful, he leaves no more impression upon the public mind in his enforced seclusion from the public service than a retiring footprint on the sandy beach, or a puff of wind upon the cheek, or a ship upon the waves of the ocean, or anything else that comes and goes in an instant. If, on the other hand, he receives the requisite number of votes in the Electoral College to carry him into the Presidency, his reputation retains its pristine glory, until he shall have exhausted all the places he has to bestow, and then—if not always, certainly oftentimes—he falls never to rise again.

But I have gone on too rapidly. We were only in the middle of a presidential canvass, and, without intending it, I have already finished the melancholy career of the aspirants. To describe fully the scenes and events which have characterised the progress of at least a few of those contests would be almost impossible: certainly it would occupy a larger space than I propose to bestow upon them in this chapter. A little later, however, I will refer to these struggles more in detail and in their regular order.

It is not wonderful that an event of such importance should in its progress produce immense excitement, when we consider the great interests involved in the issue. The future well-being and happiness of many tens of thousands of office-seekers, who have abandoned all other pursuits and whose bread is dependent upon the result, as well as the ambitious aspirations of nearly as many more, are all at stake. I will add, even at the risk of being esteemed an 'old fogey' for indulging the obsolete thought, that the great interests of the nation were also involved in the uncertain struggle.

There are, of course, very many citizens who, from really worthy and patriotic considerations, mingle in the strife, and endeavour to give to it such a direction as they believe will conduce to the general weal. But the great body of the people are stimulated by the exciting appliances which are employed to the wildest pitch of phrenzy, and the voice of sober reason is seldom listened to, and more rarely heeded.

Some of these canvasses have been signalised by great dignity during their progress; others have been equally remarkable for their frivolity; but there has been a wild excitement, amounting almost to an insanity, distinguishing nearly all which have occurred during a long series of years, utterly inconsistent with the sober realities of the duties the people were called upon to perform. The voice of reason was drowned amidst the wild passions engendered by the conflict; and the very earnestness with which they entered upon the discharge of the duty unfitted them for its judicious performance.

None may doubt who have been attentive observers of the conduct of American affairs that the great body of the people seek to do right. It comports with their wishes and their intentions, as well as their duty and their interests, to perpetuate a good Government. If they were left to their own guidance they might often err in their judgment, as other sovereigns do, but in the end no serious mischief would be likely to result; for a due regard to their own well-being would always be a sufficient guarantee of their fidelity. They would be loyal, if from no higher consideration than that their own happiness and interests would be promoted by the faithful discharge of their duties. But, unhappily, the peculiar structure of the American Government, in reference to the distribution of offices and contracts, afforded a constant temptation and invitation to enterprising citizens to abandon their ordinary vocations, and, together with all the idlers of the Republic, to engage as an occupation in the business of president-making. If the presidential office could by any means have been divested of its patronage, the election might possibly have rested with the people without exciting any well-founded cause for apprehension. But, unfortunately, this was in its very nature impossible; and the consequence was that those who had a greater and more immediate interest in the success of a party leader, than in the general good government of the country, were enabled by their superior activity to usurp the prerogatives which properly belonged to the body of the people.

I have said that no nation having a constitution was ever more essentially under the government of the few than the United States. This may seem to be at variance with the prevailing opinion that the people were the masters. But it must be borne in mind that as soon as the people placed their favourites in power, the latter immediately appropriated to themselves and their particular faction all the offices and emoluments of the Government. Though these might be displaced by a change in the popular mind, yet their successors followed closely in their footsteps, and the result still was that the few kept the control of the Government in their own hands and for their own special uses.

Are there any means which might be employed to avert this evil? Is it possible to devise any plan by which the real sober voice of the people may be heard in a presidential contest? In short, is there any process by which the demagogues and office-seekers may be rooted out, or reduced to their proper level? If there be, I confess that I have not the discernment to discover it. So long as presidents or kings, or whatever you may denominate the chief dispenser of the honours and patronage of the State, are elected by the popular voice, there may be a struggle of longer or shorter duration—a chance success may inure to the honest sober sense of the people, yet sooner or later the direction of public affairs will pass out of their hands, and the chief power is always in danger of being usurped by that class of citizens who are least worthy of confidence and least capable of discharging aright the functions of rulers.

Notwithstanding, however, the palpable faults and manifold evils of the system, it would be an error to suppose that the Presidents thus chosen have been, as a rule, bad men, or even incompetent to the discharge of their ordinary executive functions with a reasonable degree of success. In truth, the less objectionable the candidate may be, the stronger are the probabilities of a fortunate issue to the struggle; for although the people are restricted in their choice within so limited a range as two citizens, yet there are many thousands of voters who are bound so loosely by the party tie that they will give their support to the opposition candidate if they believe him to be the most worthy man. Hence, while the conventions are generally inclined to pass over statesmen who have a national reputation, for reasons which will readily suggest themselves to the mind, yet it redounds greatly to the advantage of a party if the Convention can present a man upon whose private or public character there rests no stain of reproach.

It will not, perhaps, be said by any, except the uncompromising partisan, that we have ever had a

President who employed his high position to subserve his own personal interests; and it would probably be conceded by even those who entertain the strongest prejudices against American institutions that the average capabilities of the Presidents have been not only equal to the tasks which devolved upon them, but in all qualities of statesmanship they will rank with the most distinguished of those who, under other forms of government, have occupied corresponding stations.

It may be true, also, that the indisposition of purely party leaders to place the great statesman in the executive office might be attended with compensating incidental advantages. These could be profitably employed in the Congress; and, in fact, a very large number who may be thus designated have occupied seats in the Senate, the conservative body, as well as in the popular branch of the National Legislature. Such were Mr. Calhoun, of South Carolina; Mr. Webster, of Massachusetts; Mr. Clay, of Kentucky; of whom it was the boast of their friends to say they were too great to be Presidents. In the long run liberty might be all the more secure under the guardianship of men of moderate attainments and less brilliant qualities, than under the sterner rule of greater and may be more ambitious leaders, occupying the station of chiefs of the Confederacy.

Experience has fully established the truth that the element of evil in the American Constitution did not consist wholly in the fact that under its operation wicked or incompetent men were, as a rule, called to fill the public stations. Certainly many of the very best men in the country were deterred from entering the lists as competitors for the prize of popular favour, and many unworthy men were chosen to fill public offices; but still it may not with justice be said that there was less ability among the officials of the United States Government, as a whole, than distinguished corresponding officials under other forms of government. It is undoubtedly true that the President was obliged, by an inexorable necessity, to discriminate in the dispensation of the offices in favour of members of his own party. Often he was influenced also by his private friendships, and may be enmities. Nevertheless, it would be difficult to discover evidence in the history of any nation in the past, or in the practice of any existing Government, that merit has been or is regarded by any of them as the only qualification requisite for public station. Favouritism is, and in the nature of things will in all probability continue to be, the ruling principle upon which men are selected from among their fellows as the recipients of the honours and emoluments of office. True merit may sometimes compel the dispensers of patronage to honour its claims; the exigencies of a country in times of peril may call it forth, and engage it in the public service; an urgent public necessity may induce rulers to relax somewhat the rigid enforcement of the rule. Exceptional cases may and do arise, but merit, without patronage to sustain it, may never hope to exercise a controlling influence with those who conduct the affairs of Government.

In this respect the United States constituted no exception to the other nations of the world. If there were no other evidence to establish the claims of those who filled public stations under the Government of the Union to the possession of the requisite qualifications for the discharge of the duties appertaining to their position, it is furnished upon every page of the history of the Republic, and in the unparalleled growth of the nation in wealth and power. It is certainly true that the foundation for this immense and rapid augmentation in all that constitutes the greatness of nations rested in the enormous and hitherto wholly undeveloped internal resources of the country. It would not, therefore, be fair to institute a comparison in this respect between the Governments of the United States and those of Europe, without giving due weight to the important advantages possessed by the American Government. But we may compare America with itself. We may compare the relative progress made by that portion of the continent embraced within the limits of the late Union with Mexico, with Central America, with the Empires and Republics of South America; or with the identical country itself during the long period of time in which it constituted colonial dependencies of European kingdoms.

That it has outstripped any other nation upon the American continent or elsewhere in its rapid march to greatness will not be denied, and we may therefore conclude that those in whose hands its political destinies had been placed were not deficient in some of the qualifications requisite for conducting the affairs of Government, however objectionable may have been the manner in which they attained to power.

But it proves more than this. It establishes the fact that the general influence of American institutions has been to develope in the private citizen those qualities which are requisite for the advancement of the nation. It proves, moreover, that the Government was, in principle at least, adapted to the wants of the people, and was in accordance with their sympathies. It is impossible that any nation could have advanced so rapidly under a radically bad political organisation. Evil may have existed—it did exist; but good must have been mingled with it in large proportions, or such results never would or could have ensued.

But it was not alone in the developement of the material interests of the nation that the value of its political institutions was manifested. They developed in the individual many of the best qualities which adorn human nature; they stimulated his pride by increasing his importance. He was important because he was a part of the sovereignty of the State. The higher qualities of courage, and constancy, and fidelity to their engagements in private life eminently distinguish a very large portion of the people of America in every rank of life. I do not, of course, mean to say that a very unusual proportion were characterised by the possession of these qualities; but that in these respects they will not, as a whole, suffer in comparison with the people of any other nation engaged in similar pursuits, I think will not be questioned by those who have had opportunities to know them, and to study their characters and characteristics.

If this view may seem to conflict with a proper appreciation of the barbarous manner in which the present war has been conducted by the Northern Government—with those atrocities of individual commanders and soldiers, which, though met by the universal reprobation of civilised nations, have been apparently approved and sanctioned by the public opinion of the United States—it is only necessary to consider, upon the other hand, the magnanimity, humanity, courage, and constancy which have marked the conduct of the South as a nation, as well as of the individuals comprising it throughout the terrible scenes of the cruel conflict. Other causes, it is true, have tended to increase this divergence between the North and the South ; presidential elections have been employed to cultivate and to develope the stronger and baser passions of the human heart, such as envy, hatred, malice ; local causes have contributed to magnify those evils in the North, and to soften their harshness in the South; yet, apart from the demoralising influences of presidential and other popular elections, which were by no means necessary to a proper administration of the Government, I do not believe that I have misconstrued the effects produced by the political institutions of America upon the great body of the people comprising the nation.

CHAPTER VII.

TRUE LIBERTY IS INCOMPATIBLE WITH THE EXERCISE OF SOVEREIGN POWER, BY A SINGLE WILL, WHETHER IT BE VESTED IN ONE INDIVIDUAL OR IN A MAJORITY OF THE PEOPLE, ACTING AS A UNIT—THE UNITED STATES GOVERNMENT WAS IN THEORY FREE, IN PRACTICE A DESPOTISM

WHEN the authors of the American Constitution met to establish a Government they had only two elements out of which to construct those checks and balances which are essential to the permanent security of liberty. These were *the citizens* of the States, all of whom were invested with the same political rights; and *the States as sovereignties.*

The delegates composing this Convention were not the representatives of the people of the United States, but of the States individually. They were not authorised to merge the sovereignty of the States into that of the Union, but merely to delegate certain powers to a common agent: hence, in the construction of their league, they endeavoured to provide guarantees not only for the freedom of the citizens, but the sovereignty of the States Therefore, in the distribution of the legislative powers of the Government, they invested the representatives of the people with one moiety, and the representatives of the States, as independent sovereignties, with the other. Neither could complete any act without the assent of the other. In principle they represented two distinct interests—just as the Parliament of Great Britain is composed of a House of Lords and a House of Commons—deriving their immediate authority from totally distinct sources. Upon these two divisions of power the whole fabric of the American Government rested.

Whatever may be the fundamental principle upon which the political institutions of a State may be founded, such principle must be recognised and respected in the administration of the Government. If there be two or more distinct and independent sources of power, to assail either one directly or indirectly, with a view to diminish its relative strength, is incipient revolution. To impair or to overthrow the one or the other, is revolution accomplished. The democratic principle may be admitted as a coordinate power in a monarchy, and the two may be made to act in perfect harmony. Such a combination exists in the Government of Great Britain. But if in practice the democratic principle should be permitted to act independently of the monarchical and aristocratic element the Government ceases to be a monarchy. If either one assumes to itself, and exercises supreme power, the Government may become a democracy or an unmixed monarchy, but it is revolution. The change may not be accompanied by outward violence, as has been the result of the conflict between the two elements of power in the American Confederacy; even the forms and the exterior semblance may remain unaltered, but the substance will be wanting; the Constitution will have ceased to exist, the Government will be no longer what it was before. Even the partial exercise of sovereignty on the part of either, without the cooperation of the other, under the forms and without any palpable violation of the letter of the compact, would create an antagonism between the two elements which would inevitably, sooner or later, lead to fatal consequences. The encroaching power would become arrogant and tyrannical; the other would sink in the public esteem; a conflict would ensue, in which one or the other would become supreme. Or, as has been illustrated in the history of Great Britain, the struggle would result in a reorganisation on a firmer basis of previously existing checks and balances by which neither is left supreme, and the country is thereby restored to the enjoyment of real freedom.

In the plan of Government of the United States, the States in their sovereign capacity, and the people as individuals, constituted jointly the power by which the Government was administered. It is manifest, from the internal evidence furnished by the Constitution itself, that the framers of the Government perceived the danger of collision between these two elements in the matter of choosing the President; and, in their efforts to avert it, they unfortunately furnished the readiest and surest means for producing it. The scheme they adopted, even if it had been carried out in good faith and in accordance with its spirit and intention, would not completely have accomplished their design. But, as we have already seen, its directions were complied with to the very letter, while its spirit was set at naught. The people may not justly be blamed for this usurpation, for it was a result originating in causes which they could not control. The machinery of party conventions, as practically applied, had not been in the contemplation of the framers of the Constitution; and while they could not have foretold what would be their influence, the people could not have been expected to put away the ripe fruits which the party conventions caused to fall at their feet, and for which there were no other claimants.

But this constitutional provision proves that it was not the design of its authors that the election of a President should be decided directly by a vote of the people. Moreover, it is equally clear that they did not intend that it should be exercised in the first place by the States. Hence they attempted to steer a middle course, and confided that duty to another agency which they created for that sole purpose.

We find still further proof that the framers of the Constitution intended that the election of the President should be conducted in harmony with the Federal principle, in the provision made for the performance of this function in case the Electoral College should fail to make a choice. In such a contingency it was provided that the election should be transferred to the popular branch of the Congress, which body was required to vote *by States*; that is, the representatives of the people of each State decided upon their choice and cast *one vote*. The candidate receiving the votes of a majority of the States was to be declared the President. Thus both the elements of power which entered into the groundwork of the Constitution were duly honoured. The immediate representatives *of the people* of the States were entrusted with the prerogative of electing a President; but in the very act of discharging that function they were transformed into representatives of *the States* as sovereignties.

It is probable that the framers of the Constitution believed that the presidential succession would be often settled by this contingent method, but they had not considered of the all-powerful despotism of party caucusses, in not only perverting the legitimate operation of the first trial to secure a choice, but also to avoid the necessity of resorting to the provisional expedient of a reference to the House of Representatives. The party conventions divided the nation into two parts, and the machinery was so perfect that it rarely failed to settle the question in the Electoral College.

By this means the important function of electing a President, and incidentally the dispensation of the enormous patronage of the Government, devolved upon one only of the two elements of power created by the Constitution. The States had no voice except in the rarely-occurring contingency when a majority of the Electoral College failed to agree. Practically, the presidential election was achieved in direct antagonism to the fundamental principle of the Constitution, which required both the assent of the people and the States in the completion of any act.

The consequences which followed were inevitable results flowing from the cause. The one element of power grew stronger and the other weaker in the public esteem. The natural conclusion was to elevate unduly the influence of the one, and correspondingly to reduce the other. The multitude of office-seekers, and their name was legion, worshipped at the shrine of real power; and, as is usual under like circumstances, they sought to make favour with that one which was in the ascendancy by depreciating that other element of the Government which had no patronage to dispense. The influence of these, on account of their numbers, their zeal, and their activity, stimulated by their personal interests, was very powerful. They sought to create in the public mind an interest adverse to the existence of those checks and balances which were wisely designed to protect and preserve liberty. Having dispensed in so important a particular with one of the principal of these checks, the disposition gained ground to throw off all restraints which might serve as a foil to the exercise of supreme power by the dominant element.

Many, very many, were led astray by the most egregious fallacy that the rule of a majority was synonymous with the enjoyment of liberty—that a country must be free which is governed by the people. Fatal error! which has done more to retard the developement of real freedom among the civilised nations of the earth than all the impediments which despots have been able to interpose against its progress. Many in America have no doubt become satisfied of their error in view of recent events; but there are still millions throughout the world who have faith in the delusive phantom.

True liberty can never exist in a State where a single element may exercise absolute power. It matters not where that power may be deposited, whether in a single monarch, in an oligarchy acting as a unit, or in a majority of the people, it is still despotism. In point of fact the last-named is the worst, and the first the least objectionable. Both have equal facilities for the exercise of tyranny, but it is far more easy to satisfy the demands of a single despot than many. To punish one may be accomplished, because a single hand may do it; and this fact being ever present to the mind of him who may, if he so wills, oppress his fellow-men, operates at least as a restraint upon the practice of tyranny. To punish the many is impossible, and therefore no fear of the consequences which may follow an act of oppression can deter the multitude from its commission. A slight concession from each may satisfy the demands of one supreme ruler, while the acquirement of all which a minority possesses cannot satiate the cupidity of a majority. One man naturally shrinks from the responsibility of doing a great wrong: the division of that responsibility amongst a multitude leaves so small a portion to each, that the deed is done without creating in the minds of any a feeling of moral responsibility for the act committed. At the least, there are so great a number who do not feel the influence of this restraining cause that the minority is overborne.

When mankind learn that real freedom is not to be found, and cannot exist under the rule of a power deriving its authority from a single element, whatever may be the form in which it exists—however plausible or attractive may be the garb in which it presents itself to the merely speculative mind—a greater battle than has ever yet been waged for real liberty will have been fought and won. But so long as the adversaries of that which they denominate 'the one-man power' seek to eradicate one species of despotism, in order to substitute another and a worse one, the contest will continue; or, if decided at all, the victory will almost always inure in the end to the single despot. The one man has nothing else to do but to watch the shifting tide of battle, and to shape his course in such a manner as to avoid the breakers which menace his destruction. The great body of the people are, upon the other hand, obliged to occupy themselves with other pursuits. They may, during a season of profound excitement, concentrate all their force upon the acquisition or maintenance of their power; but either reverses or successes have a tendency to cool their ardour. Sooner or later they must fall back into the channel to which the ordinary duties of life imperiously demand their recall. They entrust the management of their cause to agents, who betray them, and all is lost! If we may believe history—if we may trust the dictates of common reason—this result sooner or later is inevitable.

Those who absorb in their own hands all the powers of a State in which the principles of liberty have taken root, must live in a perpetual conflict: for the very instincts of a public sentiment, in the smallest degree enlightened in regard to the principles of freedom, are opposed to such a concentration of power. But on the other hand, where one recognised element of power is held in check by another, or by others, of coordinate force, the necessary evils incident to all government are softened, even though they may not be wholly obliterated; while the community may reasonably hope to enjoy the blessings which attend a good one. The one being jealous of the encroachments of the other protects itself by perpetual vigilance, and in guarding its own rights incidentally protects the whole community.

There is a strong incentive operating upon each to confine its action within a legitimate sphere, for the reason that it is not only under the perpetual surveillance of the other, but its moral force is thereby enhanced. If one or the other is crushed, or overshadowed, these restraints are removed, and despotism naturally and necessarily ensues. These checks and counterpoises upon the action of the Government may sometimes retard, or even wholly prevent the accomplishment of that which may in itself be right; but they much oftener prevent the consummation of evil. When a conflict of opinion arises, they may retard progress; but they leave the Government in as good a condition as they found it. After all, the power of prevention is the surest guarantee of a good Government, for there is no axiom more true, however much it may conflict with the theories of those who believe that all political and social evils may be remedied by the action of the State, than that the best governed country is that one which requires to be least governed.

It is conceded by the wisest statesmen that the laws by which a nation is governed should be few and simple, easy to be comprehended, and just in their application. The safest mode which may be adopted for the attainment of these objects consists in such a division of the powers of the Government as enforces the cooperation of different elements and interests, as a condition precedent to the passage of all laws, so that one may negative the act of the other. The fact that laws are enacted under such auspices affords the surest guarantee of their strict observance.

The art of government is not necessarily a mystery, though it may be made so by the arts of state craft. So, in passing through the mazes of a labyrinth, one may, after various windings, find himself again at the point whence he started; but if the object be simply to go over the ground necessary to be traversed in order to pass through, it is easy to make a straight road.

The entire scope, spirit, and tendency of the American Constitution was to secure this cooperation of the diverse interests which existed within the limits of the Confederacy. The whole tendency of the presidential election was to destroy that equilibrium which the Constitution sought to establish. The manner in which the President is practically chosen is in direct conflict with the Federal principle which is the foundation of the whole political edifice. The President, as we have seen, is chosen by a majority of the people of a majority of the States, containing a majority of the people of the United States. This is even worse than if it had been a consolidated sovereignty. Whereas the Government of the Union, being but the common agent of a number of sovereign States, cannot with impunity overlook or disregard the existence of the power by which it was created. In effect the President is chosen by a power, not only foreign to the States composing it, but which is absolutely unknown to the Constitution in the form in which it presents itself. The Government created by the States—the common agent of the States—is ruled over by a chief whom they had no agency in electing, and whom they have no power to depose.

But even considering that the people of the States respectively, in the exercise of this power may be regarded as representing the sovereignty of the States, still the principle of sovereignty is violated, because the larger States are thus permitted to exercise a control over the choice greater than the smaller ones, in the proportion of their superiority in population. Hence the influence of New York, or Pennsylvania, or Ohio, or Virginia even, is equal to that of half a dozen of their colleagues. This is utterly incompatible with the sovereignty of the States, because all sovereigns are and must be equals. When the Emperor of France and the King of Belgium make a compact they are considered and treated as equals. How absurd would it be to say that in case of a disagreement in regard to the terms, it should be decided according to their relative strength of numbers? When several sovereigns enter into a league, it would be impossible and absurd to give to one an influence over the other coinciding with the additional greatness of his dominions, unless there should be at least some negative check which would protect the weaker. Sovereignty is in its very nature complete, perfect, and entire. It can neither be augmented nor diminished. All other sovereignties are its equals, but none can be its superior. Sovereigns may make compacts, by the terms of which each may serve as a check upon the other, but never by which the one may have the right to control the other; for in that case the latter would cease to be sovereign.

Strictly speaking, the President, as I have before said, was elected by the sole agency of a power unknown to the Constitution. Neither in its spirit nor letter does it confer any right of sovereignty upon the people of the United States, acting as a unit, by the voice of a majority. At a superficial glance it may be difficult to discover any practical difference between an exercise of sovereignty on the part of the people, as members of separate communities and as members of the whole community—as citizens of each of the several States, or as citizens of the United States—employing the latter term according to its popular signification, for properly speaking there could not be a citizen of the United States. But a clear comprehension of the subject will satisfy the intelligent mind that the difference between the two is as vast as the difference between a good and a bad Government. There is just the difference that would exist in the usefulness of the British House of Commons, if the members, instead of being chosen by the respective districts into which the kingdom is divided, were each and all elected by the joint vote of the whole nation.

The greatest foe to liberty in any country embracing a wide extent of territory, and a consequent diversity of local interests, is centralisation, which consists in establishing one great controlling centre of power, from whence the country is governed in accordance with the requirements of one prevailing interest. Whatever may be the form of the Government, the natural effect of such a concentration, in a country so vast as the late United States, is to reduce the more remote sections to the condition of mere dependencies. It is susceptible of easy demonstration that in so far as political institutions had any agency in developing the greatness of the country that result was due, in a great measure, to the State Governments. As long as the sovereignty and independence of these were recognised and protected and cherished, the country continued to be prosperous, contented, and happy. But the moment the public sentiment of the North, under the impulse of its superior numbers, began to favour the idea of establishing a central despotism, which should govern the whole, the conflict of the two elements of power commenced.

The presidential election being resolved into a mere contest of sections, to be decided by mere numbers, afforded the temptation and the opportunity to give to the idea a practical significance. National questions, or subjects of general and common interest, were at length entirely superseded by a controversy in regard to a purely local domestic institution confined entirely to the Southern States. In regard to this question, the North had not as much right to intervene as France or England, because the former had entered into a constitutional league by which all interference was especially interdicted. In such a contest there could be but one issue at the ballot-box, for the North was numerically the strongest; and but one result following upon their success, for the South was strong enough to resist.

It seems to be almost self-evident, when we consider calmly all the facts, that the presidential election was not only the principal cause of the disruption of the Union at the time it occurred, but of the war which followed the dissolution. First, it afforded the occasion to develope the power of mere numbers, and its frequent recurrence stimulated the majority to the pursuit of objects which were constitutionally beyond its reach. At one time it was only claimed that a majority of the people of all the States might be justified in the exercise of supreme power, to the exclusion of the element of State sovereignty. It was discovered, however, at a later period, that the same object might be as readily accomplished by means of a majority of a dominant section. This was rendered easy of attainment by the adoption of what was known as the general ticket system. That is, all the people of each State voted for the number of electoral candidates to which they were respectively entitled. New York, for an example, being entitled to thirty-five electoral votes, each party nominated thirty-five candidates. In the last presidential contest the electors favourable to the election of Mr. Lincoln received each 353,804 votes. Those in favour of his adversary received 303,329 votes, consequently all of Mr. Lincoln's thirty-five friends were chosen, and he received the entire electoral vote of the whole State; just the same as though every citizen of the State of New York had desired his success; thus stifling entirely the voice of the minority. In the entire North Mr. Lincoln received 1,831,180 votes, represented by 180 electoral votes, being a majority of the electoral votes of the Union. There were cast against him in the same States 1,551,191 votes, represented by only three electoral votes

But the general result of the popular vote makes the point still more clear:—

Majority for Lincoln in the North . .	276,989
Majority against Lincoln in the South .	1,277,049
Majority against Lincoln in the whole Union	1,000,060

The entire popular vote for the Lincoln electors in the fifteen slave States, including Maryland, Delaware, Kentucky, and Missouri, was only 26,430; while in ten of the fifteen they did not poll a solitary vote!

The foregoing figures give the result of the votes actually cast in the election. The Southern States were further entitled, by express provision of the Constitution, to a Federal representation equal to two-thirds of the slave population. This could not, of course, be made to appear in the popular vote, although it was duly credited to their account in assigning their quota of electors in the Electoral College. If, however, we estimate these numbers, and add them to the popular vote against Mr. Lincoln, we find that the present President of the United States holds his office by virtue of the support of 1,857,610 votes, represented by 180 votes in the Electoral College; and against the wishes of 3,157,670 (estimating 300,000 as the additional strength of the South for the slave population), represented in the Electoral College by only 123 votes!

Is it wonderful that professional president-makers and party leaders should have struggled hard to bring the presidential elections to a contest of sections, when such results could be thereby achieved? Need we be surprised that under such circumstances the geographical division line between the North and the South should have been made to mark also the boundaries of parties? Cannot even the European Abolitionist of the sternest type imagine that there might have been a stronger impulse than love for the slave which suggested the policy of a Northern presidential party? The concoction and successful accomplishment of this complicated scheme of treachery to the people's sovereignty, of which they were themselves the instruments and the victims, affords one more striking proof of the power of mind over matter—of brains over muscle—of those who think over those who delve. Happy, indeed, will it be for the people if they will profit by the bitter lesson: if they will discover that, in the effort to perform within themselves all the functions of Government, they will be first cajoled and then betrayed by those in whom they most trustingly confide. The people never have been and never will be an equal match for the demagogues. Mind alone can meet and overcome them.

Mr. Lincoln was elected in direct conformity with all the specific requirements of the Constitution, yet it will scarcely be said that there could have been a more flagrant violation of its spirit and intention. A power unknown to the Constitution usurped all power, and a section triumphed upon an issue which was in direct conflict with the provisions of the instrument under the forms of which it was achieved; while a President was actually chosen by a minority of the only element of power which participated in the election!

Presidential elections were not only accomplished in

124 MR. LINCOLN'S PRESIDENT
But the general result of the popular
the point still more clear:—
Majority for Lincoln in the North
Majority against Lincoln in the South
Majority against Lincoln in the whole Union
The entire popular vote for the Lincoln
the fifteen slave States, including Mary
ware, Kentucky, and Missouri, was
while in ten of the fifteen they did not p
vote!

geographical division line b[illegible]
the South should have been [illegible]
boundaries of parties? Ca[illegible]
Abolitionist of the sternest [illegible]
might have been a stronger i[illegible]
slave which suggested the p[illegible]
sidential party? The co[illegible]
accomplishment of this [illegible]
treachery to the people's [illegible]
were themselves the ins[illegible]
[illegible]ords one more striking [illegible]
[illegible]tter—of brains [illegible]
[illegible] those who d[illegible]
[illegible]ople if t[illegible]
les[illegible] will [illegible]
perform within themse[illegible]
[illegible] they will be fi[illegible]
[illegible] they [illegible]

[illegible] enormous in-
[illegible]t and peaceful
[illegible] subjected the
[illegible] of revolution.
[illegible]able feuds and
[illegible]njuries inflicted
[illegible]upon the public
[illegible]he integrity of
[illegible]n its influence
[illegible]tates. Although
[illegible]ves sufficient to
[illegible]e Confederation,
[illegible]llowed without a
[illegible]ing and fostering
[illegible]orrectly speakin[illegible]
[illegible]wo sections.
[illegible]currence th[illegible]
[illegible]d by the p[illegible]
[illegible]arcely tim[illegible]
[illegible]rrived. [illegible]
[illegible]was co[illegible]
[illegible]was n[illegible]

violation of the spirit and intentions of the clause under the forms of which they were conducted—in violation of the principle of a division of power between the States as sovereignties, and the people—and in discord with the Federal principle—but in utter contempt of the will of that very power which was invoked to usurp the prerogative of undivided sovereignty.

The Constitution was cheated—the Federal principle was cheated—the States were cheated—the majority of the people were cheated—and he who, by means of all this cheating, now sits upon the throne of the Republic sends forth a million of soldiers to enslave eight millions of freemen, after having cheated eighteen millions of his own subjects of their liberties—and all for what? That greedy cormorants might riot and fatten upon the public plunder, amidst the dying groans of hundreds of thousands of their fellow-men! and oh, dearly-bought shadow of true sovereignty! that the people might exercise the right of selecting one of two men to rule over them!

CHAPTER VIII.

FATAL INFLUENCE EXERCISED BY PRESIDENTIAL ELECTIONS UPON THE MORALS OF THE PEOPLE AND THE INTEGRITY OF THE GOVERNMENT.

THE presidential election was an enormous incubus upon the proper developement and peaceful progress of American institutions. It subjected the nation every four years to the perils of revolution. It created and perpetuated irreconcileable feuds and animosities among the electors. The injuries inflicted were manifold: first, in its influence upon the public morals; next, in its influence upon the integrity of the Government; and, not the least, in its influence upon the policy of the individual States. Although these evil effects were of themselves sufficient to have produced a dissolution of the Confederation, yet this conclusion might have followed without a war, but for their influence in creating and fostering a feeling of unkindness, or, more correctly speaking, of reciprocal hatred between the two sections. The contests were of such frequent recurrence that the animosities which were cultivated by the partisan leaders during one canvass had scarcely time to subside ere the period for another arrived. With each return thereof the whole country was convulsed from centre to circumference. There was no perceptible pause when men's minds might be disposed to reflect calmly upon the probable consequences of such terrible convulsions. Nearly the entire period of a presidential term was consumed in preparations for, or active participation in, that which was to ensue. Thus, when the inevitable day of dissolution arrived—which event might naturally have given rise to sentiments of profound regret and even grief, but which should not have been the occasion of an angry emotion in the North—where they had, in effect, but the moment before announced a desire for separation—men's minds were already ripe for war and subjugation. The North, as a section, had seized upon the Government—they held the purse and sword of the whole Union; and, in defiance of the very essence of the constitutional compact—in subversion of the fundamental principle upon which their own separate Governments were founded, and as if in very mockery of their own solemn declarations to mankind, that '*any people have an indubitable, inalienable right to alter, reform, or entirely abolish their Government, whenever they believe that its existence is incompatible with their interests or their happiness*'—they invaded the territory of the South, in order to compel eight millions of freemen to become their subjects.

This revolution in the public sentiment of the Northern States startled the world by the suddenness of its announcement; but it would be a great error to suppose that the feeling which produced it was only of an hour's growth. The public mind had undergone a radical change; but the revolution had been accomplished by a silent and slow, though a sure process. The results of presidential elections had taught them that, notwithstanding the checks and balances and compromises of the Constitution, a mere majority of a section of the people, acting as a unit, could make themselves masters of the Federal Union—masters of its immense and constantly augmenting patronage—masters of all its honours, great and small, from the President to the petty postmaster in the smallest village—but, above all, masters of what had been hitherto sovereign States, and of the free citizens who inhabited them. Numbers, mere numbers, became the god of their idolatry. Property, wealth, not only ceased to be regarded as worthy of protection, but its possession became almost a bar to political promotion. The mere animal which walked erect upon two legs was considered the only legitimate source of power. The voice of these was the 'Vox populi,' and the expression of their will was the 'Vox Dei.' It was recognised as a power from whose decision there was no appeal. It was the rising sun, whose brightness dazzled every eye, and whose golden beams won every heart, and before whose opening splendours the hosts of office-seekers fell down and worshipped. The brilliancy of the light which it emitted, undimmed by a cloud, hid from the sight the blood-red tinge by which it was environed. Far away, just sinking beneath the horizon, was that declining luminary whose morning beams had once cheered the hearts of millions—whose noonday splendours were the admiration of multitudes of worshippers in every land—whose fading colours and whose dissolving form were seen and lamented by a few; but the multitude of whose former worshippers did not perceive or did not heed its rapid decline.

Is it wonderful that, in view of the immediate rewards which this new sovereign offered to his votaries, that they should regard with impatience all impediments to his undisputed sway? Were they not acting in accordance with the promptings of a principle which animates the mass of mankind—which fills the halls of the monarch—and which occupies every avenue of approach to his person with the votaries who would bask in the sunlight of his smiles?

As this power which controlled the presidential election developed its capacity to exercise the prerogatives of a despot, the natural result was that the many not only found that to support its pretensions was to be in the high road to preferment, but that to sustain the declining fortunes of the 'States' rights counterpoise' was to give mortal offence to that rising monarch who, with the prestige of present and prospective successes, would show no mercy to those who might be found in the ranks of its rival.

The ingenuity of man could not devise an ordeal which would submit the political institutions of nations—but more especially of a confederacy—to a severer test than to subject them every four years to the necessity of choosing a new chief, whether president or king. For after all president in America means nothing more nor less than emperor or king in Europe, except that the former is, probably from necessity, invested during his short reign with a far greater amount of patronage and power than falls to the lot of any other constitutional sovereign. The duration of the term seems to have been the worst that could have been adopted. If it had been longer the shock might possibly have been greater, but for the fact that the passions of the people would have had time to subside. If it had been shorter, the exasperation arising from defeat would have been less acute, because the 'outs' would sooner have had the opportunity of again trying their fortunes. If the Government had been consolidated into one, instead of being composed of many sovereignties, although liberty would have been the loser, the danger of disaster might have been less, because it would have been more difficult to create political parties in reference to geographical lines. Each community would have been divided into more or less unequal parts; but always there would have been a portion of the population, partisans of the successful candidate, whose influence might have served as a check upon any attempt of the opposition to concert a movement for the overthrow of the Government. But in a confederacy of States, exercising unrestricted sovereignty by the terms of their compact over their internal affairs—having widely different interests—containing populations rendered to a certain degree antagonistical by their diverse pursuits—the whole covering a vast expanse of territory—the presidential elections invited and enticed the party leaders into the dangerous expedient of constructing their parties upon sectional issues bounded by geographical lines. These lines once thoroughly established as a permanent basis of party organisation, an inevitable estrangement of the two sections would follow. The division line would grow broader and deeper. A feeling of reciprocal unkindness would take the place of that fraternity which should exist, and which sometimes does underlie the ebullitions of party animosities in nations having homogeneous populations. This ill feeling, by being constantly fomented to suit the exigencies of party leaders, would grow into unappeasable hatred, ready upon occasion to supplant the ballot-box by the cartridge-box. But why multiply arguments to show what might be expected to occur under a given state of circumstances? The result is before us in once happy and peaceful America! The Land of Promise has been deluged in the blood of those whose ancestors through scenes of peril and hardship first introduced the arts of civilisation, as well as of the emigrants of a later period, who sought its shores that they might bask in the enjoyment of the blessings of peace, prosperity, and presidential elections.

But for the last-named cause, the political institutions of the country could never have been subjected to such a shock. No occasion could have arisen for a general and simultaneous movement of the people. Dangerous excitements of the entire population could not have occurred at the same instant of time, or if they had, there would have been no opportunity for their developement. They would have had their day, but would soon have sunk into impotent insignificance. The sober sentiment of the nation might have been slowly and deliberately expressed through the hundreds of communities into which it was divided; and its matured will thus announced would have been honoured and obeyed. The monarch could never have worked himself up into a rage, and have executed his will, at the moment when disqualified by passion to judge aright, or to execute judgment with mercy. The nation could at least have appealed from Philip drunk to Philip sober, with a well-grounded hope that their appeal would not have been vainly made.

CHAPTER IX.

ENUMERATION OF OTHER EVILS RESULTING FROM PRESIDENTIAL ELECTIONS.

TO the mind of an intelligent stranger, unfamiliar with American customs, and institutions, and passions, the desperate expedients resorted to by the president-makers to increase the numbers of their adherents at so heavy a probable cost seems altogether inexplicable. This apparent anomaly may be, however, understood, if the observer takes an inside view of the structure of political parties growing out of the ceaseless struggle for the important post of commander-in-chief of the army and navy, and dispenser of the vast and growing patronage of the nation.

The 'immense spoils' of the Government, which, according to theory and practice, had come to be regarded as the rightful and legitimate rewards of the victors, had utterly perverted the principle upon which all government should be administered. Offices are, or ought to be, established solely for the public good. Practically, they were only held and deemed as so many prizes to be rendered for partisan services. These ever present temptations, inviting the citizen to enter into the scramble and take his chance for winning, brought into the political field, upon each recurring presidential contest, a constantly augmenting host of mere adventurers and place-seekers, who having abandoned all other avocations relied for a support solely upon the success of their respective parties. One half of these or thereabouts were sure to be disappointed by the defeat of their favourite, while the vast majority of the others were obliged to submit to a similar disappointment when the spoils were divided out, and it was found that the supply was utterly insignificant as compared to the demand.

It would probably be no exaggeration to assume that a quarter of a million of citizens devoted themselves wholly to the presidential canvasses, and an equal number participated less actively, every one of whom expected some personal reward in the shape of an office, great or small, for himself or friend, or a government contract, in the event their party was successful. He who could succeed in arousing the people to the highest point of excitement possessed a double claim upon his party on the arrival of the day of reckoning. Such topics as did not enlist the passions were regarded as too tame to be made 'available,' and they were supplanted by others which might tend to stimulate the people to the wildest enthusiasm. To keep up the agitation the most dangerous issues were evoked, and thus the public mind was kept in a constant state of tension and vague uneasiness about the probable consequences. These agitators did not seek the overthrow of the Government, but their immediate wants made them callous in regard to probable or possible results. 'Let us save the election, and God save the country,' was the rule by which their actions were guided.

For reasons elsewhere explained, the Southern States were, to some extent, exempt from the influence of many of the causes which produced excitement and agitation in the North; but the madness which attended the progress of presidential campaigns prevailed to a deplorable extent all over the country, both in the North and the South.

It would not be proper to say that all who were engaged in conducting the public affairs of the country should be ranked with the class of politicians above referred to. Many eminent men and patriots mingled actively in these contests, and for a long period of time were instrumental in softening the asperities which were the natural results of the prolonged and constantly renewed struggles of parties. There was an occasional lull when the country, wearied by unceasing agitation, seemed to seek repose; but these pauses were rare and of brief duration. They were as the fitful and transient slumbers of the maniac, resulting from mere exhaustion, who is only strengthened by his brief repose to renew his acts of violence. A new source of excitement would be opened up, and again would be resumed the never-ending, still-beginning turmoil and strife of a whole legion of Warwicks and their followers.

As a rule, to which, however, there were many exceptions, the better class of citizens withdrew themselves altogether from mingling in public affairs, where they were of less importance than the meanest grog-shop brawler, who drank rum and spouted politics to companions even more unworthy than himself. They voted—they were excited—they mingled to a certain extent in the turmoil of the contest; but only as passive actors, rarely as active agents; and when the contest was over, they buried themselves in more congenial pursuits, with the thought in their hearts if the words did not rise to their lips—'May God save the country, for we cannot.'

Not only were the offices distributed as prizes, under the inexorable rule that 'to the victors belong the spoils,' but the claimants, many of whom could establish about equal pretensions, were so much more numerous than the places, that the favoured recipients of the public bounty, before entering upon the discharge of their official functions, were in many cases pledged to surrender their positions after a given amount had been abstracted from the public crib, in order to provide for other hungry expectants for whose services no remuneration had been rendered.

The powers and patronage entrusted to the President were enormous. To him was confided the appointment of judges of the Supreme Court, and all the officers necessary in the execution of the laws. All foreign ministers, secretaries of legation, and consuls were named or removed according to his own will. The only restriction upon his power consisted in the requirement that his nominations had to be confirmed by the Senate. But a refusal to confirm his nominee in one case had only the effect of substituting another of like character.

Although this great amount of patronage increased the evils of presidential elections, yet the power of appointment could not well have been confided to other hands. To have entrusted it to the Congress, or to either branch thereof, would only have aggravated the evil by diverting the tide of place-seekers from the avenues of the White House to the halls of the Capitol, with the addition of a vast increase to its volume. The temptations to corruption would have been multiplied a hundred fold, and to the excitement of the presidential elections would have been added the party struggles in the congressional districts to secure the disposal of the patronage of the Government.

When we consider the vastness of the spoils to be distributed, the vastness of the population, and the vastness of the temptation, we can begin to comprehend something of the vastness of that army of place-seekers who filled the country with the noise of their endless clamours. When we add to these that great number who love excitement for excitement's sake, only held in feeble check by that smaller body of citizens who mingled in the fray in order to extract some little good out of the mass of evil, we may comprehend something of the pressure which was constantly brought to bear upon the vitals of the Government. The presidential contests drew hundreds of thousands into the vortex of party politics, who might otherwise have occupied themselves in useful pursuits. It made office-seeking a trade which men followed for a livelihood, as a husbandman follows the plough to gain his bread. There was more money and time wasted in electing one President than would have paid the yearly allowance of half the potentates of Europe. At every moment when we are considering these enormous sacrifices of time, and wealth, and public morals, the interrogatory again and again springs up to the lips—'And all for what?'

There was still another evil flowing from the presidential elections, which was not only seriously detrimental to the public interests, but was the occasion of much annoyance and trouble to the President. It made him at the same time a tyrant and a slave. He ruled a great and rapidly-growing nation, which already numbers thirty millions of people. He was entrusted with a larger share of power and patronage than was held by any constitutional monarch in the world, and yet the merest political charlatans—the denizen of the pot-house, the vulgar declaimer, the active electioneerer who led ignorant foreigners up to the polls to vote—all were his masters. He entered upon the discharge of his duties as the mere drudge of the party-leaders, great and small, through whose instrumentality he had won his crown of thorns. He was bound by the inexorable law of necessity to eject the greater number of those whom he found in the occupancy of the public offices, without regard to public interests or private claims, in order that he might provide places for his own expectant partisans.

I would be doing injustice even to the later Presidents, if I did not add that they often broke the bonds of party in which they were bound, and devoted themselves, as far as was in their power, to the service of the country; but the moment in which they assumed the prerogatives of President of the whole people was too often the signal for the revolt of their followers. Their inclinations of course coincided with their duty to select from amongst the best of those to whom they were indebted to fill the public stations; but in many instances they had no discretion or choice but to bestow the offices upon those whose chief qualification or claim consisted in their preeminent services in securing the election of the chief.

It was impossible, however, under the most favourable circumstances, for the President to supply one in a hundred of the claimants with the offices they demanded. And yet he was bound to discriminate amongst them, each one of whom believed his claim superior to that of the others. The successful claimant accepted the position as his due for services rendered, and consequently considered that the President and he were made even by the operation. The other ninety-nine were disappointed, chagrined, mortified, angry with the President, and at least a goodly number of them ripe for revolt upon the occurrence of the first favourable opportunity. As soon, therefore, as he had finished disposing of all he had to give, a faction of the disappointed, having nothing farther to hope or expect from the present chief, commenced vaguely or more openly, according to circumstances, to hint to their fellow-citizens that the President was 'unworthy the confidence of a free people;' and begun to organise an opposition within his own faction or party.

The irritations engendered by the distribution of the offices upon the commencement of every new presidential term were the natural and inevitable results of the system of president-making, which during the later years of the existence of the Union became the general practice. The same cause created the necessity for the expulsion from office of all those who held over, by appointment of the preceding President. These were deplorable evils; but under the operation of such a system there was no remedy. The rigid rules of party warfare, which announced as leading ideas 'rotation in office,' and 'to the victors belong the spoils,' were popular just in the proportion which the 'outs' bore to the 'ins:' that being something like a thousand to one, silenced every murmur of opposition. The 'ins' were in fact obliged to be silent witnesses of all the preparations for their own execution. They had obtained their own places by the application of the party guillotine to those who had preceded them, and after all, there was an appearance of fairness in the arrangement which satisfied the consciences, while it kept open the avenues of hope to multitudes who were looking with longing eyes to the enjoyment of perquisites which had been long sought for; but which somehow or other had always eluded their grasp.

'Rotation in office' was a rule adopted to apply to a party which might succeed in establishing itself in power during two or more consecutive terms. It was founded upon the idea that since there were not enough places for all, they should like brothers make a fair distribution amongst the greatest possible number by curtailing the term of tenure. 'To the victors belong the spoils' was only the application of one of the harsher rules of war to party politics. Upon the instant when one contesting party placed itself upon this 'platform,' its adversary was obviously obliged to do the same thing, so that politicians were compelled to acquiesce in the practice by an unavoidable necessity. It grew naturally and inevitably out of the system by which the head of the Government, who held this patronage at his disposal, was placed in power. But it was not alone upon the Government of the Union that these presidential elections exercised their baneful influence. The State Governments were corrupted by the example. If the President should be elected by the people, why not officials of lower grade—the judges of the courts of justice, the sheriffs of counties, the constables of civil districts? If the great ruler over all should only hold his office for four years and then be turned out, why should his subordinates and inferiors be suffered to linger in their places during even so long a term? The fountains of Government were thus corrupted at their very source, and the whole cry of the country was for—Change! change! change! Rotation in office!

If we may not believe that all these results were but consequences of the influence of presidential elections; and that the eradication of the great evil would be followed by a corresponding reform in the minor offices, then must we despair of establishing a permanent Government based upon the republican principle. If there is to be no change—if, when peace is restored, the people of America perpetuate the same fatal faults in their Governments which have hitherto characterised their administration—then will the history of the terrible events now transpiring describe with equal truthfulness the conflicts which will follow after. The country will only move with an accelerated pace upon that downward road which leads through anarchy to hopeless despotism.

But if 'the sober second thought of the people' should after their terrible experience induce them to cast away the great sin, then may the friends of good government indulge reasonable expectation that minor reforms of a like character will follow. All they have to do is to look to the spirit of the Constitution of their fathers, and behind that to the sentiments, and opinions, and desires of its framers—interpret in good faith the former by the latter, be guided in all things by the spirit which animated them—and all may be well.

CHAPTER X.

THE INSTITUTION OF SLAVERY WAS NOT ONE OF THE CAUSES OF THE DISSOLUTION OF THE UNION.

IN order to prove that certain results are consequences of a specified cause, it is often useful to show that other assigned causes did not, or could not, have accomplished the results named. In deciding upon the moral causes which produced the dissolution of the Union I have ranked one as a principal, and all others as accessories. More properly speaking, this one leading cause has furnished an occasion for the developement of all the others.

There are those who take an adverse view of the subject—who assign the effect to a cause which I think, was not only innocent, but which, in fact, retarded the consummation, although it may have served as a pretext for the final overthrow of the 'Model Republic.'

I am not going to discuss the rights or the wrongs, either abstract or actual, of the Institution of African Slavery, but simply to investigate its influence upon the duration and destiny of the late Federal Union.

Whether the objections which are raised by foreigners against the Institution of Domestic Slavery in the American Confederacy are well or ill founded, their opposition is most natural. Although the system was not long since almost universally adopted by the Governments of the world, yet it is now amongst civilised nations confined to a very small number. The perceptive faculties of mankind are never so acute as in discovering blemishes in the character of their neighbours, and men are never so indignantly virtuous as in the condemnation of those vices which it is no longer their interest nor within their power to commit.

Notwithstanding this, I can understand, and appreciate, and honour the opinions and sentiments of that large class of intelligent philanthropists who are opposed to the existence of a political institution which recognises property in man. Still this constitutes no valid reason for supposing that the existence of such a relation is an unmixed evil. The good may or may not be sufficient to counteract or atone for the evil, when considered as an established fact with which we have to deal; yet I cannot believe that any intrinsically worthy cause can be promoted by refusing to see anything but evil in all that opposes it. To the candid and frank adversaries of the Institution of Slavery in America I therefore address the observations which follow, in the belief that their better judgment, if not their candour, will induce them to admit the logic of undeniable facts, even though they may prove that it is possible for a little good to be mingled up with that which they consider to be in the main a very great evil.

I am well aware that, even within the narrow limits to which I propose to confine myself, there may be found those who will dissent from my conclusions, simply because they have made up their minds already that nothing but evil can spring from such a source—that none but bitter waters can flow from such a fountain. They have interpolated the sentiment into their religious creeds. Religions are necessarily, and in their nature, dogmatical. They allow of no discussion—they are unalterable—their foundations are laid in faith upon the evidence of things not seen. To doubt is to be damned. Their dogma is true, because it is in their creed—their creed is not to be questioned, because it is an emanation from an Infallible Power. Although their faith may have been born but yesterday, they none the less demand its unquestioned recognition to day. The zeal of a new convert is stimulated by the desire to atone as quickly as possible for the sins of a life-time. I may not hope to win these to my opinions, but I trust that I will say nothing to shock their sensibilities.

When the independence of the British American Colonies was achieved, it became necessary to establish a permanent Government to take the place of that one which had been repudiated. There were two classes of inhabitants—namely, Freemen and Slaves. They were of distinct races, and were as different in their physical aspect as in their origin. Their natural intellectual endowments were as dissimilar as their races or their social conditions. Many, perhaps a majority of the white inhabitants, believed, as did their ancestors, that it would have been better for them if the Africans had never been brought into the country. Others went so far as to suggest the idea that, if any means could be devised by which the two races could be separated, it would be the better policy to adopt it. Others, and vastly the greater number, considered that the system which had been inaugurated without their consent, and prosecuted by their European sovereigns against their protest, had already assumed proportions which rendered its eradication by a system of coercion impossible, even if it were desirable. They thought that they might wisely direct, but that they could not with impunity destroy. None proposed that the slave should become a citizen.

The new Government was established in accordance with these views. The freemen remained freemen—the slaves remained slaves. Men's minds were not wholly of one accord in reference to the policy of the Institution of Slavery, regarded as an abstract proposition, though they generally agreed in the determination to preserve the *statu quo.* There was an absolute and unqualified unanimity in denying to the negro the rights of citizenship, or the privileges of a social equality with the whites. The white men of that day may have been very wicked thus to have ignored the inalienable rights of man—they may have but imperfectly comprehended the truths of Divine Revelation, as expounded to-day by a Cheever or a Beecher—they may have been less pure and less holy than white men of the present day; but it is not of these things I speak, nor do I mean to defend them: I only refer to facts as they existed.

The Government was established upon a principle differing fundamentally from that on which all the other Governments of the world then rested. That principle involved a recognition of the equal political rights of all men. It was, of course, meant to be applied only to themselves; and, in constructing the details of their Government, they gave to it that specific application. They announced, as the theory upon which their political institutions were founded, that 'all mankind were created equal,' and that they were 'endowed by nature with certain inalienable rights,' amongst which was 'liberty.' Practically they applied it only to themselves, and entailed it only upon their own posterity. The Africans they left in slavery to be transmitted as an inheritance to their descendants. This may at first view seem to have been inconsistent with the theory of the Government, but nevertheless the two were in perfect accord. Certainly the application of the principle, at the very moment of its announcement, proves at least their own interpretation of their duty. It may or may not have been unjust, or unwise, or both, but there was no inconsistency between the declaration and the deed. In announcing certain general principles they meant to indicate the manner in which they proposed to govern themselves—their own race—not others. They did not mean to say that England or France should be governed in the same way. They did not even mean to say that Englishmen or Frenchmen who might come amongst them should enter upon the enjoyment of the same political rights which they had conferred upon themselves. Much less did they mean to say that Africans should be permitted to participate with them as equal partners, because they belonged to the human family. There does not exist to-day a Government of the civilised world which does not reserve to itself the right to decide whether the inhabitants of other nations, or the people of other races, should come amongst them and enjoy the political rights accorded to their own citizens. No Government could exist during a long time which had not the right to enforce this exclusion.

Nevertheless this superficial appearance of inconsistency afforded room for cavil, and was a source of disquiet to many of the citizens, who desired that their free institutions should be above reproach. The enemies of the Republic in Europe insisted that the Government could only be brought into accord with the principle upon which it was founded by abolishing slavery—elevating the African to a political equality with the citizens, and amalgamating the races. The abstract justice of the principle that all men were by nature equal, and therefore ought to be endowed with the same political rights, won the hearts and sympathies of many, who having had no practical knowledge in regard to the distinctions and antipathies existing between the black and the white races, when they are brought into contact, could not perceive why the same principle should not have a special application in America.

The establishment of the American Government, which recognised slavery as a proper legal relation between the white and the black man, thus, oddly enough, made the first converts to Abolitionism; and still more oddly, it made converts of both its friends and its enemies. It was the first formidable blow that had ever been aimed at the African slave trade. The downfall of this traffic, as a great branch of commerce, was thenceforth certain; for the Southern

Slave States, now become free from foreign control, carried into practical effect their traditional policy of refusing to permit the introduction of any more African slaves into their territory. If it be a merit, the slave-holding Confederacy of the United States may claim the honour of having been the very first and prime moving cause of the anti-slavery sentiment which afterwards became so general. Then, however, it was founded chiefly upon a political idea. African slavery was wrong, because it interposed an impediment to the developement of a certain political theory. These objections to the system were afterwards enlarged on the ground of philanthropy. As the enthusiasm increased, opposition to slavery, as before said, was interpolated by many into the Christian creed, as a cardinal doctrine of religion.

These sentiments, however, were far from being universally entertained. On the contrary, they had made no great progress beyond a very limited circle, confined almost entirely to Slave States, when the French Revolution, with its terrible upheaving of the moral and political elements of the entire European continent, fixed public attention upon the subject, and hurled all Europe into the current which swept onward to universal emancipation. If the fathers of the American Republics are entitled to the credit of inaugurating the anti-slavery sentiment, at the very moment of recognising its lawful existence, to MARAT, and DANTON, and ROBESPIERRE are due the honour of having made it universal. It may seem strange at first view, that after the removal of the pressure under which men had been, as it were, forced into the adoption of an opinion which they had never previously entertained, they should continue to move on harmoniously, and with a seeming unity of purpose, in the same direction. And stranger still, that the two parties the farthest removed from each other in their political creeds—the most Radical and the most Conservative, according to the usual signification of these terms—should have agreed in adopting the same principle, and in promoting the same object.

This seeming anomaly may be readily accounted for if we follow out the theories of both to their legitimate conclusions. The French Revolution, after many years of conflict, was quieted. It was physically dead; but its leading ideas had taken deep root in men's minds. Its enemies held the sword, but the principles which had been enunciated still lived in the hearts of the great body of the people. Its friends deplored its excesses; but they saw also the provocation: and while they refused to adopt it as a model, they cherished its doctrines. Their adversaries feared and watched, and endeavoured to check the developement of such sentiments. While they boldly confronted, they were anxious to conciliate and soften the proselytes to these opinions. The Democrats claimed the right to 'equality and fraternity,' founded upon a general principle that all men sprang from a common father. If they did not demand the same privileges for the African slaves in America, they could not clearly perceive how they might consistently accuse those of wrong who withheld from them what they claimed to be their own natural rights.

Their theory may have been founded in justice; but

they did not consider that it could only be applied to homogeneous nations as distinct communities, and not to the whole human family as a unit. In truth, they thereby abandoned, or made subordinate, the only argument which might have established the justice of their own claim. Their right to equality had no other practical foundation than their capacity to perform its duties, as well as the other members of the same community. That claim might be asserted upon the ground that they were of the same race, and that with equal advantages of education and similar political privileges, there would be found to be no difference between themselves and those who arrogated the right to govern by virtue of their descent, or by the grace of God. But when they gave to their theory a universal application — when they claimed that Asiatics, and Africans, and Europeans thrown together in the same State, were entitled to equal political rights and an equal participation in the control of the Government—they not only repudiated the only sound principle upon which their own claim rested—namely, an equal capacity with those who had taken their places above them—but they practically enforced those very distinctions in rank, and fell back upon the very same system against which they were protesting. Because, whatever may be claimed to be the natural right of one man to be the equal of his fellow-man, he can only make good his demand by being physically and intellectually able to cope with those by whom he is surrounded. This is the universal law of nature, and cannot be changed in practice by argument. There is no period of the world's history during which this invariable law has not governed the intercourse of mankind. If the most enlightened inhabitants of the Chinese empire were to-day thrown into contact with an equal number of Englishmen or Frenchmen, such an equality of political rights as existed in the American Republics could not be maintained between them for a month. It might be that neither would at first tamely submit to the dominion of the other, but either the one or the other would become the controlling power, if they remained distinct; or they would be divided into classes and castes, at least during the process of amalgamation. Equality would never have a beginning until they had been so effectually intermingled, that all traces of the original distinctions which divided them should have been extinguished. The number of generations or ages which would pass away before the final result would be achieved it would be needless to attempt to calculate. In effect many European powers have extended their conquests into Africa and Asia. They now exercise dominion over hundreds of millions of the inhabitants, yet we do not find them any more willing to concede the rights of political or social equality than upon the day when their victorious armies first entered the territory as conquerors of an unoffending race. Their Governments may not authorise the dominant race to buy and sell the people they have subdued: it is more profitable to absorb their substance—to require that a given amount of money shall be paid by each as a tribute to power. Thus, practically, the doctrine of equality is set at naught by the universal practice of mankind now and in all time past.

But when this democratic theory is pressed to its legitimate conclusion in those countries where, by external violence or from any other cause, two races so dissimilar as the white Europeans and the blacks of South Africa are thrown together, the difficulties are augmented in the ratio of the still more marked distinctions between the races. If the effort to give a practical effect to the principle of equality is attempted to be applied in a community or State, where the natural relation of master and subordinate has already been in existence from the moment when they were first placed in contact, the difficulties of such a solution are so appalling that the mind of a rational man, who has a clear and full perception of the obstacles to be surmounted, must shrink back in dismay from all further efforts to reduce such a theory to practice.

If, in the assumed case of the Englishman or Frenchman and the Arabs, an interval of so many ages is demanded before the new race formed by amalgamation could claim the right to start out upon its career of 'equality and fraternity,' how long a time would elapse before the black and the white man of the American continent would be brought to the same happy state of progress?

In the case we are considering, the first serious obstacle to be encountered is the universal feeling or sense of superiority upon the one hand, and of inferiority upon the other, which the relation of master and slave has engendered. Next we are met by the intellectual superiority, natural and acquired, of the one over the other. The difficulties to be encountered in overcoming these may be more readily appreciated when we consider of the tenacity and fixedness of purpose which in all ages of the world have animated men in maintaining the purely artificial distinctions which have originated even in the same race. The proclaimed mission of the French Revolution was to eradicate these distinctions, to elevate the masses to an equality with their superiors in social and political rank was the dream of those visionary men whose genius conceived and whose hearts prompted them to attempt the achievement. The practical difficulties which supervened, while they did not deter the chief actors in this great tragedy from the pursuit of their object, suggested its attainment by what seemed to be a straighter and a shorter road. The multitude could not, or would not be elevated: and the few would not consent that the distance between them should be diminished. The direction of the Revolution fell into the hands of the *Marats* and the *Robespierres*. It was easier for them to destroy than to build up. Easier to drag down a hundred than to elevate a thousand. Easier to kill the aristocrats, than to eradicate the principles of aristocracy from the breasts of those who had been born (and whose ancestors before them had been born) to the inheritance of its privileges. It was easier to break to pieces and remove the idols from the sight of their worshippers, than to induce the idolators to relinquish their faith. The reign of terror and of blood was inaugurated. The cities and the villages, the plains and the valleys of France, were deluged with the blood of her best and her worst citizens. The few nobles who survived escaped to foreign lands; but under all their accumulated load of misfortunes, disasters, and humiliations, they still proudly claimed to be the superiors of those who had almost annihilated their order, and driven them forth as beggars from what they claimed to be their rightful inheritance. Their followers were bound by the necessities of their position to remain under the dominion of those whom they regarded as their oppressors and their enemies ; but their hearts were with their exiled lords.

The French Revolution, so far as regards its outward manifestation, was finally brought to an end. There are none who will say that those who directed or participated in its progress exhibited any lack of vigour or energy; or that they did not upon the whole attempt to reach the goal of 'equality and fraternity' by the only means which offered any reasonable hope of prompt or immediate success. None will doubt that they did make great progress in establishing a greater degree of liberty for the masses of the people. But did they succeed in eradicating the artificial distinctions of social or political rank, either from Europe, which was the field of their labours, or from France, where they annihilated the old aristocracy? While the political rights of the great body of the people have been augmented, do the higher classes now protect their blood from plebeian contamination any less vigilantly than they did before the first gun of the French Revolution reverberated through every palace and hovel of every European empire, kingdom, and principality?

The people who were engaged in this mighty struggle, and who sustained the shock of this moral and political earthquake, and who emerged from the terrible convulsion almost or quite as far removed from social equality as at the hour of its commencement, were members of a homogeneous race. They were directed by the same passions, and the same prejudices, and the same instincts: they had the same history and traditions, and the same physical aspect. The peasant and the lord might have changed places in the cradle, changed tutors, changed the gilded trappings of the court idler and the blouse of the ouvrier, and each would have played the part of the other through life, and died without having failed in a single instance to perform the part assigned him, according to the example of those in whose society he had been cast.

Let us return to the Europeans and the Africans, whom the new and startling theory of 'equality and fraternity' found living together in harmony as master and slave in the New World. It will scarcely be denied that the political and social reformer would find on scrutinising the position, that the feeling of superiority entertained by the master, and of inferiority by the subordinate, was very strongly—I might almost say ineradicably—engrafted into the minds of both. It was certainly so in their manners. So far as related to the establishment of 'equality and fraternity,' America offered a much less hopeful field for the attainment of that chimera—that ignis fatuus, which had eluded the grasp of those who so vainly sought it with such bloody zeal through the carnage of the French Revolution.

Practically, there were three roads open, each of which offered the hope of a possible solution to those who were sufficiently infatuated to hope at all.

The first and most humane of these was by the

interposition of some foreign power, which would decree freedom to the slaves, and send its ships to take away the one or the other of the two races. Such was the plan pursued by Great Britain in the West India Islands.

The second was to preface the inauguration of the new era of brotherhood and love by placing arms in the hands of the two races, and saying to them: 'Draw the sword from its scabbard, and the brand from the fire, and never sheathe the one, or extinguish the other, until one or both shall have been exterminated.' The bloody butchery of the French province of St. Domingo achieved the work of slaughter. The whites were exterminated, and the blacks were left undisputed masters.

It is not necessary here to decide whether this was wisely or humanely done; or whether any real benefit resulted therefrom either to the African or to mankind. But it may be said that it did not inaugurate that real political independence, or that social equality, which still eluded the grasp of its pursuers. The one at the moment of its execution pleased France; the other at a little later period was accomplished in compliance with the will of England. They were the masters, and if they are satisfied, there are perhaps few now living who will complain. It may at least be said in their justification that they adopted the only means which suggested a hope of reaching the beginning of the end proposed. But it was proven by the result that to change the relations which existed between the black and the white races, required the extermination of one or the other; or the direct interposition of a foreign power.

We enter now upon the third and only remaining road left open. It has never yet been trodden. There were two nations in existence strong enough to protect themselves against internal violence, or foreign interposition, where the white and the black races lived together as superior and subordinate. The empire of Brazil—prosperous, thriving, and contented; the model government of South America, and the only one which has attained to any considerable rank—lay invitingly open to the European reformers. Strangely enough, even the anti-slavery clergymen of Europe seemed oblivious to the fact that there were there millions upon millions of European masters and African slaves. Without sending a single emissary into, and without uttering a single malediction against Brazil, they passed on to the United States of America. It was against the grievous sin of the Great Republic that the priestly proselytes of Robespierre and Marat employed their energies.*

To secure the desired result by the adoption of the plan which had been followed by England was impossible—for there was no over-ruling power which from without might dictate the measure, even if it had been possible to have transported across the ocean the constantly accumulating population. The blacks

* In an address delivered by Sir Henry Bulwer, at Constantinople, before a literary association, he made some interesting references to the origin of the anti-slavery propaganda. I regret that I have not before me the printed address, but I remember that he gave the credit of inaugurating the war upon the Institution of Slavery to Talleyrand, who, in a series of lectures, insisted that such a concession to the democratic theories of the age had, as a matter of policy, become necessary on the part of the Governments of Europe.

had neither the power nor the inclination to enact the same tragedy which had resulted in exterminating the whites of St. Domingo.

If the dominant race had therefore been prepared to adopt any suitable plan which might have offered a reasonable hope of accomplishing the end, and had schooled their minds, by proper training, to contemplate without regret the loss of their inheritance, the only means left open was by a voluntary amalgamation of their own race with that of the African. It scarcely requires an argument to prove that by this means only could the two races be brought into harmony, if the relation of master and slave should be abolished. When such were the means necessary to the attainment of the desired result, it is not wonderful that the proud and domineering Anglo-Saxon shrank back with loathing and horror from the contaminating association. To suppose that such a relation would be voluntarily assumed by any race of Europeans was, in the estimation of Americans, to discard all knowledge of their characteristics, all respect for them individually, all belief in their high destiny, and all obedience to the laws of the Supreme Ruler, who had announced His will and purpose as plainly in the intellects and aspects which He had respectively bestowed upon them as by any other law recorded in the pages of His Inspired Book.

This was, and is, the feeling of the whole American people. It is neither stronger nor weaker to-day than in the days of the Revolution. Every incident in their history bearing upon the question goes to show that there never was a foot of territory over which floated the flag of the late Union—north, south, east, or west—where such a proposition would not have been scouted as an insult. The only difference in this respect between the Free States and the Slave States is, that while in the latter it is a sentiment or prejudice which for the most part lies dormant in the breast, in the former it amounts to a fanaticism. The negro is treated in the Free States with much more rigour, and is repelled from all association or contact with much stronger evidences of disgust, than is observable in the Slave States. This, however, is not to be attributed to any radical divergence of opinion or feeling. The natural antipathy of both, under similar circumstances, would be similarly developed. But in the Slave States the white man has not hitherto had occasion to fear that the African will ever aspire to be his equal, while in the North the legal barriers have been to a certain extent removed, and the white man does not know at what hour some other change in the laws may bring them nearer together. Hence he is constantly impelled to the manifestation of that repugnance which, founded in his nature, has been magnified by education into a controlling sentiment.

Those who are curious to observe the manner in which this passion betrays itself will discover it in the conduct of Yankee armies during their invasion of the South. The unnecessary and wholly unprovoked insults which they constantly, and with impunity, inflict upon the harmless Africans are only exceeded by the wanton injuries which they perpetrate against their masters. But the statute books of the Free States furnish the most authoritative exposition of the deliberate sentiment of repugnance which pervades all classes of Northern society. It may be discovered as well in the laws of New England, before Abolitionism was employed as a means to make presidents, as in the more honest and more recent enactments of the great States of the West. These, while offering the most tempting inducements to other foreign immigrants to enter upon and occupy their unappropriated lands, repel the free negro by the most stringent prohibitions and the most exemplary punishments from any attempt to violate the laws which exclude him. At the very moment when their Government is issuing emancipation proclamations, if the African crosses their borders he is tried as a criminal and fined, and sold to pay the money penalty of his offence. While urging the poor slave to desert his home and his only protector, they refuse to him even the asylum of an open-air lodging in their vast and untenanted forests. Let not the European Abolitionist condemn too hastily the law-makers of the Free States. The chances are as a hundred to one that if he were similarly situated he would do precisely what they have done.

There are documents extant, emanating from the chief source of all power in the United States, which, echoing as they do the universal sentiment of every State, county, and township in the North, are worthy of marked consideration. I refer, amongst others of like import, to the address delivered by President Lincoln to the Committee of Negroes who waited upon him at the executive mansion in Washington, August 14, 1862, to learn what disposition he proposed to make of the Africans after he should have established their freedom. It may seem surprising that at such a moment the President should have taken such pains to dispel the delusion wherever it might exist, that he was fighting in the cause and for the sake of the African. It may seem strange that, in the very act of calling upon the slave to rise up and aid him in exterminating the white men of the South, he should have told him that he was and always would be abhorred and loathed, and refused a home upon the continent where he had been born. Yet these feelings he has expressed, and these sentiments avowed, in the name of his fellow-countrymen. He who desires to acquire useful knowledge in regard to the important subject which excited this exposition of negro philanthropy, and to discover the probable influence of the policy enunciated upon the future fortunes and fate of the Africans now residing upon the American continent, may find it eminently instructive to study this well-considered speech. The author, who occupies a more important relation towards slavery in America than any other living man—who first from choice, and afterwards from the necessities of his position, found himself confronted face to face with the reality of emancipation—who would perhaps shrink back appalled from a contemplation of the horrible fate he is preparing for the African, if it did not hold out the prospect of inflicting a greater evil upon the master, is now obliged to meet the issue he has raised.

If the real friend of the slave can find room to hope, after a perusal of this address, and others emanating from the same source, that the Africans would be benefited by the change which emancipation, under such auspices, would produce, his faith must indeed be founded upon the evidence of things not seen by the naked eye and incomprehensible to the sense.

I do not desire to be guilty of an injustice to the Northern people by assuming that to be true which the sober judgment of mankind would decide to be an error; but can any reasonable man, in the face of such testimony, believe that the Free States entered upon the conflict now raging to right the wrongs of the slave? or that they were animated by any intention or desire to better his condition? Can it be believed that the Institution of Slavery in the Southern States had any other agency in producing the present conflict than that it was employed by the North, in the first place, as a means to procure votes in a presidential election, and in the end as a flimsy pretext for the war of subjugation which they afterwards commenced? Though, in the blindness of their rage and hatred against the Southern people, they may be disposed to employ the slaves as instruments to destroy their masters, can anyone believe, who has studied their character or who has witnessed the evidences of their antipathy to the negro, that they would ever, as a nation, at any period of their whole history, have raised a finger in their cause, or breathed to them a word of encouragement or sympathy, except in so far as it might serve as a stepping-stone to the attainment of another purpose? If there had never been a presidential election to tempt the partisan leaders to employ such means to secure sectional support, is there any reason to believe that an Abolition party could have been formed in the Free States, sufficiently formidable to have carried a majority of the congressional districts in any single State of the old Union?

If we except the European powers which colonised both the black slaves and their white masters in America, the Northern States were the chief instruments in the establishment of slavery upon the soil of the South, although in doing so they violated the known will of the free inhabitants. In justification of their acts it may be rightfully urged that nearly the whole civilised world was at the same time engaged in the same commerce. I do not mean to accuse them of doing an immoral or an unchristian deed, for at that day it was regarded by the authorised expounders of the 'true faith' as a legitimate and truly Christian means of converting the heathen. All the Christian world believed that for the doing of this work of charity for the soul it would only be exacting a very moderate penalty to make the recipients of such an unspeakable blessing slaves for life, them and their posterity for ever. On the other hand, I do not mean to say that the Southerners desired to turn away the human chattels because they had a better comprehension of their duties, or were directed by a loftier code of morals. I must admit that the Southern provincials only turned their backs upon the African slave merchant because they believed upon the whole that they would be more prosperous without than with his merchandise. But slavery *was* established, and that *firmly*, and upon a basis which was evidently intended by its founders to make it perpetual. This, however, was a long time ago.*

To-day we perhaps should in charity credit Northern professions of dislike to that Institution of Slavery which they were one of the instruments in creating; for history and experience furnish us with many notable proofs that nations as well as individuals have an astonishing alacrity and a most marvellous facility in changing their principles in accordance with what may seem to be their interest. But even the fullest measure of charity would not require that we should, in the case we are now considering, give them credit for anything more than a death-bed repentance. It must also be added that the more they propose to do to aid in the slave's redemption, the more they seem to loathe him. The more they approach to the consummation of his deliverance from his Southern master, the more carefully they lock and bar their own doors, and the more vigilantly they guard their frontiers in order to prevent him from employing his liberty as a means of encroachment upon their territorial limits. In short, the more they profess to love him, the more they seem to hate him.

It is a remarkable and well attested fact, which in this connection is worthy of notice, that the African, when brought into contact with the European races, is only treated with kindness and humanity when occupying towards them the relation of slavery. The naturally broad lines which separate the two

* The facts in regard to the establishment of slavery within the limits of the present Confederacy are referred to in detail in the 'South Vindicated,' p. 195

grow deeper and clearer in proportion to the advances made towards a social or a political equality. Throughout the American continent, and upon the adjacent islands, this fact is illustrated in their intercourse. In the Southern States, where the African is held as a slave, he is treated with a degree of respect and a humanity which is nowhere else accorded to him, while in no other country is he held in such low esteem as in the Free States of the North, where the institution of domestic slavery has been abolished. By the manners and customs of the people, as well as by their laws, he is made an outlaw and held to be a vagabond, who cannot and who ought not to aspire to a higher destiny. The nearer the period of enfranchisement seems to approach, although accomplished by their own act, the more do they manifest their abhorrence of his person, and their determination to avoid the contamination of his presence, if he should presume to approach them.*

* It would be unjust in forming a judgment upon these facts not to consider and give due weight to the natural tendency of the African to become a vagabond when he is left at liberty to control his own actions. It may be that this results in part from the ignominy with which he is treated by the dominant race; but it may be clearly established that it does not proceed wholly from this cause. Whoever has visited the West India possessions of Great Britain cannot fail to discover that among the resident Europeans the local barriers which separate the two races are as thoroughly recognised as when the Africans were slaves. But an illustration of the disinclination of the Africans to adopt the tastes and the industrious habits of the Europeans is exhibited at this day in Nova Scotia. It will be remembered that in the war between the United States and Great Britain the latter carried off from the Southern States a considerable number of African slaves. These were colonised chiefly in Nova Scotia. They were kindly received by the inhabitants, and the most strenuous efforts were adopted to secure their well-being, and to lay for them the foundations of future prosperity. They were, I believe, invested with the rights of [illegible]. [illegible] At least there has been conferred upon them the right of suffrage. They

While the existence of a deeply-seated antipathy in the Northern mind to the free negro, before referred to, would of itself forbid the assumption that the Free States were tempted into the bloody path they are now following by any sentiment of benevolence towards the slave, this negative testimony is strengthened when we consider in what manner the liberation of the slaves would affect the wealthiest element in the Republican party.

That the leaders of this party designed to employ their political supremacy in such a manner as to control the destinies of the white race in the Southern States, through the instrumentality of the institution of domestic slavery, may be readily conceived. That they meant to keep the South in moral subjection by holding ever over their heads the terrible sword of Abolitionism, and that they endeavoured to weaken the power of the South by creating and fostering a spirit of rebellion amongst the slaves, may not be

vote in all elections. So far, however, from progressing, they have absolutely retrograded, and their descendants are not to-day as far advanced in civilisation as when they were released from servitude. They are ignorant, indolent, immoral, and every way degraded in their habits of life. A few employ themselves occasionally in making brooms, or in similar occupations—on election day they pocket a few shillings—for the rest they are idle, dissolute, and thriftless. Their numbers are constantly diminishing, and they are less numerous now than when they and their fathers were transplanted from the Slave States of the Union, after making due allowance for those who have emigrated. This information I have derived from various sources, but chiefly upon two occasions when I was myself in Halifax. I conversed with many intelligent gentlemen there upon the subject, and all were agreed as to the facts here stated. It would thus seem that, whether in the tropical latitudes of the West Indies—in the more moderate climate of the Free States of the American Union—or in the colder region of Nova Scotia, the freed African follows the same downward road. We may, therefore, account in some measure for the earnestness with which he is repelled by the laws and the manners of civilised communities.

questioned; but that they intended in the beginning absolutely to release the slave from the authority of his master can scarcely be attributed to more than a small number. Such a consummation would have rendered valueless their cherished system of prohibitory duties. One of the very objects which they set out to accomplish by a sectional organisation was to compel the cotton growers and agriculturists of the South to be their customers. Can we believe that they would stultify themselves by destroying the very sources of the wealth which they were endeavouring to appropriate to themselves? Can we suppose that a burglar, who has planned the robbery of a house which he knew contained a certain treasure, would voluntarily apply the torch, with a view to burn up both house and treasure, at the very moment when he had succeeded in passing the threshold, and was about to clutch the promised reward of his dishonesty? There is only a single contingency which would justify such an inference. If his presence had aroused the inmates, he might seek to make good his escape by setting fire to the premises, and running away by the light of the conflagration. This, in fact, is a solution of the present attitude of parties in the North upon the subject of the abolition of slavery. They would secure dominion over the South at the expense of slavery, if that is necessary to the attainment of their purpose; but if they could subdue the Southern people without changing the relations which have existed between the races inhabiting the South, I presume but few even among Federal partisans would assert that the Institution of Slavery would be abolished by their act.

CHAPTER XI.

THE INFLUENCE OF SLAVERY UPON THE DURATION OF THE UNION FARTHER CONSIDERED.

RETURNING to the point from whence I have been tempted to digress, I propose to consider the third and last means suggested to bring about a political and social equality between the black and white races, which, as before said, involved in its progress their amalgamation. It is scarcely necessary to adduce an argument to prove that the voluntary consent of the dominant race to such a solution could never be obtained. It is quite easy for theoretical expounders of political and moral creeds to sit down behind their books and papers and write treatises upon the rights of man, in which they may prove most clearly that a difference in colour, capacity, and race constitute no reason why the weaker should be deprived of his personal liberty. It is not necessary to controvert the abstract truth of the proposition. I might extend it further, and prove that the existence of these differences do not justify European nations in seizing upon vast territories and holding in subjection hundreds of millions of people who have never wronged them. But if we have never yet found any Government, or the subject thereof, willing to surrender their dominion over a conquered people, even upon a distant continent, how could it be hoped that when a superior and an inferior race are brought together upon the same territory the former would consent to relinquish its supremacy? The American people, whether citizens of the North or of the South, have always believed that the abolition of slavery could only be accomplished, and peace maintained, by the process of extinguishing their own race by amalgamation with the African. We have seen that it is not difficult for foreign abolitionist lecturers and European demagogues to urge the descendants of Anglo-Saxon and German and French ancestors in America to show their love for the human race, and their devotion to the principles of liberty and equality, by mingling their blood with that of a degraded and an inferior race; but there is not a kingdom nor a principality in Europe that would not scout such a suggestion, if by any possibility it might be brought home to themselves.

It is clear that the only means by which the end proposed might be reached would be through the instrumentality of an overruling external power. Suppose that such a pressure had been brought upon the Americans, and that slavery had been abolished, and that the process of absorption had been commenced among the humbler classes, who would, by the necessities of their position, have been thrown into familiar intercourse: the first effect would have been to have destroyed the Republic. It will hardly be affirmed that the same laws which might govern one homogeneous race would be applicable to a community composed in the ratio of only two to one of such different and antagonistical elements. The strong arm of absolute power, irresponsible to the inhabitants, could alone hold in due subjection such discordant materials. The peace of society—humanity itself—would, in such a case, impel the people to seek shelter and protection under the wing of just such a Government as that which the French Revolution was instituted to destroy.

Thus the theory of political and social equality, pressed beyond its legitimate boundaries, and applied to mankind as a unit, instead of to homogeneous communities, would have destroyed the only great Republic in existence, and created a despotism upon its ruins. Whether such a result will be accepted as a solution of the present devastating war remains to be seen; but that would have been the end long ago, if the political and social distinctions between the blacks and the whites had been obliterated from the laws of the country.

In considering the results which must inevitably attend the universal application of the theoretical principles enunciated by the French Revolution, we may not wonder at the coincidence of sentiment before referred to between its proselytes and the representatives of that political dogma which the revolution was instituted to destroy. The theory of the one was adverse to the existence of slavery—of the other, adverse to the existence of liberty. The practical application of the first upon the American continent would have destroyed slavery; but it would have destroyed the Republic and liberty at the same time

Was it wonderful that the politicians of the schools

of Louis XIV. and Henry VIII. should have locked arms with the Marats and the Robespierres, and said—'We will unite with you in fighting the battle of Liberty, Fraternity, and Equality for the down-trodden Africans upon the continent of America!'

There was a broad distinction between the principles enunciated by Washington and his compatriots and those which were promulgated by the French Republic. The American Republics adopted as their guide the great principles of civil and religious liberty as applied to homogeneous communities. The French Republic adopted the same principles, but sought to apply them to mankind as a unit. The former established political equality amongst its own recognised citizens, leaving it to the individual to find his own social level, according to his tastes, his habits, and his education: the latter sought to enforce not only political but social equality. The theory of the former was that each nation had a right to such a Government as might satisfy the wants and desires of its own citizens: the theory of the latter was that all mankind should be governed by uniform laws, both in their social and political relations, resting upon a democratic basis. Follow out the theory of the first to its legitimate conclusions, and it establishes liberty for each distinct homogeneous nation: the theory of the latter, in its practical application, could only end in the establishment of despotism.

Unfortunately for the cause of real liberty, the comprehensive but impracticable theory promulgated by the enthusiasts of the Robespierrean school, during a period of general delirium, has found more admirers amongst those who in Europe have assumed to be the leaders of the party of freedom than the less brilliant, though more practical scheme inaugurated by Washington and the fathers of the American Republics. Considering the radically different auspices under which the two were ushered into existence, it may not be regarded as wonderful that each, in its developement, should have partaken somewhat of the character of the circumstances and the times in which they respectively had their origin. The independence of the thirteen British colonies having been acknowledged there were none to oppose them in their onward progress. They were the architects of their own destinies, and whatever may be the fate reserved for the Confederation which they formed, the structure of the Government they created will ever remain a monument to the wisdom of its founders. They were inaugurating an experiment which had never before been submitted to a practical test. It should excite less wonder that they failed in the arrangement of some details of its complicated machinery than that they only failed in a few.

The French Republic, on the contrary, born amidst the convulsions of a continent—cradled and reared up in storm and tempest—hurled forth the firebrand of political and social equality and fraternity for all mankind, as President Lincoln has issued his proclamation of emancipation, not to enunciate a dogma, but to crush their enemies—to destroy rather than to build up—to enslave rather than to make free. It was dictated by hatred against those who opposed its progress, rather than by love for those in whose interests they professed to employ it. If the Republic had lived the dogma would have died, for the existence of the one was incompatible with that of the other. The Republic perished and the dogma has survived. From the ruins of a despotic monarchy, and the downfall of a still more despotic democracy, there has, however, emerged a Government preserving all that was really free, and rejecting all that was really despotic of both. Happy for the French people when they threw off the despotism of their tyrant kings; happier still when they cast away the bloodier tyranny of their democratic rulers; but most happy when they settled down at last to the enjoyment of that real liberty which was consistent with the prosperity, the welfare, the greatness, and the glory of the nation.

CHAPTER XII.

THE INSTITUTION OF SLAVERY RETARDED THE DISRUPTION OF THE UNION

I HAVE declared that the Institution of African Slavery did not produce the dissolution of the Union. I think that the universal and almost fanatical antipathy of the people of the North to the negro, and the extreme harshness of the laws they have enacted to repel and degrade him, and the frank recognition and acknowledgement of this by President Lincoln himself ought to be regarded as satisfactory proof that no sentiment of love for the slave, nor a desire to better his condition, prompted the North to enter upon their bloody crusade against the South. That there existed a party who urged the general Government to decree the abolition of slavery in the Southern States is true; but it is easy to show that the desire to accomplish this purpose originated in a feeling of unkindness towards the Southern white men, rather than a regard for those whom they would emancipate. It is also true that President Lincoln was the elected chief of a party existing only in the Free States, which party was pledged to an unconstitutional interference with the domestic institutions of the Southern States.

But the thoughtful student of American history cannot fail to discover that this result was brought about by other causes, stimulated to an unnatural developement by the madness which always attended presidential elections.

While it may be thus established that the Institution of Slavery did not hasten the disruption of the Confederacy, there is the strongest reason for believing that it retarded that result.

The inauguration of the American Government upon the principle of entire equality amongst its citizens, upon whom devolved the duty of conducting the Government, was an untried experiment. It had no predecessors, for the republics of former days bore scarcely any resemblance to that of which Washington was the first President. Its founders, although guided by the most profound wisdom, could not profit by the experience of others. It was in its nature subject to many dangers. The people might at times become remiss in the discharge of their duties—at other times they might prove more zealous than discreet. Admitting that the great body of the people could not have any interest which would not be promoted by a good Government, they were liable to be imposed upon and led astray by artful demagogues.

Of all the dangers which a republican Government has to encounter, the one most to be feared is the influence of the demagogue. This is true in theory, and it has proven to be so in practice. The people, however honest, cannot always distinguish between their real friends and those who pander to their passions in order to win their friendship.

However great may have been this evil in the earlier days of the Republic, it did not, during the lifetime of 'the Fathers,' assume such alarming proportions. The Revolution had drawn forth from the mass a galaxy of statesmen and patriots whose high qualities secured for them the confidence and respect of all classes of their fellow-countrymen. The wisdom with which they guided the nation may be inferred from the fact that even yet the politician can adopt no means more sure to win the sympathies of the people than by assuring them that he follows in the footsteps of Washington, Jefferson, Madison, and Monroe. When these all passed away the field for the demagogue was enlarged.

There were many causes which conspired to make the Free States the great theatre upon which this class of politicians played their parts. Although the right of suffrage was exercised alike by all citizens, yet in the South it was limited to white men. More than one-third of the population being slaves, or of African descent, were non-voters. In the North, on the contrary, the most ignorant and vicious of the population were as powerful in deciding the result of elections as the most intelligent and the most virtuous. This, however, might possibly have been an endurable evil, if it had not given birth to demagogues who employed that ignorance as a means to elevate themselves to high places of trust. They constituted the material from whence he drew his sustenance. They were an ever-present temptation, seducing even the better class of politicians into a way of life which ended by bringing the great body of those who were engaged in politics to the same low standard. The worst became finally the controlling element in all elections, and the best at last descended to the same level, as a sole resource against complete exclusion from any participation in public affairs. To secure the favour of the worst third of the population was a passport to office and power. To fail in winning their approbation was an irreversible order to the political aspirant to return to the quiet of private life. To be '*a statesman*' constituted but a very slight claim to a seat in Congress. To have been a '*rail-splitter*' was the highest boast of a candidate for the presidency.

In the South the arts of the demagogues often won the prize of political favour; but it required more skill and a higher order of talent. In the North it was only necessary to arouse the passions of the people, by calling the Southerners 'aristocrats.' In the South the candidate for popular favour had to satisfy the people that he was himself a patriot. While in the North the proverbial fickleness of the multitude often displaced the favourite of yesterday without any just cause, who had been elevated without merit; in the South they in many cases retained for a long time in office those whom they had chosen as their public functionaries. Political pursuits in the South were held in higher esteem than in the North. There was, therefore, a greater number of high-toned, educated gentlemen in the former who were willing to come forward as candidates for office. Both have degenerated in very many respects from the standard of the earlier days of the Republic, but the descent has been much greater in the North than in the South.

There was, however, a wide field for the operations of the demagogue in the North which had no existence in the South. The naturalisation laws of the United States required a residence of only five years to invest a foreigner with all the rights of a native-born citizen, whose ancestors had peopled the country in the days of its colonial dependence. Even this short period of probation was, in consequence of the exigences of parties, reduced in many of the States to a period of one year, and it has occurred that voters have been marched from the emigrant ship to the ballot-box upon the day on which they first set foot upon American soil. That many thousands of the better class of Europeans were attracted by the favourable conditions offered to them is most true. If the full rights of citizenship could have been conferred upon these, and withheld from that far larger class who also came to claim the promised bounty, the Republics would in one sense have been the gainers.

We can only realise the magnitude of this power of votes in the North by looking over the yearly reports of immigration; but without troubling the reader with these statistics, he may approximate to an understanding of the subject by considering that the population of the States of the Union has been augmented from three millions to more than thirty-three millions within about three quarters of a century.

Whatever may have been the quality of this immense influx of foreigners into the North it may easily be imagined that great changes would result in the policy, the manners, and the habits of thought and action of the Northern people. That very many thousands of these were utterly unfit, at the end of their short probation of five years, to take charge of the Government will not, I think, be questioned by those who have well considered the subject. Utterly unprepared by education and early training for the discharge of the duties which were confided to them, they nevertheless constituted in a number of the Northern States a controlling balance of power in deciding elections.

Even many of the most intelligent and best informed politicians of Europe do not fully comprehend the relations of the general Government to the individual States: how could these uninformed immigrants be expected to administer such a Government wisely? The greater number of them learned, for the first time, on their arrival in America that the country was divided into a number of independent States, united together under a league or constitution. We may conclude that even the best informed amongst them were surprised to find upon their arrival that they immediately came under the influence of the State Laws, and that they might live to old age and die without having been brought once under the operation of the laws of the United States. In their native countries they had heard only of that Government whose Capitol was Washington. The United States, to them, was like France, or Prussia, or England—a consolidated sovereignty. When, upon settling themselves down, they found that they were citizens of Indiana, or Ohio, or New York, and that they could not reside in any part of the American continent where they

There was, however, a ide
of the demagogue in the No
ence in the South. The nat
United States required a eside
to invest a foreigner wit all t
born citizen, whose ancesors ha
in the days of its colonl dep
short period of probationwas, in
exigencies of parties, reduced in
to a period of one year, and it
voters have been marche from th
the ballot-box upon the lay on w
foot upon American soil. That n
the better class of Europans were
favourable conditions offerd to the
If the full rights of citizeship coul
ferred upon these, and withheld fro
class who also came to caim the p
the Republics would in one sense
gainers.

We can only realise th magnitude
of votes in the North b looking ov
reports of immigration; ut without
reader with these statistic, he may ap
an understanding of the sbject by consi
the population of the Stes of the Uni
augmented from three milions to more t
three millions within bout
century.

Whatever may
immense influ
easily be im
in the polic

and action of the Northern p… Southern States, and the
thousands of these were … m.
their short probation of fi… hazarding too much to
the Government will not, I … age as regards natural-
those who have well conside… y guarded—if they had
unprepared by education a… ality with native-born
discharge of the duties whi… d to *reside twenty-one*
they nevertheless constitu… being permitted to
Northern States a contro… ge—they would have
deciding elections. … gard to the nature of
Even many of the mo… ederation might pos-
formed politicians of Eu… even of presidential
hend the relations of the … on longer.
individual States: how … common, I am quite
immigrants be expected t… mber of thoughtful
ment wisely? The great… ot follow, because an
for the first time, on the … epted the privileges
the country was divided … that he believes the
dent States, united to… d one. The earnest
constitution. We may c… y citizens who were
informed amongst them … conspicuously
their arrival that they i… history; but
influence of the State I… ehend that
live to old age and … States
brought once under the … gst
United States. In thei…
heard only of that Gov…
W…

could be properly designated as 'citizens of the United States,' they were not only disappointed, but many of them believed it to be a radical defect in the structure of the Government. They had been familiar in Europe with the idea of a great central head to a Government, and they thought that they would confer a service upon America if they could reform the Government of the United States according to that standard. The consequence was, when the Republican party came forward, pledged to a policy which would in its operation absorb the sovereignity of the several States into that of the Northern States, through the instrumentality of the Federal Government, it found hundreds of thousands of foreign-born voters ready to assist them in the accomplishment of their unconstitutional enterprise. They were attached to the Government of the United States, but they had of course no local attachments which would cause them to reverence the State Governments.

We may well believe that the existence of these feelings on the part of the great mass of foreign-born voters supplied at least one of the stimulants which induced the Republican party to persevere in the course they had indicated, even after it became manifest that they could only accomplish their measures by the sword. Having no respect for a system of State Governments, of which they could not comprehend the uses, but which they believed truly, operated as a check upon the despotic rule of a mere majority, they have been the most available instruments of Mr. Lincoln in fighting his battles for the subjugation of the Southern States, and the erection of a central despotism.

It would not, probably, be hazarding too much to say that if the right of suffrage as regards naturalised citizens had been properly guarded—if they had even been placed on an equality with native-born citizens, and have been required to reside twenty-one years in the country before being permitted to exercise the right of suffrage—they would have become more instructed in regard to the nature of the Government, and the Confederation might possibly have sustained the shock even of presidential elections for perhaps a generation longer.

I entertain these opinions in common, I am quite sure, with a considerable number of thoughtful foreign-born citizens. It does not follow, because an intelligent immigrant has accepted the privileges which have been offered to him, that he believes the law conferring them to be a good one. The earnest and devoted patriotism of many citizens who were born in foreign countries has been conspicuously manifest at all periods of American history; but even many of these have failed to comprehend that the surest bulwark of liberty in the United States consisted in the division of supreme power amongst the several States. They knew that in concentration there existed a greater capacity for doing good promptly; but they failed to perceive that it led directly to despotism. Still the small class referred to were patriots. They became Americans in heart when they assumed the duties of citizens. They never sought to form a 'power of foreign-born voters,' for the purpose of putting themselves in opposition to those who were born upon the soil.

There was another, and unfortunately a larger class of intelligent foreign-born citizens, who being revolutionists and demagogues at home, did not leave these characteristic qualities behind them when they went to America. Many of them were political adventurers and foes to real liberty in the countries from whence they came, and they have well sustained the same characters in the new field they have selected. Their province was rather to break down and destroy all government, than to make war upon bad Governments. Whether they were engaged, according to their own declarations, 'in securing the blessings of liberty for the down-trodden masses of Europe,' by efforts to displace those whom they declared to be their oppressors—or employing their swords to assist in reducing the freemen of the South to political servitude—was alike congenial to their principles and their tastes. Revolution was their trade. In times of peace and quiet they were restless and dissatisfied. Their occupation was gone, and they sank into ignoble insignificance. But they flourished amidst disorders, and were only happy when mingling in those scenes of violence and carnage which might bring them forth from obscurity. The leaders of these may now be found occupying the highest places in the army and the diplomacy of the Government; and—shame to the native-born citizens of the North—without the aid of these adventurers and other foreign mercenaries, who have been attracted to their standard by high bounties and a natural desire to shed blood—they could not have maintained their war against the South, notwithstanding their superior numbers, for a single month. Far be it from me to attribute this disinclination on the part of the great body of the native-born Northern people to any lack of the personal qualities necessary to make good soldiers. In a good cause, I doubt not for a moment that they would be as brave as the bravest. But their passions alone are in this war, not their hearts or their consciences, which upbraid them for the deep wrong they are perpetrating against those who have never injured them. They are willing to pay the highest rates for professional cut-throats, adventurers, and revolutionists, whether of domestic growth or foreign importation; but many of them shrink from doing the bloody work themselves.

Upon the arrival of one of these European adventurers in the United States, about the period of a presidential election, he was forthwith closeted with the professional president-makers, who discussed with him the various schemes for bringing the 'foreign element to bear upon the approaching contest.' The ignorant, and often vicious material of which the foreign-born voters were composed offered an inviting field for their machinations. They plunged at once into the arena of party politics, with all the recklessness, and vehemence, and adroitness of veterans in party warfare. They entered upon the work of pulling down the Republic with all the zeal and zest they had displayed in their pretended efforts to reform the monarchies of the Old World. At length they succeeded in combining the greater portion of the foreign element of president-making material into a unit of political power; and those who had been chiefly instrumental in the accomplishment of this result at once took a high rank as party leaders and expectant recipients of govermental honours and bounties. At a little later period they were just as ready to take a leading part in the hostile invasion of the territory of a free and an honourable people, whom they at least had never known but as friends and benefactors in the hour of their greatest need, and against whom they could not urge even the pretence of a wrong.

As long as this foreign power of votes was distributed amongst the various contestants for the prize of the presidency and the spoils of the Treasury, the one part, to a certain extent, counteracted the influence of the other. As long as the political parties maintained their national character, like the 'Whig' and 'Democratic' parties, into which the nation was during so many years divided—even though they might, to a certain extent, combine in favour of the one or the other—their power of mischief was limited and restrained. But the moment that a powerful party made its appearance, as a new contestant for supreme power—deriving its support exclusively upon one side of a geographical line, and that division being the one in which this foreign element resided—even a partial concentration of their strength, embracing as it did an overwhelming majority, turned the scale against the party which sought support from every part of the nation.

In the South this election material did not exist. The small number of foreign-born voters there, were either of the better class, or were more profitably engaged at highly remunerative wages than in the work of president-making. The great body of the Southern people were descendants of ancestors who first peopled the wilds of North America. They were not, therefore, materially affected by the radicalism of a great and constant influx of strangers. They cherished the political institutions of their fathers as something holy—something, if need be, to die for. They revered the State Governments, from which they and their ancestors before them had derived their title-deeds to their estates: they had each a local history, written and traditional. These causes made the Southern people, in the fullest signification of the term, Conservative—that is, they were rigid upholders of the Constitution and opposed to change.

This Conservatism was notably exhibited when the two sections were thrown together in Congress. Whatever divisions might exist in the South in reference to political parties, the predominating feeling amongst all, was to make as few inroads as possible upon the Constitution, or upon the original structure of the Government. This quality of Southern statesmen gave to them a powerful influence with those citizens of the North who entertained similar opinions. The respect in which they were held, and the confidence which was reposed in them, has been urged as a proof that the South has always ruled the nation. This is perhaps true in one sense, but untrue in the sense in which it is spoken. Washington was a slaveholder and a Southerner; but who would designate him, in a sectional sense, as a Southerner? Jefferson, Madison, Monroe, Jackson, Polk, Taylor, were all Southerners and slaveholders

—several of these were even opposed to the Institution of Slavery—and not one of them was chosen because he was a Southerner. In the whole history of the Union not a single citizen, either from the North or South, has been called to fill the station of President because he was a Northerner or a Southerner, except Mr. Lincoln.

The Institution of African Slavery in the Southern Confederacy may or may not be an evil in the sense in which that term is employed—I owe it to frankness to say that I do not believe it—though, as I said in the outset, I do not propose to enter into a discussion of that question. It may, or may not, have inflicted injury upon the material interests of mankind—though I am free to say that I can discover no evidences that it has. It may, or may not, have degraded the African below the position occupied by his race elsewhere, though I think that the weight of testimony is against such a supposition; but I believe that candid and unprejudiced men will decide that its conservative influence acting upon the Governments and people of the South, and from thence reacting upon the Federal Government and the Free States, has had a powerful influence in preserving the whole fabric from the domination of the radical and revolutionary elements which have for so long menaced its integrity; and that although it could not save the Union, it retarded the consummation of its final overthrow.

CHAPTER XIII.

A REVIEW OF THE EVENTS CONNECTED WITH THE FORMATION OF THE FEDERAL UNION, AND THE OPINIONS OF THE AUTHORS OF THE CONSTITUTION, IN REGARD TO SECTIONAL AND STATE SOVEREIGNTY QUESTIONS.

TO a correct solution of the causes which produced the rupture of the Federal Union, and to estimate their relative weight, it is almost essential that we should commence our investigations upon the first page of its history.

In the succeeding chapter I propose to review somewhat in detail the most prominent events connected with the progress of the presidential elections from Washington to Lincoln. These two names, constituting the extreme limits of our investigations, will no doubt suggest forcibly to the mind of the reader that it is a downward road he is invited to travel.

In the present preliminary chapter I propose once more to return to the earliest period of the Union's history, and to the opinions and acts of the framers of the Constitution, as explained by themselves, in regard to the causes which were a source of division amongst themselves, and which they feared might be productive of evil in the future.

Very great confusion in the public mind in regard

to American affairs has grown out of the fact that the history of the changes which have taken place in the Government of the United States since the first Revolution have not been understood or duly considered. Although it may be presumed that at the present day information in this respect is generally diffused, yet a brief reference to these changes may be of service to the general reader.

The First Government of the United States.

The thirteen North American colonies of Great Britain, through their delegates, in a Convention which assembled in Philadelphia, May 10, 1775, established 'Articles of Confederation and Perpetual Union' between the several colonies. The following extracts from these articles indicate the nature and objects of the league:—

ARTICLE 1. The name of this Confederacy shall be the United Colonies of North America. [On July 2, 1776, the word 'colonies' was changed to 'states' by Act of Congress, upon which day was assumed the title, '*United States of America.*' On the 4th of the same month was issued the formal Declaration of Independence. It was under the operation of this Government that George Washington was appointed Commander-in-Chief of the Army of the Confederation.]

ARTICLE 2. The United Colonies hereby severally enter into a firm league of friendship with each other, binding on themselves and their posterity, for their common defence against their enemies, for the securities of their liberties and properties, and their mutual and general welfare.

ARTICLE 3. Each colony shall enjoy and 'retain as much as it may think fit of its own present laws, customs, rights, privileges, and peculiar jurisdiction within its own limits.'

Second Government of the United States.

In the third year of Independence, that is, on July 7, 1778, the first Government was abolished, and Congress adopted other 'Articles of Confederation and Perpetual Union:'—

ARTICLE 1. The style of this Confederacy shall be '*The United States of America.*'

ARTICLE 2. Each State retains its sovereignty, freedom, and independence, and every power, jurisdiction, and right which is not by their confederation expressly delegated to the United States in Congress assembled.

ARTICLE 3. The said States hereby severally enter into a firm league of friendship with each other for their common defence, the security of their liberties, and their mutual and general welfare.

ARTICLE 13. . . . The articles of this Confederation shall be inviolably observed by every State, and the Union shall be perpetual: nor shall any alteration be made in any of them, unless such alteration be agreed to in a Congress of the United States, *and afterwards confirmed by the Legislature of every State.**

Third Government of the United States.

In the twelfth year of Independence, that is, on December 17, 1787, the second Government of the United States was abolished, as far as concerned the States which sanctioned the formation of the new Government, and was succeeded by a third.

* Many persons, by a very natural confusion of the several Constitutions, have assigned this clause to the present Constitution, and hence have concluded that this prohibition precluded the Southern States from the right to withdraw themselves from the Federal Union, whereas it was in violation of this very clause that the late Union was established; at first by nine of the twelve States which were parties to the preceding league

This was accomplished by a Convention of Delegates, representing ten of the States, at the head of which was George Washington. The States, however, not being unanimous in desiring a change, there was some discussion as to how far the last article above recited would be binding. It was decided that no restriction contained in that clause could prevent such States as might choose to do so from resuming their delegated powers and establishing a new league. They accordingly adopted an article providing that 'the ratification of the Conventions of nine States shall be sufficient for the establishment of this Constitution between the States so ratifying the same.' In effect the requisite number of States did approve the Constitution thus formed. They therefore seceded from the previous Government, and established themselves under that league from which the Southern States seceded upon the election of Mr. Lincoln to the presidency. It was not, however, until May 29, 1790, that the last of the thirteen States, Rhode Island, consented to join the new league. New York did not enter until July 26, 1789; and North Carolina did not give in her adhesion until August 7 of the same year. Thus these three States did not become members of the new Union until after the election of George Washington as the first President.

Although the powers delegated by the States to the Federal Government were more clearly defined in the last than in the two which preceded it, yet the principle of State sovereignty was as carefully guarded in the one as the other. Each one declared that the object of the league was 'to establish justice, insure domestic tranquillity, provide for the common defence, and promote the general welfare.' And the third Government, from which the Southern States withdrew, declared in the articles of the compact that 'the powers not delegated to the United States by the Constitution, nor prohibited by it to the States, are reserved to the States respectively, or to the people.'

Although the Constitution of the third and now existing Government of the United States as finally adopted bears evidence of the compromises and concessions which were mutually agreed upon by the representatives of the different interests, States, and sections, yet we can discover more clearly the ground-work of the sectional troubles which afterwards, under the stimulant of presidential elections, were employed to produce the dissolution of the Union, by examining the propositions in detail as brought forward and sustained by the respective representatives of each. If after these compromises had been achieved by mutual concessions there had never been any general elections which might serve to revive the recollection of these differences, and thus excite the popular mind, we might have reasonably hoped that the same calm councils which concurred in creating would have maintained the Constitution in its purity. The North had far greater cause to desire the perpetuation of the Union upon the compromises of the Constitution in the year 1860 than existed in 1787. Nothing short of the demoralising influence of presidential elections could ever have so blinded that shrewd, far-seeing, and sagacious people, as to induce them to forego all the advantages of a peaceful political connection with the

Southern States, by endeavouring to rob the latter of their constitutional prerogatives. In truth, I can discover no reason for believing that the Northern people as a body would ever have placed themselves in an attitude of hostility to the South, but for the influence of that army of agitators and political adventurers which was brought into being through the instrumentality of presidential contests. There did, however, exist conflicting interests, and other mutually repelling influences, which rendered the task of the agitators more easy of accomplishment.

The debates in the Convention which formed the Constitution afford us a clear view of the sectional antagonisms which were finally developed into their present proportions.

The Constitution provided that three-fifths of the slaves should be estimated in deciding upon the number of representatives to which the Slave States should be entitled in the Federal Congress, and in the assessment of direct taxes for the benefit of the general Government.

Also that those who escaped into the Free States should not be made free on account of any laws existing in said States, but should be delivered up on the application of the legal owner.

We find, by reference to the debates upon these topics in the Convention, that although there may be discovered the germ of sectionalism, founded upon the supposed pecuniary antagonisms between the North and the South, yet there was even less difficulty in effecting a compromise upon this question than upon others involving also the interests of the two sections. Some of the bitterest opponents of slavery were delegates from the South; while a few of the Northern adversaries of the South opposed the foregoing provisions—not alone because 'slavery was opposed to humanity, and was seriously detrimental to the progress in prosperity and wealth' of their Southern brethren—but because it involved the North in the necessity of expending its blood and treasure to protect the Southern people against slave insurrections! The Free States would consent to this heavy burthen, however, upon condition that the Federal Government might be permitted *to tax the exports of Southern slave labour* as an equivalent. They already exercised the right of imposing heavy duties upon foreign imports, and of transporting Southern produce by means of navigation laws, in Northern ships, to the exclusion of other competitors for the carrying trade; and if to this had been added the right (they were also in receipt of both protection and large bounties paid by the general Government to their fisheries) to tax the exports of slave labour, the South might well have prayed King George to take them back again, and do to them his will in the way of taxes, imposts, and stamp duties. It would probably be unjust to deny to the few Northern anti-slavery men of that day the merit of sincerity in their philanthropic endeavours to mitigate the evils of slavery; but the least censorious even may not deny that they mingled with this benevolent sentiment a fixed purpose to increase their worldly stores through the instrumentality of the condemned institution.

The following additional extracts from the debates in the Convention (as reported by Mr. Madison) cannot fail to be both interesting and instructive to those who desire to know the individual views and sentiments of the members:—

August 8, 1787.—*Mr. Rufus King, of Massachusetts,* could not reconcile his mind to the proposition (concerning the admission of slaves into the rule of representation). The admission of slaves was a most grating circumstance to his mind. In two great points the hands of the Congress were absolutely tied. The importation of slaves could not be prohibited. *Exports could not be taxed!* Is this reasonable? What are the great objects of the general system? First, defence against foreign invasion; secondly, against internal sedition. Shall all the States, then, be bound to defend each, and shall each be at liberty to introduce a weakness which will render defence more difficult? Shall one part of the United States be bound to defend another part, and that other part be at liberty not only to increase its own danger, *but to withhold the compensation for the burden.* If slaves are to be imported, *shall not the exports produced by their labour supply a revenue,* the better to enable the general Government to defend their masters? There was so much inequality and unreasonableness in all this that the people of the Northern States could never be reconciled to it. . . . At all events either slaves should not be represented, or *exports should be taxable.*

Mr. Gouverneur Morris, of Pennsylvania, moved to insert 'free' before the word 'inhabitants.' . . Domestic slavery is the most prominent feature in the aristocratic countenance of the proposed Constitution. The vassalage of the poor has ever been the favourite offspring of aristocracy. And *what is the proposed compensation to the North* for a sacrifice of every principle of right, of every impulse of humanity? They are to bind themselves to march their militia for the defence of the Southern States against those very slaves of whom they complain.

Without pausing to comment upon the peculiar and characteristic code of morals under which the two last speakers proposed to assist 'in the sacrifice of every principle of right, and every impulse of humanity,' provided they could be guaranteed a pecuniary compensation commensurate with the greatness of the crime they were called upon to uphold, one cannot fail to be struck with the language of exaggeration they employed in referring to the services they would be called upon to render.

If they were not speaking in irony, the sequel has been a striking commentary upon their judgment. The only occasions upon which the North has ever interfered between the blacks and the whites of the South were first clandestinely, and afterwards openly, to place the dagger in the hands of the slaves, with instructions to slay their masters. But to continue:—

Mr. Pinckney, of South Carolina, considered the fisheries and the western frontier as more burthensome to the United States than the slaves.

The motion of Mr. G. Morris (to insert 'free') was rejected—*all the States voting against it*, except New Jersey.

August 21.—*Mr. Luther Martin* proposed to vary Article 7 so as to allow a prohibition or tax on the importation of slaves. . . . Slaves weakened one part of the Union which the other part were bound to protect.* . . . It was inconsistent with the principles of the Revolution, and dishonourable to the American character, to have such a feature in the Constitution.

Mr. Rutledge, of South Carolina, would readily exempt the other States from the obligation to protect the Southern States against the slaves. He was not apprehensive of insurrections.

Mr. Ellsworth, of Connecticut, was for leaving the clause as it stands. Let every State import what it pleases The morality or wisdom of slavery are considerations *belonging to the States themselves*. What enriches a part enriches the whole, and the States are the best judges of their particular interests.

Mr. Pinckney, of South Carolina, can never receive the plan, if it prohibits the slave trade. In every proposed extension of the powers of Congress that State has expressly and watchfully

* From the moment these words were uttered up to the present the only protection afforded by the North to the Slave States was the protection which vultures give to lambs

excepted that of meddling with the importation of negroes. If the States be all left at liberty on this subject, South Carolina may by degrees do of herself what is wished, as Virginia and Maryland have already done.*

Mr. Sherman, of Connecticut, disapproved of the slave trade; yet, as the States were now possessed of the right to import slaves, as the public good did not require it to be taken from them, and as it was expedient to have as few objections as possible to the proposed scheme of Government, he thought it best to leave the matter as we find it. He observed that the abolition of slavery seemed to be going on in the United States, and that the good sense of the several States would probably by degrees complete it.

Mr. Mason, of Virginia.—This infernal traffic originated in the avarice of British merchants. The British Government constantly checked the attempts of Virginia to put a stop to it. The evil of having slaves was experienced during the late war. . . . He mentioned the instructions given by Cromwell to the commissioners sent to Virginia to arm the servants and slaves, in case other means of obtaining its submission should fail. Maryland and Virginia had already prohibited the importation of slaves. North Carolina had done the same thing in substance. All this would be in vain, if South Carolina and Georgia be at liberty to import. The Western people are already calling out for slaves for their new lands, and will fill that country with slaves, if they can be got through South Carolina and Georgia.

Mr. Ellsworth, of Connecticut, had never owned a slave, and could not judge of the effects of slavery upon character. If it was to be considered in a moral light, we ought to go farther, and free those already in the country. As slaves also multiply so fast in Virginia and Maryland that it is cheaper to raise than import them, whilst in the sickly rice swamps foreign supplies are necessary—if we go no farther than is urged, we shall be unjust towards South Carolina and Georgia. Let us not intermeddle. As population increases, poor labourers will be so plenty as to render slavery useless.

Mr. Pinckney, of South Carolina.—If slavery be wrong it is justified by the example of all the world. He cited the case of

---

* In effect, South Carolina prohibited the slave trade the same year, and from that time to the present, except during three years, the prohibition has been rigidly enforced —'South Vindicated,' p 200

Greece, Rome, and other ancient States; and the sanction given by France, Spain, England, Holland, and other modern nations In all ages one half of mankind had been slaves. If the Southern States were let alone they will probably of themselves stop importation. He would himself, as a citizen of South Carolina, vote for it An attempt to take away the right as proposed will produce serious objections to the Constitution.

General Pinckney. . . . South Carolina and Georgia cannot do without slaves. As to Virginia, she will gain by stopping the importations. The slaves would rise in value, and she has more than she wants. . . . He contended that the importation of slaves would be for the interest of the whole Union. . . . He admitted it to be reasonable that slaves should be dutied like other imports.

Mr. Gerry, of Massachusetts, thought we had nothing to do with the conduct of the States as to slaves, but ought to be careful not to give any sanction to it.

Mr. Dickinson, of Delaware, considered it as inadmissible on every principle of honour and safety that the importation of slaves should be authorised to the States by the Constitution. The true question was whether the national happiness would be promoted or impeded by the importation, and this question ought to be left to the National Government, not to the States particularly interested. If England and France permitted slavery, slaves are at the same time excluded from both those kingdoms.

Mr. Williamson, of North Carolina, thought the Southern States could not be members of the Union if the clause should be rejected.

Mr. Rufus King, of Massachusetts, thought the subject should be considered in a political light only. . . . He remarked on the exemption of slaves from duty (on importation), whilst every other import was subjected to it, as an inequality that *could not fail to strike the commercial sagacity of the Northern and Middle States.*

Mr. Gouverneur Morris, of Pennsylvania, wished the whole subject to be committed, including the clauses relating to taxes on exports and to a Navigation Act. These things *may form a bargain* amongst the Northern and Southern States.

Mr. Pierce Butler, of South Carolina, said that he would never agree to the power of taxing exports.

Mr Sherman said it would be better to let the Southern States import slaves than to part with them. . . .

Mr. Pinckney, of South Carolina, moved to commit Section 6, as to a Navigation Act requiring two-thirds of each House (instead of a bare majority).

Mr. Gorham, of Massachusetts, did not see the propriety of it. He desired it to be remembered that the Eastern States had no motive to union but a commercial one. They were able to protect themselves They were not afraid of external danger, and did not need the aid of the Southern States.

August 25.—General Pinckney, of South Carolina, moved to strike out the words 'the year eighteen hundred,' as the year limiting the importation of slaves, and to insert the words 'the year eighteen hundred and eight.'

The first part of the report was then agreed to, amended as follows:—'The migration or importation of such persons as the several States now existing shall think proper to admit shall not be prohibited by the Congress prior to the year 1808' (States voting for extension of the term for importation of slaves were New Hampshire, Massachusetts, Connecticut, Maryland, North Carolina, South Carolina, and Georgia. States voting against the extension were New Jersey, Pennsylvania, Delaware, and Virginia The remaining States were not represented in the Convention.)

The following clause was agreed to *nem. con.* viz : A tax or duty may be imposed on such importations not exceeding ten dollars for each person.

Provision for Rendition of Slaves.

August 29.—Mr. Pierce Butler, of South Carolina, moved to insert after Article 15: 'If any person bound to service or labour in any of the United States shall escape into another State, he or she shall not be discharged from such service or labour in consequence of any regulations subsisting in the State to which they escape, but shall be delivered up to the person justly claiming their service or labour'—*which was agreed to nem. con.*

There stands THE FUGITIVE SLAVE LAW, in all its length and breadth and thickness. The authors were George Washington, James Madison, Alexander Hamilton, Benjamin Franklin, and their associates in the Constitutional Convention, all of whom either voted for its enactment, or suffered it to be passed without one word of opposition. So far as we may learn from the recorded proceedings of that distinguished body of patriots and statesmen it became part and parcel of the fundamental law of the Union, by the unanimous voice of all the representatives of all the States, slave and free. More than half a century afterwards the world of Abolitionism was thrown into convulsions by the announcement that a wicked South and a truculent North had decreed the 'infamous enactment.' All Europe participated in the excitement, and joined in the hue and cry of the North against the arrogant and wicked exactions of the 'slave power.' Of course, there was not one in a thousand who filled the lecture halls of England to listen to the rhapsodies of Abolition orators, who did not believe that the constitutional provision was as recent as the excitement; and fewer still who knew that its authors were the men who fought the battles of the First Revolution, and were known in history as the 'Fathers of the Republic.' Although the wire-workers of presidential contests in the United States could not plead ignorance of this requirement of the Constitution, yet the higher-law doctrine of 'conscience before constitutions' had been already accepted as the guide of Northern politicians; and immediately the leading Abolition States enacted laws, making the attempt to enforce this provision of the Constitution a penal offence punishable as a crime of the highest magnitude. The intended effect was produced upon the public mind. Politicians eagerly mounted upon the wave of popular passions which were evoked by the discussion, and rode safely into the possession of the offices they coveted.

But there existed the germ of another sectional issue at the period of the formation of the Constitution, which was afterwards developed into a bitter controversy and struggle between the North and the South, and which for a long time, as a chief element in presidential contests, threatened to divide the Union. I refer to the protection claimed by the North for its manufactures by means of high duties upon foreign imports. The representatives of the Southern States, as will be seen, proposed to restrain the exercise of this power, but the controversy was finally adjusted by conferring upon Congress the right to tax foreign imports for purposes of revenue only. As this subject became afterwards a source of sectional agitation, scarcely second to the question of slavery itself, the discussions in regard thereto in the Constitutional Convention may not be without interest to the reader:—

Mr. Pinckney, of South Carolina, moved—'That no Act of the Congress for the purpose of regulating the commerce of the United States with foreign powers among the several States shall be passed *without the assent of two-thirds* of the members of each House.' He remarked that there were five distinct commercial interests:—1. The fisheries and West India trade, which belonged to the New England States. 2. The interests of New York lay in free trade. 3. Wheat and flour were the staples of New Jersey and Pennsylvania. 4. Tobacco the staple of Maryland and Virginia, and partly North Carolina. 5 Rice and indigo the staples of South Carolina and Georgia. These different interests would be a source of oppressive regulations, if no check to a bare majority should be provided. States pursue their interests with less scruple than individuals. The power of regulating commerce was a pure concession on the part of the Southern States. They did not need the protection of the Northern States.

General Pinckney (also of South Carolina) said it was the true interest of the Southern States to have no regulation of commerce ; but considering the loss brought on the commerce of the Eastern States by the Revolution, their liberal conduct towards the views of South Carolina (on the slavery question), and the interest the weak Southern States had in being united with the strong Eastern States, he thought it proper that no fetter should be imposed on the power of making commercial regulations, and that his constituents, though prejudiced against the Eastern States, would be reconciled to this liberality.

Mr. Roger Sherman, of Connecticut, alluding to Mr. Pinckney's enumeration of particular interests as requiring security against abuse of the power, observed that the diversity was itself security.

Mr. Pinckney replied that his enumeration meant the five minute interests. It still left the two great divisions of Northern and Southern interests.

Mr G. Morris, of Pennsylvania, opposed the object of the motion as highly injurious. Preferences to American ships will multiply them till they can carry the Southern produce cheaper than it is now carried. A navy was essential to security, particularly of the Southern States, and can only be had by a Navigation Act encouraging American bottoms and seamen.

Mr. Williamson, of North Carolina, was in favour of making two-thirds instead of a majority requisite, as more satisfactory to the Southern people. As to the weakness of the Southern States, he was not alarmed on that account.

Mr. Spraight, of North Carolina, was against the motion. The Southern States could at any time save themselves from oppression by building ships for their own use.

Mr. Butler, of South Carolina, differed from those who considered the rejection of the motion as no concession upon the part of the Southern States. He considered the interest of these and of the Eastern States to be as different as the interests of Russia and Turkey. Being, notwithstanding, desirous of conciliating the affections of the Eastern States, he should vote against requiring two-thirds instead of a majority.

Colonel Mason, of Virginia.—The *majority* will be governed by their interests. The Southern States are the *minority* in both Houses of Congress Is it to be expected that they will deliver themselves bound hand and foot to the Eastern States, and thus enable them to exclaim in the words of Cromwell—'the Lord hath delivered them into our hands.'

Mr Madison observed that the disadvantage to the Southern States from a Navigation Act lay chiefly in a temporary rise of freight, attended, however, with an increase of Southern as well as Northern shipping, and with the emigration of Northern seamen and merchants. . . . An abuse of the power would be qualified with these good effects. But he thought the abuse was rendered improbable by the provision of the two branches—by the independence of the Senate—by the negation of the Executive . . . *and by the accession of Western States,* which would be altogether agricultural.

Mr. Randolph, of Virginia, said that there were features in the Constitution so odious as it now stands that he doubted whether he should be able to agree to it. A rejection of the motion would complete the deformity of the system.

Mr. Gorham, of Massachusetts.—If the Government is to be so fettered as to be unable to relieve the Eastern States, what motive can they have to join in it, and thereby tie their own hands from measures which they could otherwise take for themselves? The Eastern States were not led to strengthen the Union by fear for their own safety. He deprecated the consequences of disunion; but if it should take place, it was the Southern part of the continent that had most reason to dread them. *He urged the improbability of a combination against the interests of the Southern States*—the different situations of the Northern and Middle States being a security against it. It was, moreover, certain that foreign ships would never be altogether excluded

On the question (to require two-thirds), it was decided in the negative—Maryland, Virginia, North Carolina, Georgia—*Aye*, 4. New Hampshire, Massachusetts, Connecticut, New Jersey, Pennsylvania, Delaware, South Carolina—*No*, 7.

There was not exhibited, however, in the Convention so much jealousy between the two sections, as distinguished by the terms Northern and Southern, as between the larger and the smaller States. The diversities of interest which might thereafter arise between the two great sections was a contingency of the future—the differences between the large and small States was a present fact. All the States agreed that the separate sovereignty of each should remain intact, in all that related to their domestic affairs, and that the general Government should only be employed in regulating their intercourse with foreign nations and with each other. The large States insisted that this constitutional provision afforded sufficient security for the protection of the small States against encroachments. The latter replied that this was well enough as far as it went; but they urged that, in right of their sovereignty, each State, as a distinct political element, should have an equal representation in the Senate. This admission of, and protection to their sovereignty conceded, they were willing that the other branch of the National Legislature should represent numbers. One reason, perhaps, why the differences which might occur between the North and the South excited but little apprehension, arose from the fact that there was no very great disparity in their relative strength, and it was supposed that the accession of Western States would still farther strengthen the South against any efforts of the Northern States to usurp the control of the Government. It must be borne in mind that the commercial antagonisms between the North and the South grew out of the difference of their pursuits. Many men were opposed to slavery both on political and social grounds; but the hostility to that institution did not extend to the master. The sternest and most uncompromising adversaries of the system of slavery were found in the Slave States. At the period of time we are now considering, the authorised teachers of religion had not announced the dogma that the slave-holder was precluded by the Divine will from entering after life upon the joys of the Christian's paradise.

Although we, therefore, find an occasional reference to the antagonisms between the North and the South, and an intimation that a combination might be formed between the Northern States which would be injurious to the interests of the South, yet the Northern representatives uniformly replied that such a concentration would in the nature of things be impossible, for the reason that the Western States would be the allies of the South; and this, too, seemed to be the opinion of the great body of the Southerners. The small States, however, were not so readily satisfied that they would not be swallowed up, unless their distinct nationality should be substantially recognised in the arrangement of the details and organisation of the Government. In illustration of the sentiments and opinions of the members of the Convention in regard to this point I will make some farther extracts from the proceedings as reported by Mr. Madison :—

Wednesday, June 27th.—Mr. Luther Martin, of Maryland, contended at great length, and with great earnestness, that the general Government was meant merely to preserve the State Governments, not to govern individuals. That its powers ought to be kept within narrow limits—that if too little power was given to it, more might be added—but that if too much, it could never be resumed. That individuals, as such, have little to do but with their own States—that to resort to the citizens at large for their sanction to a new Government would be throwing them back to a state of nature—that an equal vote in each State was essential to the Federal idea, and was founded not merely in policy but on justice and freedom—that the States, like individuals, were in a state of nature equally sovereign and free—that the States, being equal, cannot confederate or treat, so as to give up an equality of votes, without giving up their liberty. The general Government ought to be formed *for the States*, not for individuals.

Mr. Williamson, of North Carolina, thought that if any political truth could be grounded on mathematical demonstration it was that if the States were equally sovereign now, and parted with equal proportions of sovereignty, that they would remain equally sovereign. He could not comprehend how the smaller States would be injured in the case.

Mr. Madison, of Virginia, could neither be convinced that the rule contended for was just, nor that it was necessary for the safety of the small States against the large ones. Was a combination of the large States dreaded? This must arise either from some interest common to Virginia, Massachusetts, and Pennsylvania (the three large States), or from the mere circumstance of similarity of size. Did any such common interest exist? In point of situation, they could not have been more effectually separated from each other by the most jealous citizens of the most jealous States. In point of manners, religion, and the other circumstances which sometimes beget affection between different communities, they were not more assimilated than the other States. In point of the staple productions, they were as dissimilar as any three other States in the Union. . . .

Mr. Sherman, of Connecticut.—The question is not what rights naturally belong to man, but how they may be most equally and effectually guarded in society. If some give up more than others to obtain this end there can be no room for complaint.

June 29th.—Mr. Johnson, of Connecticut.—The controversy must be endless whilst gentlemen differ in the grounds of their arguments—those on one side considering the States as districts of people composing *one political society*, those on the other considering them *as so many political societies*. The fact is, the States do exist as political societies, and a Government is to be formed for them *in their political capacity* as well as *for the individuals* composing them. Does it not seem to follow that if the States, as such, are to exist, they must be armed with some *power of self-defence?* Besides the aristocratic and other interests which ought to have the means of defending themselves, *the States, as such, have their interests*, which ought to have the means of defending themselves. On the whole, he thought that in some respects the States are to be considered in their political capacity, and in others as districts of individual citizens—in *one* branch *the people* ought to be represented, and in the *other* the *States.*

Mr. Gorham, of Massachusetts.—The States as now confederated *have no doubt a right to refuse to be consolidated*, or to be formed into any new system. But he wished the small States to consider which are to give up most—they or the larger ones.

Mr. Madison entreated the gentlemen representing the small States to renounce a principle which was confessedly unjust. He prayed them to ponder well the consequences of suffering the Confederacy to go to pieces.

Mr. Alexander Hamilton.—It has been said that if the smaller States renounced their *equality*, they renounced at the same time their liberty. The truth is, it is a contest for power, not for liberty. He admitted that common residence within the same State would produce a certain degree of attachment, and that this principle might have a certain degree of influence on public affairs. He thought, however, that this might by some precautions be in a great measure excluded, and that no material inconvenience could result from it, as there could not be any ground for combination amongst the States whose influence was most dreaded. *The only considerable distinctions of interests lay between the carrying and non-carrying States*, which divides instead of uniting the largest States.

Mr. Pierce, of Georgia, considered the equality of votes under the Confederation as the great source of the public difficulties. State distinctions must be sacrificed as far as the general good required, *but without destroying the States.*

Mr. Gerry, of Massachusetts. . . . The States and the advocates for them were intoxicated with the idea of their sovereignty. He was a member of Congress at the time the Federal articles were framed. The injustice of allowing each State an equal vote was long insisted on. *He voted for it*, but it was against his judgment, and under the pressure of public danger, *and the obstinacy of the lesser States.*

[Upon the vote which was taken at the close of this discussion it was decided that the rule of suffrage in the first branch of the Legislature should be in accordance with the populations of the different States.]

Mr. Ellsworth, of Connecticut, moved—'That the rule of suffrage in the second branch [the Senate] be the same with that established by the Articles of Confederation [that is, that the States should be equally represented]. He was not sorry, on the whole, he said, that the vote just passed had determined against the rule in the first branch. They were partly national, partly Federal. The proportional representation in the first branch was conformable to the national principle, and would secure the large States against the small. An equality of voices was conformable to the Federal principle, and was necessary to secure the small States against the large. To the eastward he was sure that Massachusetts was the only State that would listen to a proposition for excluding the States as equal political societies from an equal voice in both branches. The others would risk every consequence rather than part with so dear a right. The power of self-defence was essential to the small States. Nature had given it to the smallest insect of the creation. He could never admit that there was no danger of combination amongst the large States. They will, like individuals, find out and avail themselves of the advantage to be gained by it. *It was true the danger would be greater if they were contiguous and had a more immediate and common interest.** The existing Confederation was founded upon the equality of the States in the article of suffrage.

Mr. Baldwin, of Georgia, would vote against the motion of Mr. Ellsworth, though *he concurred with those who thought it would be impossible for the general Legislature to extend its cares to the local matters of the States*

Mr. Wilson, of Pennsylvania, in an elaborate speech, insisted that the representation in the Senate should be in accordance with the populations of the respective States. The rule of suffrage ought, he said, on every principle, to be the same in the second as the first branch. Much has been said of an imaginary combination of three States. It would be easy to prove, both from reason and history, that rivalships would be more probable than coalitions; *and that there are no coinciding interests that could produce the latter. If the motion should be agreed to, we shall leave the United States fettered precisely as heretofore* under

---

* Although this distinguished citizen of Connecticut did not judge rightly in regard to the combination which was the object of his immediate fears, yet he seems thoroughly to have understood the encroaching disposition of his countrymen, when he intimated that if contiguous States could be united upon any common interest, they would not respect the constitutional rights of the weaker members, but would combine to overthrow them

the Confederation.* He thought the States necessary and valuable parts of a good system.

Mr. Ellsworth.—No instance of a confederacy has existed in which an equality of voices has not been exercised by the members of it. *The danger of combinations among the States is not imaginary.* Although no particular abuses could be foreseen by him, the *possibility* of them was sufficient to alarm him. He appealed to the obligations of the Federal compact, which was still in force, and which had been entered into with so much solemnity.

Mr. Madison contended that the States were divided into different interests, not by their difference of size, but by other circumstances, the most material of which resulted partly from climate, but principally from the effects of their having or not having slaves. These two causes concurred in forming the great division of interests in the United States It did not lie between the large and small States. It lay between the Northern and Southern , and if any defensive power were necessary, it ought to be mutually given to these two interests. He was so strongly impressed with this important truth, that he had been casting about in his mind for some expedient that would answer the purpose. . . . *He would preserve the State rights as carefully as the trial by jury.*

Mr. Bedford, of Delaware, contended that there was no middle way between a perfect consolidation and a mere confederacy of States. The first is out of the question, and in the latter they must continue, if not perfectly, at least equally sovereign. . . . Are not the large States evidently seeking to aggrandise themselves at the expense of the small? They think, no doubt, that they have right on their side, but interest has blinded their eyes. The small States are willing to observe their engagements, but will meet the large ones on no other ground but that of the confederation.

Mr. Ellsworth.—Under a National Government we should

* The motion was agreed to in substance, and the Government was so 'fettered,' notwithstanding which the combination then deemed impossible did afterwards take place—the North against the South—with an avowed purpose which, if accomplished, would despoil the Southern States of their constitutional rights Can it be believed that the South did not possess the right by the very letter and spirit of the compact to resist?

participate in the national security, but that was all. What he wanted was domestic happiness. The National Government could not descend to the local objects on which this depended. It could only embrace objects of a general nature. He turned his eyes, therefore, for the preservation of his rights to the State Governments. From these alone he could derive the greatest happiness he expects in this life. This happiness depended on their existence, as much as a new-born infant on its mother for nourishment.

Mr. King, of Massachusetts.—As the fundamental rights of individuals are secured by express provisions in the State Constitutions, why may not a like security be provided for the rights of the States in the National Constitution?

Mr. L. Martin, in reply to a suggestion that a committee should be appointed to devise 'a compromise,' said that no modifications whatever could reconcile the smaller States *to the least diminution of their equal sovereignty.*

Mr. Randolph, of Virginia, reminded the small States that if the large States should combine, some danger of which he did not deny, there would be a check in the revisionary power of the Executive; and intimated that, in order to render this still more effectual, he would agree that in the choice of an executive each State should have an equal vote.

The States'-rights party finally triumphed, and the Convention adopted the rule that, in the senatorial or second branch of the National Legislature, *each State should have an equal vote.*

These extracts from the proceedings of the Convention of States, which seceded from the second Confederation and established the late Union, enable us to obtain a clear insight into the thoughts, the passions, the interests, and the sympathies of those who framed the compact of the Union. It is true that, by a perusal of the provisions of the Constitution itself, the mind is led almost irresistibly to the conclusion that they were the results of concessions and compromises between adverse opinions and interests; but here we enter into the very thoughts of the actors, and are by this means enabled to discover more clearly the meaning of all its various parts, by the detailed expression of the individual sentiments of those who embodied them into a Constitution.

We discover that a certain number would have favoured the absorption of the State Governments into a general Government, and the establishment of a monarchy; but they accompanied the announcement of their individual opinions by a distinct disclaimer of any intention to press their views upon the Convention in opposition to the almost unanimous public sentiment. Upon a single point, with the few exceptions before referred to, the entire body of members was agreed—namely, *the preservation of the sovereignty of the State Governments*, except in such cases as certain powers might be *specifically delegated* to a Federal Government, limited to the regulation of the foreign and domestic intercourse of the States.

There was a severe struggle between the large and the small States in regard to the principle of representation. The large States insisted that they should be allowed an influence in the Federal Government proportioned to their relative wealth and population; yet they at the same time repelled the idea that they wished to infringe in the slightest degree upon the sovereignty of the individual States. But the majority insisted firmly that the States were not only sovereign, but equally sovereign—that they would not enter into a union unless that sovereignty and equality were admitted—and that it must be recognised by the admission of each State to an equal voice in the senatorial branch of the National Legislature. It is made clear by the debates that the Convention would have adopted other safeguards for the protection of the weak States against the encroachments of the stronger, if it had not been believed that it would be impossible to form a combination of States sufficiently powerful to menace seriously the independence or the liberties of the others.

In reference to the power of *coercion* centred in the Federal Government, it will be observed that it was only intended to be applied within the States in aid of the constituted State authorities. It would assist in putting down a rebellion *within* a State; but the idea of applying the force of the Federal Government against a State needed only to be hinted at to be scouted by the entire Convention. When this point came to be incidentally discussed, upon a resolution empowering the Government *to call forth the force of the Union against any member of the Union failing to fulfill its duties under the articles thereof*, Mr. Madison observed:—

> The more he reflected on the use of force, the more he doubted its *practicability*, *justice*, and *efficacy*, when applied to people *collectively* and not *individually*. A union of the States containing such an ingredient, *seemed to provide for its own destruction*. The use of force against a State would look more like a declaration of war than an infliction of punishment, and would probably be considered by the party attacked as a dissolution of all previous compacts by which it might be bound.
>
> *Colonel Alexander Hamilton* remarked that a certain portion of military force was absolutely necessary in large *communities*, but how can this force be exerted on the States collectively? *It is impossible.*

In effect, the motion of Mr. Madison to postpone the section referred to, in order that some system might be framed to render the application of force unnecessary, *was unanimously adopted* (see 'Madison Papers,' vol. ii. p. 761). Here we have proof positive that the entire Convention, embracing every State, repudiated the bare intimation that the Government of the United States might apply force against a State, even though the latter '*might oppose the carrying into execution the acts or treaties of the Federal Government*' (see also 'Madison Papers,' vol. ii. p. 863).

Mr. Jefferson, in a letter to Colonel Humphries (March 18, 1789), properly defines the nature of the league between the States in the following words:—'The best general key for the solution of questions of power between our Governments is the fact that every foreign and federal power is given to the Federal Government, and to the States every power purely domestic.' About the same time he wrote: 'The Federal is in truth our foreign Government, *which department alone* is taken from the sovereignty of the several States.'

It is manifest in every act of the Convention that the allegiance of the citizens was regarded as primarily due to the States to which they respectively belonged, and only secondarily to the Government of the Union. Just as individuals of a nation are bound by the treaties of their own Government with foreign States, so were the citizens bound to the Government of the United States. But the moment that a State, through its regularly constituted authorities, repudiated the authority of the Federal Government, that very instant the citizen of such State was released from his legal obligation to the Government of the Union. How could it have been otherwise? Could the citizen serve two masters who were at war with each other? The *States*, through their representatives, formed the Union, each one having an equal voice without reference to wealth or population. They voted upon each and every article as *States*, not as representatives of the people of the Union as a single community. The State laws operated constantly upon the citizens—the United States laws rarely, and then only in the exceptional cases which might arise between themselves and foreigners, or, what was the same thing, between citizens of different States. Under the State laws they derived their title to their lands—under the State laws they were protected in their rights or punished for their offences: the State laws provided for the transmission of their estates to their descendants. In short, all the functions of internal Government were performed by the States, while the Government of the United States had no authority, nor did it even exercise any authority over the individual or his property, except in the rarely occurring instances specifically designated in the Constitution. To avoid all misconstruction, the Constitution provided in a separate article that *all such powers as were not specifically granted to the general Government were reserved to the States* respectively, and the people

Whatever may have been the merits of the controversy between the Federal and State authorities, the responsibility of the individual for acts committed against the Government of the Union was merged and lost in that of the State by whose authority and command he acted. How, then, is it possible that a citizen of a State, acting in obedience to the laws of his State, could be released from his obligations as a citizen? Even admitting that he owed a certain fealty to the two Governments, yet, when they were at war with each other, he must serve one and oppose the other; and in serving his own State, he could not, by virtue of any law, human or divine, be regarded, in the proper legal signification of that term, as in rebellion against the Federal Government. Hence, when the latter power decreed the confiscation of the property of citizens of the Southern seceding States, and inflicted grievous and degrading wrongs against their persons, because they were acting in obedience to the requirements of the Governments to which they owned allegiance, it was nothing less than an act of brigandage, as wholly unjustified by the laws of the country or the usages of civilised nations, as it was repugnant to every principle of justice or humanity. How far one nation may be justified in attempting or accomplishing the subjugation of another, will probably be decided in the future, as it has been in the past, by the sword; but after the passions engendered by the conflict shall have subsided, the moral sentiment of the world must unite in condemning that nation which in effect conducts even a war of conquest upon the same principles which govern highway robbers.

Mr. Madison's View of the Federal Compact.

As to the right of the Southern States to withdraw from the Union, the questions involved have been so thoroughly discussed that but little is left to say. Yet it may not be inappropriate to refer to the opinions of those who framed the Constitution, and who ought to have understood the effect and meaning of their own acts. We again quote from a speech of Mr. Madison—who may be said to have been at least a Father of the Constitution—delivered before that Convention, of which he was a leading and most influential member:—

> It has been alleged (said Mr. Madison) that the Confederation, having been formed by unanimous consent, could be dissolved by unanimous consent only. If we consider the Federal Union as analogous to the fundamental compact by which individuals compose one society, and which must, in its theoretic origin at least, have been the act of the component members, it cannot be said that no dissolution of the compact can be effected without unanimous consent. *A breach of the fundamental principles of the compact by a part of the society would certainly absolve the other part from their obligations to it* If the breach of any article by any of the parties does not set the others at liberty, it is because the contrary is implied in the compact itself, and particularly by that law of it which gives an indefinite authority to the majority to bind the whole in all cases *This latter circumstance shows that we are not to consider the Federal Union as analogous to the social compact of individuals;* for if it were, a majority would have the right to bind the rest, and even to form a constitution for the whole. If we consider the Federal Union as analogous, not to the social compacts amongst individual men, but *to the conventions amongst individual States,* what is the doctrine resulting from these conventions? *Clearly that a breach of any one article, by any one party, leaves all the other parties at liberty to consider the whole convention as dissolved.*

It would be impossible to define in clearer language the plain intent and meaning of the Constitution than this exposition by one who aided in its construction, and which was addressed to his colleagues, who approved his views. I presume that there will not be found any disinterested persons who will say that the spirit of the compact had not been broken by the North before the secession of a single Southern State. The entire body of Northern States had combined together to usurp the exclusive control of the Government of the Union, and were pledged to an unconstitutional interference with the domestic institutions of the Southern States. Clergymen and politicians of the North had been during a number of years engaged in stimulating the fanaticism and the passions of the multitude against the Southern States, until they were wrought up to such a pitch of fury and madness as rendered it apparent that there was no longer any safety for the South in the Union. The Southern States did not attempt to revolutionise the Government. They merely withdrew from a Union which had become hateful to them, and from a people who cherished against them the bitterest feeling of rancour. They felt that their safety and happiness were no longer to be hoped for in a political union with the North, and they said to their Confederates: 'The great continent of America is broad enough for both of us: let us part in peace.' The answer to this just demand is known to the world.

To return from this partial digression to the point which I set out to establish, I will only add that, whatever may be the judgment of mankind in regard to the wisdom which governed the councils of the framers of the Convention in the adjustment of its compromises, it is clear that they should not have been afterwards subjected to the trying ordeal of periodical presidential elections. By this means they reopened every four years, before a tribunal composed of the whole body of the people, the same sources of discord which were with difficulty adjusted by the small body of statesmen and patriots who composed the Convention. Often during the progress of that work the difficulties of compromising all the questions at issue seemed almost insuperable, and even the most sanguine at times despaired of ultimate success. Eventually they succeeded in agreeing upon terms of union. Each conceded something in order to obtain guarantees for other rights or interests; and although no party, or section, or interest was wholly content, yet they agreed to adopt the Constitution as the best that could be done under the circumstances. But how could it be hoped that the compromises and bargains which they made would stand the test of a resubmission to the people twenty-five times in every succeeding century?

When we consider that every four years, under the system of presidential elections, the nicely-balanced compromises of the Union were submitted to the operation of such an ordeal—with such an ever-augmenting population from foreign countries, a large portion of whom were of different races, speaking different languages, operated upon by different motives, with different tastes, habits, and principles, who, without any practical knowledge of such a Government, entered almost at the moment of their arrival into the business of king-making for the Republic—our only wonder should be that the Federal Union was not sooner overthrown.

Tabular Statement of Presidential Elections.

Popular Vote in Presidential Elections from 1824 *to* 1860.

Year	Names of Candidates	North	South	Total	Majority and Minority
1824*	John Quincy Adams (Democrat) E.	82,863	22,458	105,321	No election by Electoral College
	Andrew Jackson (Democrat) .	74,786	78,113	152,899	
	Wm. H. Crawford (Democrat) .	17,398	29,867	47,265	
	Henry Clay (Democrat) . .	19,361	27,726	47,087	
1828	Andrew Jackson (Democrat) E. .	417,871	232,157	650,028	maj. 137,870
	John Quincy Adams (Whig) .	411,162	100,996	512,158	
1832	Andrew Jackson (Democrat) E. .	487,730	199,772	687,502	maj. 137,313
	Henry Clay (Whig) . . .	449,229	104,565	550,189	
1836	Martin Van Buren (Democrat) E.	550,880	211,269	762,149	maj. 25,413
	All others (chiefly Whig) . .	520,024	216,712	736,736	
1840	William H. Harrison (Whig) E. .	900,346	374,437	1,274,783	maj. 138,472
	Martin Van Buren (Democrat) .	809,705	318,997	1,136,311	
	Birney (Abolition) . . .	7,609	...		
1844	James K. Polk (Democrat) E. .	924,632	411,202	1,335,834	min. 23,469
	Henry Clay (Whig) . . .	910,860	386,173	1,359,303	
	Birney (Abolition) . . .	62,270	...		
1848	Z. Taylor (Whig) E. . . .	970,165	391,866	1,362,031	min. 152,102
	Lewis Cass (Democrat) . .	847,842	374,613	1,514,133	
	Martin Van Buren (Free Soil) .	291,379	299		
1852	Franklin Pearce (Democrat) E. .	1,147,375	443,115	1,590,490	maj. 54,605
	Winfield Scott (Whig) . .	1,044,347	364,242	1,535,885	
	Hale (Abolition). . . .	156,856	440		
1856	James Buchanan (Democrat) E. .	1,232,783	618,177	1,850,960	min. 369,553
	Millard Fillmore (American) .	407,843	478,117	2,220,513	
	J. C. Freemont (Republican) .	1,333,306	1,247		
1860	Abraham Lincoln (Republican) E.	1,831,180	26,430	1,857,610	min. 1,000,050
	Douglas (Democrat) . . / Breckenridge (Democrat) .	1,480,033	786,496	2,857,660	
	Bell (Southern Peace candidate) .	74,658	515,973		

* The very small number of votes cast in this election, compared with those which follow, was owing to the fact that up to the election of 1828 many of the States chose their presidential electors by the Legislature. Up to 1824, the States adopting this method were, Delaware, Georgia, Louisiana, New York, Vermont, and South Carolina. In all subsequent elections, however, every State except South Carolina submitted the choice of election to the popular voice. This latter State is, therefore, not estimated in this table except in the last election, where I assume what would have been the vote if the election had gone before the people.

E. Elected President.

Table of Elections by the Presidential Electoral Colleges, from Washington to Lincoln inclusive.—1788 *to* 1860.

Year	Names of Candidates	Votes cast for each Candidate			Whole No. of electoral Votes	Distributed		No. of States in the Union	
		N.	S.	Total		N.	S.	Nrn.	Srn.
1788	*George Washington*	38	31	69	* 73	38	35	5	5
1792	*George Washington*	73	59	132	135	73	62	8	7
1796	*John Adams* (Federalist)	59	12	71	138	73	65	8	8
	Thomas Jefferson (Democrat) †	14	54	68					
1800	*Thomas Jefferson* (Democrat) ‡	20	53	73	138	73	65	8	8
	John Adams (Federalist)	53	12	65					
1804	*Thomas Jefferson* (Democrat)	85	77	162	176	95	81	9	8
	C. C. Pinckney (Federalist)	9	5	14					
1808	*James Madison* (Democrat)	50	72	122	176	95	81	9	8
	Pinckney (Federalist)	39	8	47					
1812	*James Madison* (Democrat)	40	88	128	218	121	97	9	9
	De Witt Clinton (Federalist)	80	9	89					
1816	*James Monroe* (Democrat)	93	90	183	221	124	97	10	9
	Rufus King (Federalist)	34	...	34					
1820	*James Monroe* (Democrat)	128	103	231	235	129	106	12	11
1824	*J. Q. Adams* (Democrat) §	8	5	13	24 States			12	12
	Crawford & Jackson (Democrats)	4	7	11					
1828	*Andrew Jackson* (Democrat)	73	105	178	261	147	114	12	12
	J. Q. Adams (Whig) ‖	74	9	83					
1832	*Andrew Jackson* (Democrat)	132	87	219	288	165	123	12	12
	Henry Clay (Whig)	26	23	49					
1836	*Van Buren* (Democrat)	113	57	170	294	168	126	13	13
	W. H. Harrison (Whig)	45	28	73					
1840	*W. H. Harrison* (Whig)	156	78	234	294	168	126	13	13
	Van Buren (Democrat)	12	48	60					
1844	*James K. Polk* (Democrat)	103	67	170	275	167	108	13	13
	Henry Clay (Whig)	58	47	105					
1848	*Z. Taylor* (Whig)	97	66	163	290	169	121	15	15
	Lewis Cass (Democrat)	72	55	127					
1852	*Frank. Pearce* (Democrat)	158	96	254	296	176	120	16	15
	Winfield Scott (Whig)	18	24	42					
1856	*James Buchanan* (Democrat)	62	112	174	296	176	120	16	15
	J. C. Freemont (Republican)	114	...	114					
	Millard Fillmore (American)	...	8	8					
1860	*Abe Lincoln* (Republican)	180	...	180	303	183	120	18	15
	Douglas (Democrat)	3	9	12					
	Breckenridge (Democrat)	...	72	72					
	Bell (Peace candidate)	...	39	39					

* There were only ten States in the Un'on, and hence the small number of electoral votes. New York, North Carolina, and Rhode Island had not, at the time referred to, agreed to secede from the previous Confederacy.

† To avoid confusion I designate this party by the name it soon afterwards assumed, though at first it was called 'Republican' or 'Democratic Republican.'

‡ The electoral vote is here given, as indicating the relative strength of parties; although, in consequence of the occurrence of a contingency not provided for in the Constitution, it became necessary to refer this election to the House of Representatives. At that time the electors voted for two persons, one of whom should be President and the other Vice-President, depending upon which should have the largest aggregate vote. In this election all who voted for Mr. Jefferson voted also for Aaron Burr, intending that the latter should be Vice-President. Mr. Jefferson not having, therefore, obtained a majority, the election was carried to the House of Representatives, when Aaron Burr *was put up by the Federalists, and voted for, for the first office.* After a long struggle, however, Mr. Jefferson was electvd.

§ This is the vote by States in the House of Representatives, the Electoral College having failed to choose.

‖ For reasons stated in note †, this offshoot of the Democratic party is not designated by the title of 'National Republican,' which it at first assumed.

CHAPTER XIV.

A SURVEY OF THE PRESIDENTIAL ELECTIONS FROM WASHINGTON TO LINCOLN CONSIDERED IN REFERENCE TO THE APPLIANCES EMPLOYED BY THE PARTIES AND FACTIONS TO OPERATE UPON THE PUBLIC MIND

PREFATORY.

IN preceding chapters I have explained the circumstances and the manner in which presidential elections originated. I have culled from the reports of the proceedings of the Convention which framed the Constitution all that was necessary to prove that the almost unanimous sentiment of that august body was adverse to the election of Presidents by the popular voice. Perhaps even many Americans will be surprised to discover from the debates growing out of this subject that a prevailing opinion amongst a number of 'the Fathers of the Republic' was favourable to the creation of a limited monarchy. Some freely expressed their convictions in words, others in actions, others by their silence. The obstacles to its accomplishment were, however, frankly admitted to be insurmountable, and they therefore adopted the only alternative which remained. They believed that they had devised a means by which the President would be chosen by an intermediary body between the politicians and the people. The intention was good, but its execution was impossible.

I have shown, also, the manner in which the party-leaders, with the aid of the people, frustrated this wise purpose by the instrumentality of nominating conventions.

In the present chapter I propose to refer somewhat in detail to the practical application of the system, as illustrated by the presidential contests, in order by a reference to facts and events to show the influences exercised by these contests upon the public mind, the public morals, and the integrity of the Government.

Before the commencement of the war between the North and the South there were perhaps few citizens of the 'Model Republic' who ever permitted their minds to dwell longer than a mere transient interval of time upon the full measure of evils resulting to the country from the contests growing out of presidential elections. Not that they could have doubted their existence, for they have been manifest to all intelligent observers during a long series of years; but they regarded the disease as incurable. They could discover no peaceful means by which it might have been eradicated. The monarch had been made drunk, madness had supervened, and the frequent and strong libations which were administered to him by the courtiers, left him no lucid interval in which he would have listened with complacency to any warning from any source. Therefore it is that even the most patriotic and sober citizens were silently, yet anxiously awaiting the unavoidable end.

We may, however, suppose that at the present moment there are very many whose thoughts revert to the events which signalised these contests with anything but pleasurable emotions, when they survey the parts which they themselves have played in these grand national farces, followed so swiftly by that bloody tragedy which has for the present at least furnished the material for an excitement even more general than that which attended the struggle of factions for the possession of the presidency and the spoils of office. There are many who, perhaps for the first time, have had both leisure and inclination to review the past, and to reflect with calmness upon the causes which have consigned these to a prison, those to an enforced exile from homes which have been plundered or confiscated. Conscious of no crime, nor even a fault—unless, indeed, it be criminal to be faithful and true to the Governments under which they live—they find themselves hunted out as malefactors by those who never had the semblance of a moral or legal claim to govern or in any way control their actions. While these causes may communicate a degree of bitterness to their reflections, it will increase the probabilities of their arriving at conclusions unbiassed by an undue reverence for that Government by which they have been oppressed, and whose faults in times past they might have desired to overlook.

A review of the various presidential elections, in the order in which they have occurred, considered solely in reference to their influence upon the general public sentiment and manners and morals of the country, presents such strange and startling features that the philosophical mind must be interested in the survey, whether or not it suggests a method by which the evil may be discarded from the system.

For reasons which I have already stated, it is necessary in analysing these contests to divide them into two classes—namely, those which occurred during the lifetime of the actors in the Revolution, and who were present and participated in the rebellion against British rule and the establishment of the Government; and those which took place after these had all passed away, and their places had been supplied by a new generation. The point of time dividing the two epochs may be fixed at 1825.

Washington, the elder Adams, Jefferson, Madison, and Monroe, occupied consecutively the office of 'Chief Magistrate' during the first period; and during the last, Adams the younger, Jackson, Van Buren, Harrison (Tyler, after his death to the end of the term), Polk, Taylor (Fillmore after his death), Pearce, Buchanan, and lastly Lincoln. From Washington to Adams the second was thirty-six years; from Adams the second, inclusive, to Lincoln was thirty-six years.

At the formation of the Government there was, it is true, as we have already seen, a North and a South; but the antagonisms which had always existed between them had been much softened by the events of the long war through which they had just passed, as well as by that law of necessity which enforced a union of their strength as against foreign powers in consideration of their individual weakness.

The geographical division line was the same then as it is to-day; but it is worthy of note that it could not have been wholly produced by the Institution of Slavery, because slavery existed in both. It was likewise true at that day that the chief opposition to the slave trade, as well as to the Institution of Slavery itself, was found in the South. We must, therefore, look to other causes to account for the developement of that sectionalism which was afterwards so carefully nurtured by the president-makers of the North, and which in the end was made to yield such deadly fruits. This feeling of reciprocal animosity, or antipathy, or repugnance, or whatever name may more properly designate the relation referred to, found occasion for developement even in the midst of their common defence against a common enemy. It manifested itself more strongly than elsewhere amongst the soldiers, when the necessities of war threw them together upon the same field, or in the same camp. Notwithstanding the earnest exertions of the leading men upon both sides, they often deported themselves rather as allies from necessity than friends from choice, or brethren of the same family.

Whatever local or transient causes may have tended to increase this estrangement, much of the feeling thus manifested had its origin in Europe before they or their ancestors had emigrated to America.

It is not necessary in this connection to decide which was the most worthy of esteem or respect, but only to denote the adverse causes which repelled them the one from the other. Each was devotedly attached to its own favourite form of despotism, but the foundations upon which these despotisms respectively rested were as antagonistical as those of liberty and slavery.

The Northerners were the first of English subjects to welcome the reign of cant and Cromwell; the Southerners were the last to desert the royal standard of the Stuarts. So resolute were these in their loyalty to the fallen fortunes of their monarch, that Cromwell, on finding they were the only British subjects who resisted his despotic rule, gave orders that the slaves should be armed and turned against their masters. The Northerners were the last, and the Southerners the first to welcome back the Stuarts to the throne. Few enlightened friends of liberty of the present day would be inclined to look with favour upon either of these contestants for supreme power; yet it is difficult to imagine any two phases of human character existing in the same race and under the same form of civilisation more utterly at variance than these. During the last quarter of the last century a common desire for independence, a common danger, and a common necessity united them together in the same Government; and although they subsequently approached much nearer to each other than before the war, yet to this day, and through all the past days, the distinction continued to be strongly and clearly impressed upon their manners, and to some extent upon their local laws.

Still there was not such an incompatibility as would have precluded them from continuing under a common confederacy, if their mutual antipathies had not been constantly stimulated by presidential contests, which led inevitably to the attempt of the stronger to tyrannise over the weaker, and to reduce the latter to a condition of political vassalage. If this ever-active cause had not existed there might not have been an opportunity for the gratification of that domineering propensity of the Northern mind which finally severed the bonds of their union. But the very freedom and independence which were secured to the citizens by means of the State Governments made them the more tenacious of their liberties, and more united in defending them against encroachmennts.

FIRST PRESIDENTIAL EPOCH—FROM 1789 TO 1825.

It will only be necessary to refer briefly to the events of the nine first presidential elections, which covered a period of thirty-six years. At its close the last of the men of the Revolution who served as President retired into private life.

Washington was chosen the first President in 1789, being the fourteenth year of the independence of the United States. There was no corresponding office under the two preceding Confederacies. At the expiration of his first term he was re-elected (1793) without opposition. At the close of his second term he withdrew altogether from public life, and John Adams was elected for the third term. It was during this period that the Federal and the Democratic parties—the latter then and for some years afterwards known as the Republican party—made their first great issue upon the proper interpretation of the provisions of the Constitution. The 'Federalists,' under the lead of the President, and many of the most distinguished public men of that day, were in favour of construing all doubtful questions which might arise in regard to that instrument in a manner favourable to the general Government. The latter, under the lead of Jefferson, Madison, and others, insisted that when a power was not in direct terms conferred upon the Federal

Government it remained with the States. The margin allowed for a controversy was certainly very narrow, since both parties proposed to be guided entirely by the very explicit terms of the Constitution itself. Nevertheless, a most fierce party warfare commenced in regard to the constitutionality of two laws which were passed by Congress, entitled the 'Alien and Sedition Acts.' These were thought to involve the issue in question, and hence the immediate effects of the enactment of those laws was to arouse the whole nation to a pitch of fury, which at the present day appears to have been wholly out of proportion to the significance of the Acts themselves. It was upon this occasion the celebrated Virginia and Kentucky resolutions of 1798, prepared respectively by Mr. Jefferson and Mr. Madison, were adopted, and soon after incorporated as the fundamental and perpetual doctrine in the platform of the Democratic party; and from that day to this, through all the vicissitudes of its eventful career, it has adhered to that interpretation of the meaning and requirements of the Constitution.

These resolutions declared that 'the Government of the United States may only exercise such powers as are specifically delegated by the States; and that whensoever it assumes other powers its acts are unauthoritative, void, and of no force; and that each State had a right to judge for itself, as well of infractions as of the mode and manner of redress.'

The Legislatures of Massachusetts, Vermont, and other New England States, passed resolutions in opposition to these. In 1800 the question was referred to the arbitration of the people in the contest between Mr. Adams and Mr. Jefferson. The States'-rights doctrine carried the day, and Mr. Jefferson was chosen President. Mr. Adams was therefore obliged to retire, after having served but a single term. This was the first time that the important question of State sovereignty was decided upon in a presidential election; but from that period up to the year 1860 it was the recognised doctrine of the dominant party. No President could be elected who stood upon any other platform. As long as that principle was recognised as the policy of the party in power, a war between the Federal Government and the States was impossible; but upon the instant when the Federal idea of the last century acquired the ascendancy in 1860 the conflict of arms commenced.

Mr. Madison succeeded to Mr. Jefferson in 1809, and Mr. Monroe succeeded to Mr. Madison in 1817. After having served two terms he retired in 1825.

Thus, during thirty-two out of thirty-six years, the presidential office was filled from the single Southern State of Virginia. The Federal party had never recovered from its first discomfiture; and although it made a show of opposition for several years subsequent to the defeat of Mr. Adams, it became weaker and weaker, until during the administration of Mr. Monroe it disappeared for ever from the political stage, without even leaving a successor. When the last of the Presidents belonging to the era of the Revolution disappeared, the Democratic party was without a single rival. Not even a formidable faction raised its head in opposition. To all outward appearance there was an entire unity of political sentiment all over the Union. All subsequent contests for the presidency were between a new people and upon new issues. The institutions of the country were for the first time put upon their trial, divested of the influence of the great statesmen who had formed the Government and had for thirty-six years guided and directed it safely through every peril. Henceforth they must stand or fall upon their own merits.

It would be an error to suppose that the country was entirely exempt during this period from the evils which subsequently attended the presidential contests. Party spirit divided and menaced the tranquillity of the nation, while faction within the parties embittered the lives of all who had the direction of public affairs. This grew naturally out of the fact that there were then, as afterwards, a great number of aspirants to presidential honours of nearly equal and irreconcileable pretensions. Although Washington himself was not exempt from the annoyances which naturally attended such a condition of affairs, yet it was not until his withdrawal from public life that these rivalries assumed a malignant form. Mr. Adams, his successor, addressed a series of letters to a Boston journal, in the year 1809, being eight years after his retiracy from the presidential office, in which he reviews the state of public affairs during his administration of the Government. He refers also to his private grievances, and complains with far more bitterness against the conduct of those who were among the leaders of his own party than of others who were his open and avowed adversaries. His experience, as reported by himself, affords the most conclusive evidence that there was a radical defect in the organisation of the Government which imposed such an insupportable burthen upon the shoulders of the chief on whom the nation bestowed its highest honours. In one of these letters he refers to one of the unpopular measures of his administration in the following terms:—

> To me as a public man it was fatal, and that only because Alexander Hamilton [a rival leader of his own party] was pleased to wield it as a poisoned weapon, with the express purpose of destroying me. Though I owe him no thanks for this, I most heartily rejoice in it, because it has given me eight years incomparably the happiest of my life. Whereas, had I been chosen President again, I am certain I could not have lived through one year more of such labours and cares as were studiously and maliciously heaped upon me by the factions.

Alexander Hamilton, as well as Mr. Adams, was a prominent leader of the Federal party—one of the most distinguished amongst the great actors in the Revolution, and amongst the number of those who were regarded as aspirants for the presidency. His career, however, was cut short in the zenith of his popularity, having been killed in a duel by Aaron Burr.* At the epoch of Mr. Adams's administration the wars occasioned by the French Revolution made a deep impression upon the public mind in America. Public sentiment was much divided. Mr. Hamilton took the side of the British; many of the leaders of the Republican party favoured the French, while Mr. Adams, as President, proclaimed a strict neutrality between the belligerents. This was probably the part of wisdom, but it failed to satisfy either party; and it afforded the opportunity for presidential aspirants

* 12th July 1804.

upon both sides to strengthen their own pretensions, while assailing him. Presidential elections brought all such questions before the people, and it is not wonderful that Mr. Adams was made to suffer for his negative course before such a tribunal, stimulated by the eloquent appeals of partisan leaders. Mr. Hamilton had also other grounds for complaint against Mr. Adams. Upon one occasion he wrote—'The outset of Mr. Adams's administration was distinguished by a speech which his friends lamented as temporising. It had the air of a lure for the favour of his opponents at the expense of his sincerity.' To this attack Mr. Adams, in one of the letters referred to, made the following reference:—

> That address sprang from a very serious apprehension of danger to our country, and a sense of injustice to individuals, from the arbitrary and exclusive principle of faction which confines all employments and promotions to its own favourites. . . But I soon found myself shackled. I could not name a man who was not devoted to Hamilton without kindling a fire. The Senate was now decidedly Federal During President Washington's whole administration of eight years, his authority in the Senate was extremely weak. I have great reason to believe that President Jefferson came into office with the same spirit that I did—that is, with a sincere desire of conciliating parties, so far as he possibly could consistently with his principles. In the House of Representatives, in General Washington's time, the majority of Federalists was very small In my time it was somewhat larger, but still small. In Mr Jefferson's time the majority of Republicans was immense. Consciousness of their strength had the same effect upon Republicans as it had upon Federalists in my time. It made them confident, exclusive, and presumptuous. Mr Jefferson, as I did, found it impossible to follow his own inclinations

These brief disclosures of the ex-President inform us that even at that early day the influence of presidential aspirants, and their attendant trains of office-seekers, precluded the actual occupant of the chief executive office from pursuing the policy in regard to appointments which his judgment dictated. He was obliged to employ the powers of his office in reference to future presidential elections, and to satisfy the clamours of his own partisans.

The last extract I will make from these letters, although written in a humorous vein many years after the writer had been relieved from the cares of State, affords very conclusive evidence that amidst the contentions of parties and factions, and the struggles of ambitious men to obtain place and power, the President was not suffered to repose upon a bed of roses:—

> When I look back (wrote he) on the opposition and embarrassments I had to overcome from the factions, I have in some of my jocular moments compared myself to an animal I have seen take hold of the end of a cord with his teeth, and be drawn slowly up by pulleys through a storm of squibs, crackers, and rockets flashing and blazing around him every moment; and though the scorching flames made him groan and roar, he would not let go his hold until he had reached the ceiling of a lofty theatre, where he hung some time, still suffering a flight of rockets, and at last descended through another storm of burning powder, and never let go till his four feet were safely landed on the floor.

All those upon whom rest the weighty cares of State must at times feel that they have a grievous load to bear. To adjust conflicting interests, and to settle rival pretensions under any form of government, is the most difficult and delicate duty that the chief of a State is called upon to perform; but under the Government of the United States, where every citizen who aided by his vote in the elevation of that chief might set up a claim to be rewarded with an office as a *quid pro quo* for services rendered, it embittered the whole life of the President; and his efforts to conduct the affairs of the Government aright were in many instances thwarted and overruled by those whom he had been obliged to disappoint. We will see how this evil increased in magnitude as the country grew in greatness, and how finally the business of president-making became the active and only employment of hundreds of thousands of citizens.

SECOND PRESIDENTIAL EPOCH—1825 TO 1860.

Election of John Quincy Adams.

Inauguration of the New Era, by the Commencement of the 'Bargain, Intrigue, and Corruption Mania'—Year 1825.

At this epoch—this turning point in the conduct and management of the Model Republic—from whence every step was a descent from the high ground occupied by the 'Fathers of the Republic,' it is right that we should linger for a moment before entering upon that downward road from whence we will never again deviate until we reach the bottom and the end. Whatever may have been the faults of the past, they were in the main errors of the head and not of the heart. Great statesmen were the leaders, and it was the pride of the people to place great statesmen in power. Men rarely aspired to reach stations above their capacity, or if they did they were rebuked by the people. Men of education, and refinement, and wealth were regarded by the masses of the people with favour. The possession of these qualities constituted ever a claim to be employed in the public service, while at the same time a humble origin or occupation, coupled with natural ability and capacity to serve the public, constituted no bar to political promotion. Merit, wherever it might be found, was sure to win the favour of the people. They might err in their judgment, but they sought to do right.

At the point of time we are now considering the Constitution was, as we have seen, only thirty-six years old. True, the last of the Presidents who assisted in its creation had withdrawn from the public councils; yet it would not have seemed unreasonable to hope that the influence of their example would not have been wholly lost upon the men and the people who were their immediate successors. The enthusiastic devotees of Republican freedom might possibly have expected that, aided by the light of experience, they would have advanced higher and higher. Even the less sanguine admirers of democratic institutions might have thought that presidential elections would turn upon questions of public policy involving the weal of the nation—its advancement in prosperity, power, and happiness. Let us turn from speculation to the realities of fact.

The presidential contest of 1824, as we have said, opened a new era in the history, conduct, and management of presidential elections. Hitherto there had been an organised opposition to the dominant party. The nation had been divided into two very unequal parts as regards the mere strength of numbers: still the different parties were arrayed against each other upon issues involving great principles. There had been much jarring—great asperity in the progress of the contests; but withal they were not without dignity. The Federal party, crushed beneath the overpowering load of popular disfavour, had disappeared even in name, and had left the great Democratic States'-rights party undisputed master of the political field.

In the contest we are now considering there was, therefore, no party issue to be discussed or decided in advocating the rival pretensions of the different aspirants. The four candidates were John Quincy Adams of Massachusetts, Gen. Jackson of Tennessee, Henry Clay of Kentucky, and William H. Crawford of Georgia. They were all members of the great political party whose power everywhere predominated. There being no enemy to combat, the people busied themselves in discovering which of the four was farthest removed from the taint of Federalism. Upon this point there was not a sufficient number of people who agreed to elect either one over all the others, so that the Electoral College failed to make a choice. In compliance with the provisions of the Constitution, in view of such a contingency, the decision of the question was referred to the House of Representatives. The result was favourable to Mr. Adams; but the circumstances which attended and followed the election satisfied the American people of all parties that if a popular election before the whole body of the people was attended by evil consequences, an election by the popular branch of Congress was very many degrees worse. If a contest before the people caused the superstructure of the Government to tremble, a reference of the question to the partisan politicians of the House of Representatives shook the whole edifice to its very foundations. The magnitude of the popular convulsion which attended and followed this election may be conceived when we consider that during nearly an entire generation the incidents of this struggle of a few days duration formed a principal ingredient in the excitement of political struggles. In 1844 the contest which resulted in the choice of Mr. Polk turned in part upon the personal issues growing out of the election of Mr. Adams upon the occasion referred to; while the same questions were again revived, and made to play an important part in the canvass of 1857, which resulted in the election of Mr. Buchanan.

The political events of the epoch following immediately upon the election of Mr. Adams constitute one of the most curious as well as one of the most inexplicable phases of American history. One scarcely knows whether to be more astonished at the bitterness of the animosities it engendered—the long duration of the excitement—or the insignificance of the causes by which they were produced. They can only be accounted for upon any rational hypothesis by attributing them to the unnatural and unhealthy influence engendered in the public mind by the presidential elections.

The origin of this great madness grew out of the part borne by Mr. Clay in the election of Mr. Adams. Although Mr. Clay was himself a candidate before the people, he did not receive a sufficient number of votes in the Electoral College to carry his name into the House of Representatives. He was, however, a delegate in Congress from the State of Kentucky; and consequently the undesirable duty devolved upon him of assisting in the choice of a President from amongst his three competitors. This position was rendered even more delicate when it was ascertained that the result would turn upon the vote of Kentucky, which it was supposed would be controlled by him. He supported Mr. Adams, who was thereby chosen President; and then Mr. Clay committed one of the grave errors of his life by accepting from Mr. Adams the post of Secretary of State.

Immediately thereafter charges were preferred against Mr. Adams and Mr. Clay, not only in the public journals, but in the halls of Congress, which were described by the expressive and comprehensive words, 'bargain, intrigue, and corruption.' The whole nation became at once divided into two great factions; for it would be a misapplication of terms, according to the usually-accepted definition, to call them political parties. The newspapers wafted the charge or the defence to every mansion, and every counting-house, and every hamlet throughout the land. The people caught up the wild excitement of the hour, and upon every lip was heard, either in bitter accusation or derisive scorn, the now familiar phrase, 'bargain, intrigue, and corruption.'

At this moment was ushered upon the political stage that great personal controversy between the two master spirits of their day and generation—Andrew Jackson of Tennessee, and Henry Clay of Kentucky—which, during a long series of years, and almost without a single lull, convulsed the entire nation from one extremity to the other. All other questions were held in abeyance, all other issues postponed, all other subjects of controversy neglected or forgotten, in deference to the all-absorbing passions which this life-time struggle engendered in the very heart's core of the people. It was the War of the Roses fought with the pen and the tongue, instead of the sword and the long-bow; but none the less uprooting the foundations of society and breaking into fragments even the most cherished family ties.* It was as baseless a cause of quarrel as that between the Montagues and the Capulets, but in its progress it involved half a continent—divided a great nation—divided States—divided cities, villages, neighbourhoods, friends, and kinsmen. It was an insanity, a madness, in which reason was dethroned—objectless, aimless, in which the victory of the conqueror was a defeat and the defeated became the victor.

It was a controversy which, in its very nature and essence, was of such a character that there could never be a decision—in which a confession of the facts charged would not necessarily have implied guilt—and which at the most, under ordinary circumstances, would not have supplied a week's

* The contest was not always a bloodless one. Very many duels were fought by the respective partisans of the principal chiefs The one of most note was fought by Mr Clay himself with the distinguished Virginian, John Randolph of Roanake Mr Randolph, in his place in the Congress, alluded to the alliance between Mr Clay and Mr. Adams as 'a corrupt league between the puritan and the blackleg.' For this Mr Clay challenged him to the field of honour Mr. Randolph accepted They went upon the ground and exchanged shots. Upon the third shot Mr. Randolph fired into the air The affair was thereupon adjusted, as Mr Clay refused to continue a duel in which his adversary refused to fire at him. It appeared subsequently that Mr Randolph, before going upon the ground, had informed a confidential friend (Mr. Thomas H. Benton) that he would in no event aim at Mr. Clay's person.

material for sensation newspapers. Mr. Clay stood so high in the estimation of his countrymen that it was no advancement for him to be Secretary of State. Any other President would have been only too proud to have had him accept the same position, so there was not the smallest possible motive for bargain, and without bargain there could have been no corruption. But suppose the charge to have been true in the sense in which it was uttered, what an utterly insignificant cause for the convulsion of a whole nation during a quarter of a century, and how trivial a point upon which to elect or defeat a half-dozen Presidents.

It lasted during an entire generation, and was discussed during the greater portion of the time with unabated virulence. The two great political chieftains of this mighty struggle, which convulsed the entire Union, entered upon the contest when they were still in the prime of manhood. They both lived to a good old age, and died, in the usual course of nature, at the head of their respective hosts—still defiantly confronting the one the other—still, with their last breath, contesting—still accusing, still denying. Thus they lived and died. Thus fretted, quarrelled, fought through life and died the people who were their followers.

Mr. John Quincy Adams was the last of the Presidents who, as a rule, retained the appointees of his predecessors in office. Even in selecting his Cabinet he continued, as far as possible, those who had filled the same stations under Mr. Monroe. To Mr. Crawford, one of his defeated competitors, he offered the place of Secretary of the Treasury. If this had been accepted, every member of his Cabinet would have been taken from those he found in office at the time of his election. Removals, except for cause, were rarely made. What a change was afterwards wrought by the universal practice of the later Presidents? Yet how could it have been otherwise? When two candidates were announced for the presidency, one of whom declared that he would not remove those whom he found in office, and the other promised to turn out all and fill the vacancies by appointments from among his supporters, the success of the latter was of course certain. Hence, when the system of distributing the places amongst the partisans of the successful candidate was once inaugurated it became universal.*

Protective Tariffs as an Issue in Presidential Contests.

The student of American history who desires to be thoroughly informed in regard to the active causes

* It was during this term that Thomas Jefferson and John Adams, the second and third Presidents, died, each at an advanced age. They were distinguished for high qualities of statesmanship, though they were of very different schools, and by their great moral influence over their countrymen they contributed powerfully to the success of the revolutionary cause.

Jefferson said of Adams 'that a more perfectly honest man never issued from the hands of the Creator,' and their friendship survived even the estrangement produced by presidential rivalries. The parties which sprang into existence simultaneously with the establishment of the Constitution found Jefferson at the head of the 'States'-rights,' and Adams at the head of the Federal party, soon to be rival aspirants for the presidency. After Adams had served one term he was displaced, as we have seen, by Mr Jefferson, who established his party permanently in power Both died upon the same day, and by a coincidence, which at the time excited much interest, they both died upon the 4th July (1826), the anniversary of the Declaration of American Independence.

which were employed to widen the breach between the South and the North should not overlook the important relation which this subject of duties on foreign imports bore to the question. I shall therefore briefly survey the history of the struggle it engendered from its first introduction into Congress as a sectional as well as a party issue.

The appliances employed in presidential contests were of three kinds. First, the appeal to reason and the justice of the cause espoused; second, the appeal to the passions, such as envy, hatred, malice, ambition; and third, the appeal to the personal, pecuniary, or sectional interests of the voters. These were not always effective or employed in the order in which they are placed. In fact, the second and the third were most often found in combination, and the first was only employed to smooth over the deformities of the latter.

The system of protection to domestic manufactures by means of high duties upon foreign imports was supported not only by an appeal to the personal and sectional interests of the voters, but to the passions which sectional controversies evoked. It will be necessary to consider briefly the action of the general Government upon this subject, to understand how it was finally resolved into a mere struggle between the North and the South—the one to fasten the incubus of this oppressive system of taxation upon the country—the other to relieve itself from the unjust burthen thus imposed.

It was not until the year 1828 that the policy of levying duties, with the primary object of protection to domestic manufactures, became the doctrine of a section as well as of a political party, although hitherto it had been made to play an important part in presidential contests. The agitation may be said to have commenced during the presidential canvass of 1816. A higher duty was established in 1820—a still higher in 1824—and in 1828 it was sought still farther to increase the duties, and to perpetuate the policy under the attractive appellation of the *American System*. At this date, also, it became altogether a sectional issue between the North and the South. It will be observed that upon each of the occasions referred to the subject was thrust before the people, at intervals of four years, coinciding in point of time with the canvasses for the presidency.

At first, New England only sought to obtain protection for her shipping and fishing interests. The latter was protected by heavy and increasing bounties which have been perpetuated to the present day. But the main purpose of the early tariffs was to produce a revenue, although there was at the same time a very general inclination to subserve incidentally the interests of their infant manufacturers.

The sagacity exhibited by the New England manufacturing interest in isolating the Southern planting States from all participation in the benefits of the Government, and in compelling that section to contribute a large share of its earnings to the enrichment of the North, was worthy of a better cause. In one sense, however, it was not wise, for it laid the foundations of an augmented antagonism between the sections, which necessarily grew and expanded with the causes which produced it. It divided the nation into two parts; one of which claimed and received constant bounties from the Government, and thus placed the other under the necessity of paying them.

This was clearly contrary to the plain intention and spirit of the constitutional compact, as may be readily discovered, both by the provisions of that instrument and by the views expressed by those who were its authors. The power to levy duties was specifically limited to revenue purposes. But whether the duties were twenty, one hundred, or three hundred per cent. the protectionists might, and in fact did claim that they were for revenue. It was only a matter of conscience, for there was no mode by which the question could be brought before any legal tribunal.

The tariff of 1828 was set on foot for the benefit of only one branch of manufactures, namely, the woollen. Soon, however, by the system known by the designation of 'log rolling,' it was made to embrace all the leading manufacturing interests of the entire North. This was not sufficient to carry it through Congress; and it was then made to embrace *lead*, for the benefit of Illinois and Missouri—*hemp*, to secure Kentucky—and *sugar*, to add Louisiana to the formidable array. Thus, a sufficient number of votes were secured to bid defiance to the Southern States.

Indigo had been one of the leading productions of the South, but it had fallen off to a mere nominal amount after the protection which had been extended to it by the British Government had been removed. It was first planted in Georgia and North and South Carolina about the year 1740. A premium of sixpence sterling per pound was paid during the reign of George II. which in a very short time increased very greatly the production. There was exported

In the year 1760	. .	220,000	pounds
„ 1779	. .	1,100,000	„
„ 1800	.	400,000	„
„ 1814	. .	40,000	„
„ 1818	.	700	„
„ 1826	. .	5,000	„

Here was presented a wide and important field for the application of the protective principle. True, the South was opposed to it; but their representatives in Congress said, 'if we must have protection, let it cover alike the South and the North,' but all in vain.

The terrible drain upon the wealth of the South produced by the enormous bounties demanded by Northern manufacturers was clearly set forth by many of the wisest statesmen of that day. Amongst others who spoke upon this subject was Mr. Benton, of Missouri, a Western man, whose prejudices were not often favourable to the South. He delivered in the Senate of the United States in 1828 an able speech, in which he proposed to restore indigo to the list of protected articles. He urged this as a measure of equal justice, if the policy of protection should be permanently established, though he opposed the whole system. I cannot communicate so readily the influence exercised by this question upon the final separation between the North and the South as by quoting a few extracts from the speeches of leading statesmen upon the subject:—

Extract from Mr. Benton's Speech—Year 1828

I expect a unanimous vote in favour of my amendment (to protect indigo). The North should vote for it, to secure the life of the 'American System' [thus the protective policy was denominated by its party supporters], and to give a proof of their regard for the South—to show that the country south of the Potomac is included in the Tariff Bill for some other purpose besides that of oppression. The South itself, although opposed to the further increase of duties, should vote for this duty, that the Bill, if it passes, may contain one provision favourable to its interests. The West should vote for it through gratitude for fifty years of guardian protection, generous defence, and kind assistance, which the South has given it under all its trials. I feel for the sad changes which have taken place in the South during the last fifty years. Before the Revolution, it was the seat of wealth as well as of hospitality. Money and all it commanded abounded there. But how now? All this is reversed.

Wealth has fled from the South and settled in the regions north of the Potomac; and this in the midst of the fact that the South in four staples alone has exported produce since the Revolution to the value of eight hundred millions of dollars, and the North has exported comparatively nothing. Such an export would indicate unparalleled wealth, but what was the fact? In place of wealth a universal pressure for money was felt—not enough for current expenses—the price of all property down—the country drooping and languishing—towns and cities decaying—and the frugal habits of the people pushed to the verge of universal self-denial for the preservation of their family estates. Such a result is a strange and wonderful phenomenon. It calls upon statesmen to enquire into the cause; and if they enquire upon the theatre of this strange metamorphosis they will receive one universal answer from all ranks and all ages, that *it is Federal legislation which has worked this ruin.* Under this legislation the exports of the South have been made the basis of the Federal revenue. The amount annually levied upon imported goods to defray the expenses of the Government are deducted out of the price of their cotton, rice, and tobacco, either in the diminished price which they receive for these staples in foreign ports, or in the increased price which they pay for the articles they consume at home. Virginia, the two Carolinas, and

Georgia, may be said *to defray three-fourths of the annual expense of supporting the Federal Government; and of this great sum annually furnished by them, nothing or next to nothing is returned to them in the shape of Government expenditures* That expenditure flows in an opposite direction—it flows northwardly in one uniform, uninterrupted, and perennial stream. This is the reason why wealth disappears from the South and rises up in the North. Federal legislation does all this. It does it by the simple process of eternally taking away from the South and returning nothing to it. If it returned to the South the whole or even a good part of what it exacted, the four States south of the Potomac might stand the action of this system, but the South must be exhausted of its money and its property by a course of legislation which is for ever taking away and never returning anything.

Every new tariff increases the force of this action No tariff has ever yet included Virginia, the two Carolinas, and Georgia, within its provisions, except to increase the burthens imposed upon them. This one alone presents the opportunity to form an exception, by reviving and restoring the cultivation of one of its ancient staples, one of the sources of its wealth before the Revolution. The tariff of 1828 owes this reparation to the South, because the tariff of 1816 contributed to destroy the cultivation of indigo—sunk the duty on the foreign article from twenty-five to fifteen cents per pound.

The amendment proposed by Mr. Benton was seconded by Mr. Hayne, a senator from South Carolina, accompanied, however, by the following disclaimer:—

I am opposed (said Mr. Hayne) to this Bill in its principles as well as in all its details. It could assume no shape which would make it acceptable to me, or which would prevent it from operating most oppressively and injuriously upon the Southern States. With these views I had determined to make no motion to amend the Bill; but when such motions were made by others, and he was compelled to vote upon them, he knew no better rule than to endeavour to make the Bill consistent with itself. With a fixed resolution to vote against the Bill, I still consider myself at liberty to assist in so arranging the details as to extend to all portions of the country, as far as may be practicable, equal protection, and to distribute the burthens of the Government equally, in order that its benefits as well as its evils may be fully tested. As a Southern man, I would ask no boon for the South; but I must say that protection of indigo rests on the same principle as every other article proposed to be protected by this Bill.

But the protectionists had already secured as many votes as were necessary to carry their measure—and possibly enough electioneering material to carry the presidency—and hence the amendment of Mr. Benton was rejected, and the duty on indigo was diminished still farther, on the ground that such reduction would still farther protect the Northern manufacturers of woollen cloths. In the House of Representatives, Mr. McDuffie, of South Carolina, gave expression to the exasperation of the Southern members by a speech which is interesting as portraying the effect of such a system of sectional legislation even at that early day:—

Extract from Mr. McDuffie's speech—Year 1828.

Sir, if the union of these States shall ever be severed and their liberties subverted, the historian who records these disasters will have to ascribe them to measures of this description. I do sincerely believe that neither this Government nor any free Government can exist for a quarter of a century under such a system of legislation. Its inevitable tendency is not only to corrupt the public functionaries, but all those portions of the Union and classes of society who have an interest, real or imaginary, in the bounties it provides, by taxing other sections and other classes. What, sir, is the essential characteristic of a freeman? It is that independence which results from an habitual reliance upon his own resources and his own labour for support. He is not, in fact, a freeman who habitually looks to the Government for pecuniary bounties. I confess that nothing in the conduct of those who are the prominent advocates of this system has excited more apprehension and alarm in my mind than the constant efforts made by them all to impress upon the public mind the idea that national prosperity and individual wealth are to be derived, not from indidual industry and economy, but from Government bounties. An idea more fatal to liberty could not be inculcated. The days of Roman liberty were numbered when the people consented to receive bread from the public granaries. From that moment it was not the patriot who had shown the greatest capacity and made the greatest sacrifices to serve the Republic, but the demagogue who would promise to distribute most profusely the spoils of the plundered provinces that was elevated to office by a mercenary and a degenerate populace Everything became venal, even in the country of Fabricius, until finally the empire itself was sold at public auction. And what, Sir, is the nature and tendency of the system we are discussing? It bears an analogy but too lamentably striking to that which corrupted the republican purity of the Roman people. God forbid that it should consummate its triumph over the public liberty by a similar catastrophe, though even that is an event by no means improbable if we continue to legislate periodically in this way, *and to connect the election of our chief magistrate with the question of dividing out the spoils of certain States amongst the influential capitalists of the other States of the Union.*

Sir, when I consider that by a single act like the present so large an amount of money may be transferred annually from one part of the community to another—when I consider the disguise of disinterested patriotism under which the basest and most profligate ambition may perpetrate such an act of injustice and political prostitution—I cannot hesitate to pronounce this very system of indirect bounties the most stupendous instrument of corruption ever placed in the hands of public functionaries. Do we not perceive at this very moment the extraordinary and melancholy spectacle of less than one hundred thousand capitalists, by means of this unhallowed combination, exercising an absolute and despotic control over the opinions of ten millions of citizens? Sir, I will not anticipate or forebode evil. I will not permit myself to believe that the presidency of the United States will ever be bought and sold by this system of bounties and prohibitions—but I must say that there are certain quarters of this Union in which if a candidate for the presidency were to come forward with this tariff in his hand, nothing could resist his pretensions, if his adversary were opposed to this unjust system of oppression Yes, sir, the Bill would be a talisman which would give a charmed existence to the candidate who would pledge himself to support it; and although he were covered with all the multiplying villanies of nature, the most immaculate patriot and profound statesman in the nation could hold no competition with him, if he should refuse to grant this species of imperial donation.

In the course of the proceedings on this Bill, Mr. Webster, the great champion of New England manufactures, proposed to strike out the duty on hemp, under the belief that the protectionists could get along very well without Kentucky; but the majority thought otherwise, and retained it. Without that provision, of course Kentucky would have been opposed to a protective tariff. Now, mark how the independence of senators and representatives was destroyed by this odious system of bribery. Mr. Rowan, of Kentucky, while bitterly denouncing the policy of the Bill, nevertheless announced to the Senate that because of the protection given to hemp he was constrained to vote for the measure.

Extract from Mr. Rowan's Speech.

I am not opposed to the tariff as a system of revenue honestly devoted to the objects and purposes of revenue; *but when perverted by the ambition of political aspirants*, and the secret influence of inordinate cupidity, to purposes of individual *and sectional ascendency*, I cannot be seduced by captivating names or terms, however attractive, to lend it my individual support.

It is in vain, Mr. President, that it is called the 'American System.' There is but one American system, and that is delineated in the State and Federal Constitutions. It is the system of equal rights and privileges, secured by the representative principle—a system which, instead of subjecting the proceeds of the labour of some to taxation with the view of enriching others, secures to all the proceeds of their labour, exempts all from taxation, except for the support of the protecting power of the Government. As a tax *necessary* to the support of the Government, I would vote for it—call it by what name you please; as a tax for any other purpose, and especially for the purposes to which I have alluded, it has my individual reprobation, under whatever name it may assume.

It might be supposed from what I have said that I will vote against the Bill; *but I am not at liberty to substitute my individual opinion for that of my State.* I am one of the organs here of a State that by the tariff of 1824 has been chained to the car of the New England manufacturers*—a State that has been from that time, and is now groaning under the pressure of that unequal and unjust measure—a measure from the pressure of which, owing to the prevailing illusion throughout the United States, she now saw no hope of escape by a speedy return to correct principles, and seeing no hope of escaping from the ills of the system she is constrained, on principles of self-defence, to avail herself of the mitigation which this Bill presents, in the duties which it imposes upon foreign hemp, iron, and molasses. The hemp, iron, and distilled spirits of the West will, like the woollens of the Eastern States, be encouraged to the extent of the tax indirectly imposed by this Bill upon those who may buy and consume them. To this tax upon the labour of the consumer, my individual opinion is opposed; but as the organ of the State of Kentucky, I feel myself bound to surrender my individual opinion and express the opinion of my State.

The reader will perceive with what consummate skill the sagacious manufacturers of the North, by the most palpable system of bribery and bounties, divided the nation into two unequal parts, and then set to work to fleece the South of all its earnings. There was a deliberate premeditated robbery involved in the system, which was not even disguised by any attempt at subterfuge. Taxes were notoriously imposed upon one section, to be placed in the coffers of the other section; and upon the approach of every recurring presidential election the same system was

* This Tariff Bill, after a protracted debate of ten weeks, was carried through by a vote of 107 to 102 in the House of Representatives, and by 25 to 21 in the Senate.

augmented, in order to operate upon the cupidity of the States to whom bounties were promised out of the proceeds of Southern plantations.

During the colonial dependence of the country the Southern provinces, under the rule of Great Britain, had been the great centres of wealth and prosperity. Thus it had been for more than a century preceding the War of Independence. At the time of which we are now writing all this had been changed, notwithstanding the domestic institutions had remained the same. The lands were the same—the people, bond and free, were the same—the exports were of the same kind, though, except indigo, enormously increased in quantity. When we look to the table of imports before and after the establishment of the Government of the United States, and consider that during the entire period between 1760 and 1860 the exports have gone almost exclusively from the South, we cannot wonder at the determination of that section to cast off, at all hazards, the oppressive system which transferred her wealth to other States. In the colonial condition the South, as before said, was far more prosperous than the North; but very soon after the establishment of protective tariffs all this was changed, as may be seen from the following figures:—

1760—Imports into South Carolina and Virginia	£1.405,000
1760—Imports into New York, Pennsylvania, and all New England . . .	£735.100
1832—Imports into South Carolina and Virginia	$1,750 000
1832—Imports into New York alone . . .	$57,000,000
1859—Imports into Northern States . . .	$306.000 000
1859—Imports into Southern States . .	$34,000,000

Wealth, under the operation of protective tariffs,

had flown in a continuous stream from the South to the North. The reader has but to make an estimate, founded upon Mr. Benton's speech, before quoted, to see that the result of the system was obliged to bring ruin upon the planting States. Assuming that they only paid twenty millions of dollars per annum for the support of Northern manufactures, which never returned to them, the gross drain in fifty years upon the wealth of the South would amount to one thousand millions.

Under the eternally increasing load of taxes, so hid away beneath the plausible delusion of 'protection to home industry,' it is not wonderful that the grass commenced to grow in Southern cities—which during the preceding half-century had been the chief marts of prosperous trade—and that Southern citizens became borrowers of money from the rich North. It seems almost incredible that the South was able to sustain for three-quarters of a century such an insidious and ceaseless drain upon her wealth. Her immense resources alone enabled her to exist under the heavy pressure. But it may readily be conceived that the North would enjoy boundless prosperity so long as it could induce the South to pay to them this enormous annual tribute.

Without the aid of constantly recurring presidential elections this system could never have been fastened upon the South. No senators would have been driven to support the measure against their own convictions, as we have seen was true with regard to the senator from Kentucky, and as Mr. Benton, the senator from Missouri, also admits was his own case, under the apprehension that the people of their States might not be willing to relinquish the bone which was thrown to them by the manufacturers of the North.

But not only did this grinding system favour a particular class, and that the wealthiest, but, as we have seen, it deliberately divided the nation into sections, one of which was permitted to prey upon the other.

Never, after the year 1828 passed, had the Southern or planting States any reason to hope that in the future they would be regarded in any other light than as mere provinces assimilating to those which were held by the old Roman Government—merely to be plundered. The more sagacious statesmen then beheld, though obscurely, the year 1860; but the great body of the oppressors were blinded by present gains, and could not see that inevitable future. If there were any who saw that the only hope of a change consisted in a change in the manner of filling the office of chief magistrate, they did not dare to say so in direct terms. The multitude rushed madly on, and the sanguine hoped for some 'interposition of Providence;' but the wise must even at that early day have seen the foreshadowing of the end.

In order to group in a connected way the proceedings of the Congress in reference to the protective policy, it is necessary to pass over another four years. As in 1816-20-24 and 1828, so in 1832, the subject was again revived, with a view to operate upon the then pending presidential election. A presidential canvass was always the signal for offering another slice of Southern wealth to propitiate the stronger section; and hence, in the long session of 1832, the subject of protection was again brought up with renewed zeal by the manufacturers, and resisted with ever-increasing bitterness by the South.

Extract from the Speech of Gen. Smith, of Maryland—Year 1832

We have arrived at a crisis. Yes, Mr. President, at a crisis more appalling than a day of battle. I adjure the Senate to pause, to reflect on the dissatisfaction of all the South. South Carolina has expressed itself strongly against the tariff of 1828—stronger than the other States are willing to speak. But, Sir, the whole of the South feel deeply the oppression of that tariff. In this respect there is no difference of opinion. The South, the whole South, and every State of the South considers it oppressive. They have not all spoken, but when they do speak, it will be with a voice that will not implore, but will demand redress. I am. Mr. President, one of the few survivors of those who fought in the war of the Revolution We then thought we fought for liberty—for equal rights. When the Senate met there seemed to be a strong disposition with all parties to ameliorate the tariff of 1828, but now I see a change which makes me almost despair of any effectual modification. I am told that the lobby members (agents of the manufacturers) have reprobated all change whatever. These interested men hang upon the committee on manufacturers like an incubus I would say to that committee, depend upon your own judgment—discard sectional interests—study only the common weal, and thus relieve the oppressions of the South.

Extract from the Speech of Mr. Hayne, of South Carolina—Year 1832.

Let not gentlemen so far deceive themselves as to suppose that the opposition of the South to the protective system is not based on high and lofty principles. It has nothing to do with party politics, or the mere elevation of men. It rises far above all such considerations. Nor is it influenced altogether by calculations of interest; but is founded upon much nobler impulses. The instinct of self-interest might have taught us an easy way of relieving ourselves from this oppression. But, Sir, we have scorned in a contest for our rights to resort to any but open and fair means to maintain them. The spirit with which we have entered into this business is akin to that which was kindled in the bosoms of our fathers when they were made the victims of oppression; and if it has not displayed itself in the same way, it is because we have ever cherished the strongest feelings of confraternity towards our brethren, and the warmest attachment to the Union. If we have been in any degree divided amongst ourselves in this matter, the source of that division, let gentlemen be assured, has not arisen so much from any difference of opinion as to the true character of the oppression, as from the different degrees of hope of redress. All parties have for years past been looking forward to this crisis for the fulfillment of their hopes or the confirmation of their fears. And God grant that the result may be auspicious. Sir, I call upon gentlemen from every section of the Union to meet us in the true spirit of conciliation and concession. Remove, I earnestly beseech you, this never-failing source of contention. Dry up at its source this fountain of the waters of bitterness Restore that harmony which has been disturbed. It is in your power to do it this day; but there is but one means under heaven, namely, *by doing equal justice to all.* And be assured that he to whom the country shall be indebted for this blessing will be considered as the second founder of the Republic.

I will close my extracts from the debates attending this prime first cause of perpetual estrangement between the North and the South by quoting a remarkable passage from Mr. Clay's great speech upon this occasion. Mr. Clay, as is well known, was the leader of the protectionists, and the author of the so-called 'American System.' It will be seen that while the South proclaimed its unwillingness to submit to such partial legislation, and intimated a determination to resist, if all constitutional means of redress should fail, Mr. Clay took the ground that the great North would not tamely submit to being deprived of the right of fleecing the South through the agency of protective tariffs:—

Extract from Mr. Clay's Speech—Year 1832.

The danger to our Union does not lie on the side of persistence in the protective system, *but on that of its abandonment* If, as I have supposed and believe, the inhabitants of all north and east of James River, and all west of the mountains, including Louisiana [sugar protected], are deeply interested in the preservation of that system, *would they be reconciled to its overthrow? Can it be expected that two-thirds of the people of the United States would consent to the destruction of a policy believed to be indispensably necessary to their prosperity?* In estimating the degree of peril which may be incident to two opposite courses of human policy, the statesman would be short-sighted who should content himself with viewing only the evils, real or imaginary, which belong to that course which is in practical operation. He should lift himself up to the contemplation of those greater and more certain dangers which would inevitably attend the adoption of the alternative course. What would be the condition of the Union if New York and Pennsylvania, those mammoth members of our Confederacy, were firmly persuaded that their industry was paralysed, and their prosperity blighted by the enforcement of the British colonial system, under the delusive name of free trade? They are now tranquil, and happy, and contented—conscious of their welfare, and feeling a salutary and rapid circulation of the products of home manufactures and home industry throughout all their great arteries. But let that be checked—let them feel that a foreign system is to predominate—let New England and the West and the Middle States all feel that they, too, are the victims of a mistaken policy, *and then indeed might we tremble for the continuance and the safety of the Union.*

Nothing short of the overpowering influence of presidential elections could ever have induced the great and good Clay to give utterance to such sentiments. He declares, in effect, that the North (constituting with the protected West two-thirds of the whole Union) must be permitted to exhaust the substance of the South in the future as they have in the past; or *they must be expected to rebel* against the Government. He does not deny that the South is the victim of oppression; but he believes that the Northern States, constituting a majority, will not remain tranquil if they are denied the privilege of taxing the South for their benefit.

When such sentiments and opinions were openly avowed by the purest and the best of the politicians of America, was not the Union in effect already dissolved in the hearts of the citizens? Could any people having the power of resistance be expected to submit to such an exercise of despotic power, with the threat openly proclaimed, that if the Congress of the nation should attempt to relieve them of their grievous burdens, the protected States would make war upon the Government? And yet the patient South bore this, and tenfold accumulated wrongs, for more than thirty years after this plain avowal made by the leading champion of protection! Unfortunate for the South that she did not then meet the issue and apply the only efficacious remedy.

South Carolina Resists the Tariff by an Act of Nullification—Year 1832.

Six months after the delivery of the speech from which I have extracted the foregoing paragraphs, a crisis had arrived which demanded a prompt change in the policy of protection, or the alternative of disunion. The exasperation of the South had culminated in the act of nullification by South Carolina. The President had threatened to reduce the 'rebellious State' to subjection by the force of arms; but South Carolina remained firm in her purpose to resist. At this moment, the only living man who could induce the Northern manufacturers to relax their hold was Mr. Clay, and he had the boldness to come forward and discharge this duty. He introduced a Bill which he called a compromise, and which was in fact a compromise. It conceded the principle for which the South contended, but gave to the manufacturers a declining scale of protection for a period of ten years. He proposed to reduce the rate of duties upon all articles paying more than twenty per cent. by a gradual reduction of one-tenth of the excess for ten years. At the end of that time there were to be no duties exceeding that amount, and more than one hundred named articles were then to be relieved of all duty:—

Extract from Mr. Clay's Speech—Year 1832.

In presenting the modification of the tariff laws which I am now about to submit, I have two great objects in view. I believe the American (protective) system to be in the greatest danger, and I believe it can be placed upon a better and a safer foundation at this session than at the next I heard with surprise my friend from Massachusetts (Mr. Webster) say that nothing had occurred within the last six months to increase its hazard. I entreat him to review that opinion. Is it correct? Is the issue of numerous elections, including that of the highest officer of the Government, nothing? Is the explicit recommendation of that officer in his message at the opening of the session nothing? Is his declaration in his proclamation that the burdens of the South ought to be relieved nothing? Are the increasing discontents nothing? Is the tendency of recent events to unite the whole South nothing? What have we not witnessed in this chamber? Friends of the Administration bursting all the ties which seemed indissolubly to unite them to its chief, and with few exceptions south of the Potomac, opposing (and vehemently opposing) a favourite measure of the Administration! Let us not deceive ourselves. Now is the time to adjust the question in a manner satisfactory to both parties. How, I ask, is the system to be sustained against the whole weight of the Administration, against the united South, and against the increased impending danger of civil war?

This proposition was accepted by the South, although the great body of the advocates of protection in the North opposed it with earnestness, and recorded their votes against any reduction whatever. As an illustration of the spirit in which it was received by the South I will make a brief

Extract from Mr. Calhoun's Speech.

I will make but one or two observations. Entirely approving of the objects for which this Bill was introduced, I will give my vote in its favour. He who loves the Union must desire to see this agitating question brought to a termination. Until it shall be terminated we cannot expect the restoration of peace or harmony throughout the country. The general principles of this Bill received my approbation. I believe that if the present difficulties are to be adjusted, they must be adjusted on the principles embraced in the Bill. It has been my fate to occupy a position as hostile as any one could to the protective policy, but I will never give my vote to suddenly withdraw all those duties by which capital was sustained in the channel into which it had been directed There are some of the provisions of this Bill to which I object, but I look upon these minor points of difference as points in the settlement of which no difficulty will occur, when gentlemen meet together in that spirit of mutual compromise which I doubt not will be brought into their deliberations, without yielding the constitutional question in regard to the right of protection.

But the proposition of Mr. Clay met with the most violent opposition from those who had been for so long a time the recipients of this Southern bounty that they felt themselves entitled by prescription to the chief profits of southern plantations. Mr. Webster, of Massachusetts, as well as the representatives of that State and of the New England party generally, employed every means in their power to defeat the measure:—

Extract from Mr. Webster's Speech.

It is impossible that this proposition of the honourable member from Kentucky (Mr. Clay) should not excite in the country a very strong sensation; and in the relation in which I stand to the subject I am anxious at an early moment to say that, as far as I understand the Bill, there are principles in it to which I do not at present see how I can ever concur. If I understand the plan the result of it will be a well-understood surrender of the power of discrimination, or a stipulation not to use that power in the laying duties on imports after the eight or nine years have expired This appears to me to be matter of great moment. The honourable member admits that though there will be no positive surrender of the power, there will be a stipulation not to exercise it—a treaty of peace and amity, as he says, which no American statesman can hereafter stand up to violate. For one, Sir, I am not ready to enter into the treaty. I propose, so far as depends on me, to leave all our successors in Congress as free to act as we are ourselves. The honourable member from Kentucky says the tariff is in imminent danger. This may be so, Sir; but if it be so, it is because the American people will not sanction the tariff; and if they will not, why then it will not be sustained at all. But I know nothing which has happened within the last six or eight months changing so materially the prospects of the tariff. *I do not despair of the success of an appeal to the American people* to take a just care of their own interest, and not to sacrifice those vast interests which have grown up under the laws of Congress.

Mr. Clay, as I have before said, was the great leader of the protective policy, called by his party the 'American System.' He was in favour of protection as a general system, and desired as far as possible to make it embrace the leading interests of all the States—North and South. Unfortunately, there was but a single product of the South (indigo) which could be protected, and the North was strong enough to vote that out of the tariff.

Mr. Calhoun, upon the other hand, was the champion of a precisely opposite system. Not exactly free trade, but as near an approximation to it as was possible.

Mr. Webster was the champion of protection to New England manufactures, and for that very reason was opposed to protecting indigo in the South and hemp in Kentucky—the latter of which he made a strong effort to strike from the list of protected articles. The reckless earnestness with which his party clung to these bounties from the agricultural and planting interests is exhibited in his remarks above quoted. It will be remembered that at the very moment when he proclaimed his determination to hold on to the last penny of exactions, South Carolina had already virtually withdrawn from the Union, and but for the vast influence of the then President Jackson the whole South would have been in a blaze. As it was, the failure of Mr. Clay's Bill would have resulted in war or disunion; and yet, as will be seen from the foregoing extract, even the statesman Webster desired to postpone any action upon the subject until after the question should have been re-submitted to the people at another general election for the presidency, in order to ascertain the will of the majority. Twenty millions of people were to be called upon to decide a question which in its very nature could only be adjusted by a small number upon a principle of compromise under the guidance of the Constitution. A subject of enormous details, involving the nicest discrimination, and a thorough knowledge of constitutional law, ought to be again submitted, according to Mr. Webster, to the decision of a majority of the people, before

Congress should take any farther cognizance of the question.

Certainly, Mr. Webster was right in saying that one Congress could not absolutely prevent a succeeding Congress from the exercise of its constitutional powers. Still they could advise, and this they did in the section of Mr. Clay's Bill which provided that, '*after the 30th of September*, 1842, *duties shall only be laid for raising such revenue as may be necessary for an economical administration of the Government.*'

The Bill passed, and became the law of the land. The more moderate protectionists accepted the boon of a ten years longer lease of bounties, and the South agreed to continue them for the stipulated time, in the hope that after that period they would be relieved altogether from the incubus of the protective system. Both sides made sacrifices, and it might be readily proved that both acted inconsistently with their previous professions. But this was an inevitable result of a compromise upon the then existing state of facts.

Peace and harmony were restored for a certain time; but even before the period arrived when, according to the stipulation, '*duties were to be laid for revenue only*,' the whole question had been submitted to the people at a presidential election, and September 30, 1842, dawned upon one of the most extravagantly protective tariffs that had ever before existed. Still the great agricultural West was growing daily in power and wealth; and it soon became manifest that, unless the New England manufacturing interests could break up the natural alliance between the South and the West, in opposition to the protective policy, the whole system would soon tumble to the ground. Then was called to their aid the negro question, and by this means the alienation between the South and the West was consummated and perpetuated. If there had been no presidential canvasses to disturb the legitimate course of events, the tariff question would no doubt have been permanently settled, with due regard to the rights and interests of the whole people. Unfortunately, however, the great leaders, Clay, Webster, and others, were respectively at the head of parties which aspired to govern the country by means of presidential elections. Many of them possessed high and noble qualities. Many honoured the country which they served; but all no doubt had political careers very different from those which would have signalised their lives, but for the influence of these periodical contests for supreme power.

I have thus briefly glanced at one of the great sectional issues which disturbed the tranquillity of the country, from the very foundation of the Government, and which at last brought the Union in 1833 to the very verge of dissolution, when it was saved by the influence of Mr. Clay. If this compromise had never been disturbed by another presidential election, the principle thereof might and probably would have continued to be the policy of the Government. For the purpose of combining the events connected with the subject of protection I have passed over a number of interesting incidents connected with presidential contests. I will now return to the contest which followed the administration of Mr. J. Q. Adams.

Election of General Jackson.

Continuation of the 'Bargain, Intrigue, and Corruption Mania'—Year 1828.

The contest between Mr. Adams and General Jackson for the presidency during the next term may be said to have commenced nearly four years before, upon the day when Mr. Adams was chosen President by the House of Representatives. It was attended during its entire progress with an acrimonious personal bitterness hitherto unparalleled in the history of political squabbles. The struggle ended in the defeat and final overthrow of Mr. Adams as a presidential aspirant. There was no sectional issue introduced in the canvass which was not drowned by the excitement growing out of the personal issues. General Jackson received a majority of the electoral votes of the North, and almost a unanimous vote in the South. Although Mr. Adams could not properly ascribe his defeat to the South, for if the South had not cast a vote in the election he would have been defeated by his own section, yet the bitterness which from that day forth he manifested towards the South showed that he regarded that section as the chief promoter of his political overthrow. He was subsequently chosen by the people of his district to a seat in the representative branch of Congress, where for many years he devoted his great talents and acknowledged ability in fomenting discord between the sections, and in laying the foundation for that political party which rested entirely upon geographical lines, and which has since acquired such a terrible notoriety. Generally, however, his conduct was tempered by that dignity of character which signalised his deportment as a man. He was acrimonious and often unjust to the South in his oratorical efforts; but on more than one occasion, when called upon to vote on a question involving the constitutional rights of the South, he refused to comply with the requirements of his section. Certainly but few public men ever had stronger provocation to retaliate upon their foes than Mr. Adams. He was unjustly accused of a high crime, and pursued with a vindictiveness and a success which pulled down his friends with him into irretrievable ruin. Those who were his chief supporters were never again successful in replacing themselves in popular favour. Many of them were the most eminent statesmen of the Republic, and their names are impressed upon its history amongst those who served it most faithfully. But the majority of the people never announced their forgiveness to those who had been guilty of the crime of having elected Mr. Adams to the presidency. No wonder he was embittered against those whom he regarded as the authors of his and his friends' misfortunes. It was not in human nature to submit quietly to such accumulated personal insults and wrongs. He could not destroy all his enemies; but he could plant a thorn in the side of the South, which his strong good sense and clear-sighted sagacity might have taught him would rankle there long after he should have paid the debt of nature. It can scarcely be presumed, however, that he sought to penetrate so deeply into the future. The influence of presidential contests appears almost to have deprived men of the capacity to foresee the inevitable consequences of their acts.

At least, a great number, even amongst the leading politicians, seemed to act alone in reference to the passing moment, and an immediately hoped for result.

General Jackson was installed into the presidency, but the 'Bargain, Intrigue, and Corruption' agitation was not suffered to slumber. The great body of his supporters believed that he had been defrauded out of his just rights by the election of Mr. Adams, and their previous attachment for him was thereby converted into an enthusiastic devotion, which made them regard almost as personal enemies all who did not share their sentiments. The office-seekers were, of course, not disposed to surrender such a potent weapon of party warfare after only a single success. In 1832 it was the controlling issue made in the contest between General Jackson and Mr. Clay, and again the result was in favour of the assailants. In 1833 General Jackson entered upon his second term, and the 'Bargain and Corruption Mania' upon the ninth year of its uninterrupted career.

For a period of brief duration there was a comparative lull in the terrific gale which, during so long a period, had swept over the land with resistless fury. In truth, the party which defended Mr. Clay had been so utterly discomfited and overwhelmed by the long series of disastrous defeats which they had sustained, that they were incapable of continuing the contest with any hope of success. Mr. Clay did not surrender—he never surrendered—it was not in his gallant nature; but his struggle for the presidency was for the time being abandoned, and the many-edged sword which had been employed against him and his friends was returned to its scabbard for a season, because there remained no combatants upon whom it might be employed. But it was only for a season. It was unsheathed again at subsequent periods, when it was as before eminently successful in accomplishing its mission as a president-maker. In summing up its achievements, we find that it was the chief instrument in making one president in 1829, another in 1833, and another indirectly in 1837. It was a prominent issue in 1845, and came near defeating Mr. Buchanan in 1857, just thirty years from the day when an obscure member of Congress, from Pennsylvania, first breathed into it the breath of life. In every case, except the last, the decision amounted to a condemnation of Mr. Clay, who is to-day justly regarded by men of all parties, with all his admitted faults, as one of the purest patriots and one of the most noble-hearted men whose name is recorded in American annals.

Not the least curious feature of this most strange history remains to be told. Mr. Clay lived to a ripe old age; and, after having served his country faithfully in the Senate for a long series of years, he died a disappointed man. Not for himself, but for the sake of his friends he desired to be the President; but he went down to the grave with the stain of an infamous charge, confirmed by the repeated verdicts of his countrymen, resting upon his memory and embittering the last moments of his eventful life. And yet, upon the day when it was announced that his spirit had taken its flight to another world, upon that very instant, by the universal public sentiment of his countrymen, he was acquitted altogether of the offences which had been laid against him. None were left who believed that he had ever been corruptly guilty, as set forth in that grievous charge which had embittered so many years of his life. Now, it is never referred to, except to be scouted and derided, even by those who in the phrensy of the excitement produced by presidential elections were the chief agents in its propagation. It is a singular fact that all those whose testimony was relied upon to give a colour to the accusation, recanted at some period of their lives; and the principal witness made a death-bed confession of the wrong he had done to Mr. Adams and Mr. Clay. We may well believe that posterity will find the history of the 'Bargain, Intrigue, and Corruption Mania,' one of the most inexplicable phases of that insanity which presidential contests produced.

In order to trace out more distinctly the tendency and operation of the causes we are considering, it is necessary to recall once more the condition and names of the two great parties which emerged from the contest of 1824. Although Mr. Clay was always defeated before the people upon every trial where his name was brought forward, yet he continued to be the acknowledged chief of the opposition party up to the day of his death. As I before said, all the candidates in 1824–5 were adherents of the Democratic party. After the split produced by that election, the part headed by General Jackson being the victor, of course retained the old name, while the defeated fragment organised themselves under the lead of Mr. Clay into what was known throughout the greater part of its history as the '*Whig*' party. At first the difference between them may be said to have been purely personal At a later period there were fierce dissensions in regard to the re-charter of the Bank of the United States. General Jackson boldly throttled the monster money-dealer, and for a long time the result of the contest was doubtful. The money of the Bank was freely employed as a counterpoise to the patronage of the Government; but in the end the indomitable unconquerable Jackson planted his foot upon the prostrate body of his antagonist. It is here worthy of special remark that the great body of the people took their stand upon the one side or the other in this controversy, according to their personal partialities or prejudices for or against General Jackson or Mr. Clay. If they believed the charge of 'Bargain, Intrigue, and Corruption' to be true, they went with General Jackson against the Bank. If they believed it to be false, they went with Mr. Clay in favour of the re-charter. In reference to a protection tariff, the influence of the Northern manufacturers swerved the policy of the party in that direction; and once, as we have seen, they seized upon a temporary success and adopted very high duties. But if their platforms be examined now, it will be found that both parties avoided as far as possible a direct issue. The Whigs were in favour of a 'revenue tariff, with incidental (insidious) protection,' while the Democrats favoured a 'judicious constitutional tariff.'

Throughout the whole of these long years, however, it is plainly observable that before the great body of the people all political questions were made tributary to the bitter personal contest between Clay and Jackson. It seemed as though these were the heads of rival dynasties for the chief office of the Republic, and it is doubtful whether any two civilians in the history of the civilised world ever exercised for so long a time so great an influence over the wills of so many millions of people. Even after General Jackson's retiracy, the prestige of his name continued. Though withdrawn from active participation in public affairs, from his 'Hermitage' in Tennessee he signified his opinions, and his party deferred to them. His wishes were commands, and his commands were obeyed without a murmur or a token of disapprobation amongst the great body of his hundreds of thousands of followers. The politician who faltered in his fealty, no matter how high he may have climbed upon the ladder of fame, tumbled headlong to the bottom, never to rise again. It was wonderful, marvellous the power exercised by that man over the wills of his fellow-men. He served but two terms as President, yet for a series of years he exercised a despotic influence over the destinies of parties. Mr. Clay, the leader of the Whig party, may be appropriately described as one of 'nature's noblemen.' Combining within himself the attributes of a statesman, the highest gift of oratory, and all the qualities of a high-toned gentleman, he was during his whole life the idol of his friends, who loved him with a devotion that never faltered; and the terror of his adversaries, who respected while they feared, and honoured while they maligned him. Though mingling actively in party politics during a period longer than that which is assigned as the duration of a generation, he did not leave a real stain upon his reputation as a gentleman. Though always defeated in his aspirations for the presidency, his friends never deserted him; but in all his bitterest disappointments they clung to him with a self-sacrificing devotion which has never been exhibited by American politicians for any other unsuccessful leader. He towered so high above all his life-long misfortunes that even in defeat he looked and was the conqueror. So far as related to the attainment of the great object of his personal ambition, it was his misfortune to have lived in the days of Jackson. With this man of iron will he struggled for a lifetime; and though his adversary was always the gainer and he always the loser in every contest for political supremacy, yet it would be difficult to decide which of the two exercised the greater influence over the minds of the people and the destinies of the nation. Jackson may be said to have been the bone and the sinew of the country—Clay, the head, the intellect. Neither had any rival but the other.

Martin Van Buren, of New York, Elected President in 1837.

The force of General Jackson's popularity carried Martin Van Buren into the presidency in 1837. The old charge of 'Bargain' was still sufficiently formidable to keep down any successful opposition. But the Democratic party had now held their lease of power continuously since the election of Mr. Jefferson in 1801 Their long tenure of office had been attended with the usual results; and there is no doubt but great corruptions had crept into the administration of the Government. In truth, it may be said that official corruption was the rule, honesty the exception. Defalcations of public officers became so common as scarcely to excite attention. These were but the legitimate fruits of presidential elections.

For a long series of years to the ordinary rancour of party-spirit was added the bitterness of personal animosities. The discussion of the simplest question of State policy fell into the usual train of ferocious invective; and whether the subject was one of internal improvement, tariff, or bank, a stranger would have supposed that the decisions involved the personal characters of those who were arrayed upon the one side or the other. Everything connected with party politics was always serious when it was not bitter or malignant. But every excitement must have an end, as well as all available issues in presidential elections. A new one became necessary, and the closing months of Mr. Van Buren's term found the nation plunged headlong into another madness.

The 'Log Cabin and Hard Cider Mania' in the Canvass between Martin Van Buren, of New York, and William Henry Harrison, of Ohio—Year 1840.

There are very many Americans who would, if they could, draw the veil of perpetual oblivion over the canvass of 1840 between Mr. Van Buren and General Harrison—the former being the Democratic and the latter the Whig candidate for the presidency. And yet whatever may have been its influence in bringing presidential elections into disrepute, it was in itself the most amiable, although the least dignified, of all the party squabbles by which it had been preceded. Surely such a sudden and overwhelming revulsion in party tactics was never before witnessed. The transition from the grave to the gay—from the serious to the absurd—from tragedy to buffoonery, was but the work of an instant. It was really funny—very funny. It was, in fact, neither tragedy nor comedy: it resembled nothing which had ever before been put upon the stage. It might be likened to a kind of sensation spectacle farce, gotten up and performed by the inmates of a lunatic asylum, in which the actors all changed their usual characters. The buffoon played tragedy—the high comedian low comedy—while the tragedian tickled his nearest neighbour with a straw to make the audience laugh. The inconsiderate did laugh—they laughed immoderately—and all the time. Wit, or the absence of it, was alike a provocative of merriment. The judicious essayed to look grieved, but anon they broke forth into boisterous mirth. To be betrayed into such an exhibition of undignified weakness made them angry of course—angry with themselves—angry with the political charlatans around them—angry with the world—but the more angry they became the more they laughed. Can anything be imagined more funny or more curious than a scene which causes anger, tears, and mirth at the same instant? The press participated in the general delirium, and contributed its due share to the propagation of the prevailing madness. Imagine the London 'Times' converted into a huge daily 'Punch,' and 'Punch' putting on the airs and strutting about in the castaway garments of the great 'Thunderer:' and the Englishman may have a glimmering conception of the American press in the memorable year 1840.

'We have never yet won a single battle: let us stoop to conquer!' said the Whig leaders, and never was a programme more rigidly adhered to. The Convention nominated for the presidency a plain, obscure, excellent old gentleman, whose home, so far as New England was concerned, was in the Far West. He had never done any harm—he had never before jostled anyone off the track—though his nomination did now exclude Mr. Clay at the only period of his life when he might have been elected. If he had but few friends he had no enemies. In searching through the musty records of his early history it was found that he had been at one time a general in the army of the Republic—he had fought the Indians at the battle of Tippecanoe, and the English somewhere else. And although it was said, though I know not with how much of truth, that the ladies of his native town in Ohio had bestowed upon him the rather dubious compliment of voting him a 'petticoat' in honour of his military achievements, yet, in the absence of wars, or even rumours of wars, there was thought to be sufficient material, if skilfully combined with the fancy touches of a real artist, to fashion at least a passable hero. There could be said of him what might with the same propriety have been said of ten thousand other citizens: he was, without doubt, an excellent gentleman, a true patriot, and a brave soldier.

The vast body of the Whigs, who were devoted to Mr. Clay, were indignant, almost rebellious, when it was announced that the Convention had set aside their favourite, for an obscure individual, whose name even was unfamiliar to their ears, notwithstanding he had once before been a nominal candidate for the presidency, because the prominent leaders of the party did not court the honour of a defeat. But there was no use lamenting. The fiat had gone forth from the caucus of politicians assembled in solemn conclave, and from their judgment there was no appeal.

Moodily, grumblingly, angrily—with drooping heads and sinking hearts—the Whig masses set about the performance of the unpalatable task which had been assigned them by their masters, the professional president-makers.

The Democrats laughed outright. It seemed to them so irresistibly ludicrous, they could scarcely credit the messengers who conveyed to them the tidings that the great Clay had been superseded by Harrison. 'What!' said they, 'to set aside the gallant chieftain who has raised them up from a handful to a host! whose clarion voice has so often cheered them in the hottest of the battle!'

Never did combatants seem so unequally matched as those who now marshalled their armies to take the field; and never did a result furnish a more impressive illustration of the unreliability of human calculations, the deceitfulness of appearances, the fickleness of fortune, the uncertainty of presidential elections.

As I intimated before, it was intended by the leaders of the Whig party to run General Harrison through as a military hero. But one single sneer, accompanied by one burst of laughter, emanating from an obscure letter-writer, whom nobody knew, and who has never been heard of but once since, changed the whole aspect of the struggle. There is a deep significance in this truth, and a moral might be deduced from it which ought to convey a useful lesson to enthusiasts of the 'vox populi vox Dei' school of politicians.

'How very odd!' wrote this unknown correspondent: 'William Henry Harrison a candidate for admission into the White House! A man only fitted by nature and education *to live in a log cabin and drink hard cider!* Ha! ha! ha!'

It was enough. The deed was done—the battle was in effect already fought and won. The Whigs took up the gauntlet which they pretended to believe had been thrown down in derision by their adversaries, and from that moment their success was sure. They laughed—the joke was so good a one they were obliged to laugh—but they were, nevertheless, very much in earnest. They inscribed the words 'Log Cabin and Hard Cider' upon all their banners, in letters of silver and letters of gold. They constituted the burthen of all their speeches—they were printed im glaring capitals in all their newspapers; and, more potent than all, they were incorporated into all their songs. They laughed and sang—in time and out of time—in place and out of place: they would n't be serious a single moment. They peremptorily refused to designate their opponents any longer by their ancient title of 'Democrats.' They said it was too sober, too grave—the very sound made them melancholy; and they never applied the word 'democrat' to their adversaries again. They called them '*Loco-focos*'—said there was something light as well sulphurous about that name which pleased them; and ever afterwards they refused to recognise their adversaries by any other title. Their coat of arms was a log cabin, with the string of the door-latch upon the outside, a jug of hard cider, a 'coon *rampant*, regarding with a sardonic grin a 'loco-foco' *couchant*.

The Democrats were bewildered: in fact, utterly disconcerted. They knew not which way to turn, or what to do, or where to go. 'People of America,' said they, 'have you become so drunk upon hard cider that you will no longer listen to the voice of sober reason?' The response was a laughing chorus, descriptive of the transcendant virtues of log cabins and hard cider.

'Meet us as of yore,' implored the now despairing Democrats, 'with solid argument and biting wit. Take any other shape but that, and if we must fall, let us fall like men; but do not, for the honour of our common country, laugh and sing us to death.' In response the Whigs only laughed and sang the more.

But the 'spectacle' at a 'grand mass meeting' was the oddest of all. A long procession of queer-looking objects, resembling nothing that had ever before been invented or conceived by man, came slowly forward towards the spectators. In the distance it reminded the beholder of the descriptions recorded in Eastern story of some grand pageant prepared to honour the coronation day of a potentate of the olden time. They are all moving on, up hill and down hill, and yet they seem so very huge! One wonders what can be the motive power to draw them. A nearer view detracts somewhat from the brilliancy of the moving mass, but adds to the wonder. The vast line seems now to be composed of vehicles, but of such very odd proportions and of such vast dimensions, that it is impossible to conjecture the uses to which they might be applied. They appeared to be a sort of cross between hackney coaches and country churches in the back woods; and in their uses to subserve in some measure the purposes of both. At length the procession approaches within full view, and the mystery is solved: they are log cabins on wheels! Upon the outside there are "'coon-skins,' and other emblems of back-wood life, while upon the roof the living raccoons are peering curiously upon the scene below. Within are the performers, sitting upon barrels marked in large letters 'hard cider.' Each one waves aloft a 'gourd,' filled to the brim with the muddy fluid, and sings at the top of his voice some doggrel rhymes, the burden of which is—

> Up, Tippecanoe, and Tyler, too,
> And down with the Loco-foco crew!

As the novel spectacle moves slowly forward the excitement grows apace. Men are not drunk, but seem to be so. Judge and jury, attorney and prisoner, rush from the court-room into the street to witness the scene. The merchant abandons his desk, the carpenter his plane, the farmer his plough, the clergyman his study, to join the curious throng. The 'Loco-focos,' in spite of their vexation, mingle with the crowd, annoyed and angry, cursing the folly of all mankind, but more especially the absurd insanity of the 'ciderites;' but even they laugh—laugh hysterically.

Slowly, but still onward, moves the quaint pageant. The inmates of the wheeled cabins distribute gourds of hard cider to the crowd without. The voices of the singers grow in volume with every new accession to their ranks, until at length the multitude join vociferously in the swelling chorus—

> Hurrah! hurrah! for Harrison and Tyler!
> A good log-cabin and a barrel of hard cider!

The famous national air of 'Yankee Doodle' became obsolete. The stirring notes of

> Hail, Columbia! happy land!

were no longer heard, and even the star-spangled banner paled before the opening splendours of the log cabin and 'coon-bedecked flag of the ciderites, which proudly floated from the windows of every hovel and mansion of the now-triumphant Whigs. Liberty poles, whose summits reached almost to the clouds, were planted in the principal streets of all the towns and villages. All the ordinary avocations of life were suspended—all classes and conditions of men mingled in the turmoil—vast bodies of citizens, numbering sometimes tens of thousands, at other times almost hundreds of thousands, assembled daily in different parts of the country to organise what they denominated 'grand national councils of the real people,' at which the orators made speeches, and the masses drank hard cider. For anyone to be sanely sober during this great and universal madness would have been regarded as the strongest evidence of insanity.

Mr. Van Buren entered upon the contest with the prestige of a previously successful career. He had already been the President during one term, and he appeared before the people for a reelection as the acknowledged head and representative of a party which, since the foundation of the Government, had never known a defeat and scarcely a discomfiture. But all would not do. The people were seized with an insanity which swept away all previous party ties. The 'log cabin and hard cider mania' bore down all opposition. 'Tippecanoe, and Tyler, too,' were the high priests of this new worship; and in due time the plain honest old farmer was transplanted, upon the shoulders of his fellow-countrymen, from the midst of the congenial scenes which surrounded his humble abode upon the banks of the Ohio to the gilded sepulchre of the White House. And still as they bore him on to that goal, the attainment of which has been for many of those who have reached it at once the fruition of their ambitious hopes and the graves of their happiness, they sang—

> Hurrah! hurrah! for Harrison and Tyler!
> A good log cabin and a barrel of hard cider!

Unfortunate man! The change was too great for his feeble frame. Scarcely had he placed foot in his new abode, ere his palace was besieged by a crowd of hungry office-seekers and congratulating friends, who left him no single moment of repose. Amongst others came the identical letter-writer, whose sneer had made him President, claiming a recompense for his unintended services. They talked to him until his very brain reeled and all his senses were bewildered. They shook him by the hand, and shook him until they had shaken the life out of his body. In one month and a day from the hour when he entered the door of the White House, the elected sovereign of twenty millions of people, a funeral *cortége* passed out, bearing back to their last resting-place, upon the banks of the Ohio, all that remained of William Henry Harrison, the ninth citizen who occupied the post of chief magistrate of the United American Republics. It cannot be said, in legal parlance, that he was murdered, because it was not the intention of his persecutors to take away his life. But if ever a truthful record of the cause of his untimely end shall be inscribed upon his tombstone it will be: '*Killed by the clamours of the office-seekers, within the space of thirty days after he became the President of the Model Republic.*'

Mr. Tyler, the Vice-President, became by the provisions of the Constitution the President during the remainder of the unexpired term. It was the first success which the opposition branch of the great Democratic party had ever achieved. A log cabin and hard cider excitement had brought them into power; but, when the leaders settled themselves down to the sober work of conducting the affairs of the Government, they found themselves composed of such antagonistical ingredients that the 'administration' was a failure. The party lost so much ground during its four years tenure of power, that even the great genius and popularity of Mr. Clay, who was their next candidate, was unable to keep them in power.

The responsibility for this failure was visited upon the luckless head of Mr. Tyler, an honourable man, a high-toned gentleman, and withal a statesman of no ordinary capability. The Whigs insisted that what they meant by the 'log cabin and hard cider' campaign was to express metaphorically their admiration for a United States Bank, for the distribution of the public lands, and for protective tariffs. Mr. Tyler, who had always been opposed to these measures, protested very naturally that he could not view the affair in that aspect. He could discover no link of connection between 'log cabins' and a bank, or 'hard cider' and a tariff. This divergence of opinion between the Vice-President and many of the party leaders produced an open rupture as soon as Mr. Tyler, by the death of General Harrison, became the President.

Never perhaps in the annals of political squabbles, even in the Model Republic, was there poured forth upon the head of any other President such a torrent of vulgar denunciation and malignant vituperation as emanated from the party leaders and the party press against the man whose name but a few short weeks before was a talisman employed to arouse the Whig masses to the highest pitch of enthusiasm. His picture adorned alike the palace and the hovel. The people sang aloud in every town, in every valley, and upon every hill-top the praises of 'Tyler, too,' while the music of Meyerbeer and Rossini was banished from the *salons* of the rich to be superseded by the popular melodies which told of the love they bore for Harrison and Tyler—the great, the good, the incorruptible champions of the denizens of log cabins and the drinkers of hard cider. Mr. Tyler had few defenders. The wounds that had been inflicted upon his defeated adversaries in the late memorable campaign were too recent to have even commenced to heal. It was not in human nature for the Democrats to interpose a word or an act which might avert a single blow aimed by the Whigs at their late popular leader. The only single reproach which they had the semblance of a claim to utter against him was that in accordance with his honest convictions and long-cherished principles, he refused to give his official sanction to the charter of a United States Bank! They had no reason to doubt then, and none doubt now, but that he acted conscientiously. Every purely personal consideration which might have exercised an influence over his judgment would have prompted him to yield to the desires of his own party leaders, while to oppose his own convictions of right to the popular clamour afforded evidence of a moral courage rarely possessed by the leaders of political parties. But nothing could save him from the fury of his late admirers. His name was coupled with that of Benedict Arnold, the traitor of the War of Independence. Though he went up with the velocity and the brilliancy of a rocket, it was only for an instant that he rested poised in mid air—the adored, the honoured, the idol of the multitude—ere he came down like a stone which had been cast forth by some convulsion of nature.

How wonderful is the influence exercised by the principle of ambition over the mind of man! The fate of Mr. Tyler has been the fate of almost all the party leaders who have during nearly a quarter of a century risen to power upon the tide of popular favour. Unable to satisfy the wants of greedy partisans, they have been made to pay the penalty of their ephemeral honours by a descent only equalled in rapidity by the suddenness of their elevation.

Their only consolation in too many instances consisting in the reflection that though they arose without merit they fell without a fault.

Shadows of Approaching Evils.

It was during the remarkable political campaign which resulted in the election of General Harrison that two distinct elements began to develope themselves into such a formidable power that they attracted no small share of attention from thoughtful citizens, who were not carried away by the whirl, and excitement, and delirium of the 'log cabin and hard cider mania.' Party politicians, also, with the proverbial sagacity of their trade, begun to discover the new elements which, by judicious cultivation and training, might be reared into powerful agents in the ever beginning, never ending work of monarch-making for the great and growing Republic.

European emigrants had been for many years pouring into the country in a continuous stream. In many districts they constituted a majority of the population; and in all the large cities of the North and West they were a formidable ingredient. The term of residence necessary to invest them with all the rights of native-born citizens was only five years, and it was found that in the critical emergency of a doubtful election even this brief period of probation might be shortened. They had not up to this time organised themselves as a unit of political power; but a common sentiment and a common sympathy amongst a large number of them produced a certain uniformity in their political tendencies. Many of them became excellent, worthy, and patriotic citizens, and conducted themselves accordingly; but others seemed only intent upon opposing themselves to all the conservative checks and balances of the Constitution, in order that they might reconstruct it upon that radical basis which their theory taught them was essential to the full developement of democratic power. The descendants of revolutionary fathers were knocked down and driven away from the ballot-box by strangers, who only a brief season before had placed foot for the first time upon American soil.

The other element was the 'Abolition,' or Anti-Slavery party. The great excitement between the North and the South in 1820, which originated upon the application of Missouri for admission into the Union, shook the Government from centre to circumference; but with the settlement of that question the flame of discord was immediately extinguished, the insanity subsided, and the subject passing into temporary oblivion was only referred to as a point in history, noting a brief interval of an inexplicable popular madness. With the exception of an occasional fitful and purposeless start from its slumbers, as if only to show that though buried it still lived and breathed, it never sufficiently aroused itself during a long series of years to take an important position as a president-maker. We may well imagine that the childish, silly, frivolous canvass of 1840 was calculated to arouse the cold, plodding, earnest Puritan to some effort to restore presidential contests to something of their original seriousness. 'We have had a season of puerile frivolity and mad folly,' he would naturally exclaim: 'let it be followed by a stern and terrible retribution.'

Even in the North, however, the ultra-Abolitionist could scarcely shelter himself against the indignation of his own countrymen. The measures he proposed to inaugurate were so utterly revolting to the moral sense, and so vindictive and atrocious in their proposed application to the slave-holders, that the country turned away from him with loathing and horror. Fortunately, up to the period of which I am now speaking, no political party was willing to identify itself with this dangerous element, and hence its leaders were obliged to content themselves with the accessions they might make from the ranks of disappointed politicians, who had abandoned all hope of promotion if they continued in the service of the old parties. The professional president-makers saw clearly that the occasion was not opportune—the public *heart* was not ready to entertain, much less adopt, the bloody programme of the Abolitionists. Men's minds must be schooled by long training before they can be brought to contemplate with satisfaction the consummation of such a purpose as that which was shadowed forth by this handful of fanatics and madmen. Besides, 'Sectionalism,' which was a necessary prerequisite to the successful execution of such a scheme—saving in the matter of a tariff, which was after all only a money issue—had not as yet suggested itself, except spasmodically, to the attention of the king-makers. A little later we will discover the causes which, at a subsequent period, enabled the Abolition party to take rank as a leading contestant for the coveted prize of the presidency and the spoils.

Canvass between James K. Polk, of Tennessee, and Henry Clay, of Kentucky.

Revival of the Bargain and Corruption Charge—Texas Annexation Consummated—Year 1844.

Mr. Clay—ever unfortunate as to time when he appeared as a candidate for the presidency—now entered upon the canvass at a moment when his party was demoralised by the internal dissensions which had destroyed its harmony during the entire period in which they had held the reins of Government. The Democrats, with a vivid recollection of the 'log cabin and hard cider' campaign, commenced the canvass in imitation of the songs and buffoonery of the Whigs in 1840. The Whigs essayed to do likewise. But in a short time both parties abandoned to a great extent this undignified manner of conducting the canvass. The game seemed to have been played out. It was impossible to reach again the unapproachable folly of the preceding farce; and besides, the people seemed for the moment weary of the nonsense. Neither of the candidates was adapted to play a leading part in such frivolous orgies. They were made of sterner stuff. Although Mr. Polk had not hitherto appeared as one of the prominent contestants for the candidacy and leadership of his party, yet those who were familiar with his character knew him to be a man of superior abilities, varied and extensive acquirements, a most sagacious politician, and combining with these advantages the characteristic qualities of a gentleman. To be placed in opposition to the veteran statesman and orator of Kentucky, who had maintained his reputation and rank during an entire generation, was to subject any citizen of the Republic to a most trying ordeal; but Mr. Polk sustained himself as well, at least, as would any of the members of his party who were his rivals for the post of leader. Regarded as men and as politicians, either one of them would have worthily filled the high station to which they were aspiring.

With such candidates, the conductors of the canvass were obliged to preserve a certain degree of dignity; and both being citizens of Southern States, the rabid Abolitionists could only be spiteful towards both. Mr. Clay's friends entertained strong hopes of his success. In truth, they scarcely regarded the result as doubtful. The old story of bargain and corruption was brought up, and probably influenced the votes of many of General Jackson's more devoted followers, because it revived the memories of bitter animosities; but Mr. Clay was doubtless at the moment of his nomination the most popular citizen of the Republic.

Suddenly a new question, 'the annexation of Texas,' was skilfully brought forward, upon which he was, by the force of circumstances, constrained to take not only the unpopular side, but one which was, without doubt, in opposition to his own personal inclinations. The Democratic party was relatively stronger in the South than in the North. It was this party which proposed the measure, or rather adopted it after Mr. Tyler had brought it forward. The Northern Anti-Slavery party, strangely enough, if we may believe that they were honestly concerned about the welfare of the slave, took the opposite side. The Whig party of the North committed themselves so strongly in opposition to annexation, that Mr. Clay gave a reluctant consent to adopt their views as a part of his own programme. But his attitude was considered by the Anti-Slavery opponents of the scheme of annexation as at least equivocal, and they abstained in a great measure from participation in the contest between Mr. Clay and Mr Polk, and voted for a member of their own faction. Thus Mr. Clay's unfortunate position lost him not only the supporters, but the radical opponents of annexation.

Mr. Clay was really adverse to making the subject of annexation a party question. He thought very properly that it should be brought forward as a national measure, altogether independent of party politics. If Texas could have been added to the States of the Union by the voice of the nation, the measure would probably have had no warmer friend than Mr. Clay.

It is interesting to note the difference in the means by which such Anti-Slavery men as Mr. Clay proposed to benefit the slave and to abolish slavery in the Border States, and those of the Yankee Abolitionists. Mr. Clay thought, with many other citizens of the Border States, that if the radical Abolition party would cease to meddle in Southern affairs, slavery would gradually and imperceptibly pass on in the direction of the South, and finally disappear from several of the larger States, by the operation of the same causes which had already transferred it from the Northern States. As soon as slavery should have disappeared from the present Border States, other Border States would, according to their belief, take the same course. Texas offered a wide field for this absorption of the African population of Kentucky, Maryland, and Virginia. Another generation might possibly find other territory still farther south, still inviting the owners of slaves to transfer them on and on, until, by the operation of natural laws and by an imperceptible process, the two races would have been separated, and each one would dwell in the latitude best adapted to his constitution, his habits, his nature, and his tastes. This, it is true, may be regarded as but the dream of the enthusiast; but it offered the only possible solution of the question of slavery in the States of the Confederation which would not entail misery and disaster upon both races. The annexation of Texas was desired by many, who believed that it would drain the more Northern States of their slave population.

The Abolitionists opposed annexation, because they supposed that by some means or other it might be beneficial to the Slave States. There were also many citizens of the North who, though not of the rabid Anti-Slavery faction, opposed the acquisition, because it would add to the political power of the South in the Senate. Upon the whole, the strength of the Abolitionists, as a political sectional organisation, was much augmented during this period. Still they were too weak in numbers to be able to dictate terms to either of the two great parties. The foundations of the party, several years afterwards known as the Republican party, were, however, permanently laid during this canvass. The fatal truth began to make itself known, that sooner or later the president-makers would discover the irresistible power which would fall into their possession if they could succeed in combining the whole North. The vultures had already from afar off scented the prey. It was not yet ready to be devoured, nor were they ready to devour it. They had not only a remnant still left of the aliment upon which they had previously fed, but new events were developing a new source of supply, amply sufficient, as they believed, for present necessities.

Mr. Polk was elected, and during his administration the war with Mexico, which grew out of the annexation of Texas, postponed to an indefinite period in the future the developement of the now growing sectional party of the North.

Contest for the Presidency between General Taylor (Whig), General Cass (Democrat), and ex-President Van Buren (Free Soil)—Year 1848.

Mr. Benton, who was the warm friend and partisan of Mr. Van Buren, makes the following remarks in his 'Thirty Years in the Senate,' in reference to this contest:—

'Party conventions for the nomination of presidential candidates had now become an institution and a power in the Government; and, so far as the party was concerned, the nomination was the election. No experience of the evils of this power had yet checked its sway, and all parties went into that mode of determining the election for themselves! The Democratic convention met as heretofore at Baltimore, and was numerously attended by members of Congress and persons holding office under the Federal Government, who would be excluded by the Constitution from the place of electors, but who became more than electors, having virtually supreme power over the selection of the President, as well as his election, so far as the party was concerned. The two-thirds rule was adopted [that is, it required two-thirds of the Convention to make a nomination], and that put the nomination into the hands of a minority and of the trained intriguers. Every State was to be allowed to give the whole number of its electoral votes, although it was well known that there were many of them which would not give an electoral vote for the nominee of the Convention. Massachusetts, which had never given an electoral vote [for the Democratic candidate], now in convention gave twelve [in the selection of a candidate].

'The Whig nominating convention met at Philadelphia. The nomination of General Taylor was avowedly made on the calculation of *availability*; setting aside Mr. Clay and Mr. Webster, in favour of the military popularity of Buena Vista, Monterey, and Palo Alto.

'The third convention, growing out of the rejection of the Van Buren Democratic delegates, nominated Mr. Van Buren for President and Mr. Charles Adams for Vice President. The watchwords of this party, to be inscribed upon their banners, were "*Free soil—Free labour—Free speech—Free men.*"'

Thus the Mexican war, which had just been brought to a successful close, furnished the Whigs with the material for a candidate. General Taylor, a gallant officer, but previously unknown to fame, had proven himself to be a good soldier, and had thereby won the hearts of the people, who are always carried away by a successful military career. Four years before, his name had never been heard by one in a thousand of the American people, yet the lately discomfited Whigs at once seized upon him and his blooming honours as their own property, and placed him in nomination as their candidate for the presidency. He was, as usual upon such occasions, interrogated in reference to his views upon the party politics of the day; but he replied frankly that he was a soldier, and knew nothing at all about party politics or the government of States.

He was only a favourite military commander before his nomination, but after he became a candidate he was the idol of vast multitudes of people, and his praises were upon the tongues of many a politician, who discovered new beauties in his character, and new qualities of statesmanship, as the prospects of a successful issue of the canvass grew brighter.

Even his war-horse, known by the most unromantic name of 'Old Whitey,' participated largely in the fame and popularity of his master. The poor old animal was almost denuded of his mane and tail by enthusiastic admirers of his master's military genius; and the Democrats went so far as to say that they scarcely knew which to consider as their most formidable competitor, the General or his steed.

Although the name and fame of this new hero and really estimable gentleman added hundreds of thousands of votes to the ranks of the declining Whig party, yet he might have failed to restore its fallen fortunes but for the unanticipated withdrawal from the Democratic party of that large and formidable faction in the North who were discontented with the nomination of General Cass, for the reason that they favoured the pretensions of another aspirant. This defection from the hitherto united ranks of the Democracy, headed by Martin Van Buren, the late President, deserves more than a passing notice. It was the first fatal blow that had ever befallen it. The process of disintegration was thus commenced in the very section where its united strength was necessary to preserve for it the character of a great national organisation. To add to the mortification of the Conservatives, he who was placed at the head of the seceders was once the trusted and petted leader of the Democratic party. They had made him their President for one term, and tried unsuccessfully to elect him a second time. He was then abandoned for a more available candidate. In the bitterness of disappointed ambition he permitted himself to be employed as an instrument of discord in the ranks of his former adherents. The originators of this movement did not probably intend to destroy permanently the unity of the Democratic party, which was at this moment necessary to the very existence of the nation. They merely designed to defeat it in the then pending election, in order to avenge a personal disappointment, and to give themselves the balance of power in the next nominating Convention. But, unfortunately, the issue they made was intended only to secure Northern votes, and hence, while professing to differ from the Abolitionists, they sought to place themselves upon a platform which would attract to their support this dangerous and desperate faction.

The Abolition party, in its crude state, would not

have answered their purposes, even if they had been disposed to employ so wicked a means for the accomplishment of their revenge. Its doctrines were so odious, and its settled purpose to break up the Union and deluge the country in blood, were so transparent, that the great body of the people of the North, up to that moment, turned away with loathing from all party affiliation with its leaders. But the New York politicians, under the guidance of their accomplished chief, discovered a means by which they might mould this party into a different shape, and thus adapt it somewhat to the prevailing sentiments of the people. They satisfied the conscientious scruples of the timid after the following manner:—

'The Constitution,' said they, 'clearly prohibits us from any direct interference with the Institution of Slavery in the States of the South. We have neither the power nor the right to abolish slavery in the Southern States, then what benefits may be expected to flow from the organisation of a party which announces no practical issue? But we may prevent its farther progress by denying to Southerners the privilege of emigrating with their slaves into the unoccupied "territories" belonging to the United States. These are under the control of Congress: Congress may be very readily brought under the control of the North, by means of its numerical superiority at the ballot-box; and thus we not only do God's work by confining slavery within its present boundaries, but we secure for ourselves and our posterity, to the entire exclusion of the South, the vast wealth of that almost boundless breadth of country which is embraced within the unoccupied lands belonging to the Union. Let us, therefore, abandon the palpably unconstitutional programme of Abolitionism, and establish ourselves upon a "Free Soil platform," which will not only in the end accomplish the purpose you seek, but will at the same time redound to our pecuniary advantage, add greatly to our relative power, and secure for ourselves the exclusive control of the Federal Government.'

To which the national branch of the Democratic party replied:—'Your scheme is but a subterfuge to cheat the Constitution and the South. If the money taken from the common treasury of the Union is employed to purchase territory from adjoining nations, you cannot justly exclude any single State or any class of States from any privileges in regard to the lands thus acquired which are accorded to the others. The North sold its slaves to the South, and by this means, and this alone, the Northern States became free, and made a heavy profit by the process. Why should we now deny to the Border Slave States the like privilege of banishing slavery from their midst? Let slavery and the slaves go on farther and farther from our borders, by the gradual process of migration, which has already relieved the Northern States from the presence of both; but do not increase the hardships of the African by closing up his only avenue of egress. True, if the South will agree to this exclusion, you may become in one sense richer, by appropriating all the property of the whole nation to your own uses; but the Southern States will never submit peaceably to such an unconstitutional discrimination against them. Remember, that if the States of the North may appropriate all the common wealth of the Union to their own use, the States have not equal rights. If they are not equals, then our whole system of Government is overthrown. We are at sea without compass or rudder; and a disaster sooner or later is inevitable.'

But there are few people who are disposed to trouble their consciences about nice points of constitutional law, after they have been passed upon by those whom they have appointed to be the judges—especially when the judgment rendered is in accordance with their inclinations or their feelings of self-love, or if they believe that they have a great personal or pecuniary interest in sustaining the opinions thus announced.

Very few persons who have attempted to explain the causes which produced a rupture of the Union have given the proper weight to the enormous interests comprised in this controversy. To the South it involved the issue of political life or death; for if the principle had been admitted in the practice of the Federal Government, that the North might lawfully exclude the South from a common participation in the benefits which might be derived from the common territory, their constitutional rights would be ever thereafter at the mercy of their enemies. If they could not claim this common privilege, what rights were left which might not be withheld? To the Southerner, who desired the abolition of slavery within the limits of his own State, it would have closed for ever the only door through which slavery has ever passed out, even from Massachusetts itself, to say nothing of Pennsylvania, New York, and New Jersey. Under this process of depletion Maryland

and Missouri were fast approximating to the practical abolition of slavery, without even the intervention of a legislative enactment. It is true that the South had but little pecuniary interest in the result of the controversy, for she had far more territory within her own limits than she could profitably occupy for generations yet to come. But the future of such an exclusion loomed up darkly before her, and her most sagacious and far-seeing statesmen believed that a final decision against her would be the turning-point in her destiny—the epoch in her history from whence she could look forward to nothing but humiliations, and a gradual absorption of her substance, by the greedy cormorants who swayed the majority of the North in presidential elections.

On the other hand, the Northerners had not only a prospective, but an immediate and a very large pecuniary interest in the exclusion of the Southern States from these vast tracts of territory by means of legal prohibitions.

The process by which this pecuniary interest had so enormously increased within a few years was as follows. The general Government, through the influence of speculators, had, under pretence of 'allowing every poor man the opportunity of buying himself a home,' exposed for sale many millions of acres of public land, long before a necessity existed for opening them up for cultivation. The price under such circumstances was, of course, established at a very low rate, in order, as they declared, to meet the necessities of the poor, who had not the means to pay a large sum. The result was that the speculators either bought up the lands from the Government, or purchased the preemption rights of actual settlers. Thus, enormous tracts of territory, equal in extent to a European principality, fell into the hands of single individuals. Many tens of thousands of Northern citizens were engaged in these speculations. Without labourers these lands were valueless. Labour was therefore capital, and the question arose how was this capital to be procured?

These land speculators entered the European market to obtain the commodity they wanted, and which could not be obtained in sufficient abundance on the American continent. In order to facilitate their purposes, and to preserve the unappropriated lands as a mine of wealth for their exclusive benefit, they sought by legal prohibition to exclude the South. They endeavoured by this means also to conciliate the prejudices of the European labourer, by the assurance that he would never be brought into direct contact with the Institution of Slavery.

The reason may thus be readily conceived why the army of land speculators in the North and West should have manifested so much eagerness in 'securing the continent of America for the uses of white men.' To the influence of these were of course added the Abolitionists, and many others, who sought by this means to gratify a feeling of sectional animosity against the South.

When, then, the influential chieftain, Mr. Van Buren, placed himself at the head of the Free Soil party, it at once sprang into formidable dimensions. The consequence was that hundreds of thousands of honest well-meaning citizens fell into the trap which had been set for them by the political land jobbers.

They took that fatal step, which was but the forerunner of a series, which has led them on by a natural and unavoidable sequence to that disastrous end to which their very instincts might have taught them that they would have arrived if they pursued that road.

The defection of the Free Soilers from the Democrats, under the leadership of the 'Sage of Kinderhook,'—ex-President Van Buren—achieved the immediate purpose which this disappointed and discomfited leader had in view. General Cass, the Democratic nominee, was defeated, and General Taylor, his successful competitor, bade adieu for ever to the camp and the field, and took up his abode in the White House.

What a change for the excellent old gentleman who had passed a long life upon the distant frontiers with no other companions than his sword and his messmates! He was, of course, as innocent as a child of all the arts of State craft, as well as of the wiles and tricks of party hacks. Imagine his bewilderment when he was first confronted with the crowd of eager office-hunters and oily-tongued flatterers who surrounded him—fawned upon him—pressed with the apparent fervour of true affection his honest outstretched hand—and with beseeching looks, seconded by interminable recitals of the important aid they had rendered him at the most critical juncture of the canvass, begged of him some speedy recognition of their services to meet their pressing necessities! See the wily, cautious, smooth-tongued politician, Seward! Bred in the most corrupt school of New York party tacticians—priding himself rather upon his skill in arranging and perfecting the details of a political campaign, than upon his statesmanship—what protection was the honesty, and simplicity, and inexperience of the soldier President against the insidious approaches of such a veteran in party management.

It must not be supposed that 'Old Whitey,' the gallant steed of the elected chief of the great Republic, was suffered to disappear at once from the public eye, after having played so conspicuous a part in the presidential contest. The same newspapers which announced the advent of the President in the Capitol of the nation made known also the simultaneous arrival of 'Old Whitey.' Very soon the journals throughout the country informed their readers that this celebrated animal might be visited by his admirers any bright day at one of the public gardens, where he was suffered to graze *ad libitum* upon the green grass plots, and in the midst of the perfume of the sweet flowers which adorned the shady walks. 'Old Whitey's' mission was, therefore, not yet fully achieved. The public grounds in which he held his court were larger than the circumference of the walls of the White House, and many a needy office-seeker, who could not press through the throng into the presence of the master, was fain to content himself with a manifestation of his loyalty to the beast. There was a drop of comfort in the reflection that by the merest chance fidelity to the horse might be a sort of passport to the heart of the man. It was probably with some such thought as this that a number of citizens of New York assembled in that city to consider in what manner they might most appropriately manifest their gratitude to the noble steed which had so proudly borne upon his shoulders the gallant chieftain of the late war to battle and to victory. They finally adopted a plan as ingenious in conception as it was appropriate in the manner of its execution. They voted unanimously to employ the most skilful artist in the city to construct a curry-comb of solid silver, to be enclosed in a rosewood case, which they forwarded by a committee, as a slight testimonial of gratitude and regard for one of the most justly celebrated war horses whose back had ever been pressed by a warrior rider.

The work was soon executed, and the fortunate gentlemen who were selected to compose the committee were soon installed in a first-class hotel in the Federal capital ready to execute the pleasing duty assigned to them by their fellow-countrymen. Mr. Seward, the present premier of Mr. Lincoln's Cabinet, was then a senator from the State of New York. His political adversaries affirmed that he was nervously anxious to get the reins of Government into his own hands, and the present occasion offered at least the opportunity of seizing upon the bridle of 'Old Whitey.' It was therefore arranged that the committee should be formally presented to the President by the distinguished senator from New York. This was accordingly done in the midst of imposing ceremonies, and the committeemen, having discharged their functions, returned to their homes to await the results of the hoped for impression they had made upon the Executive heart. Soon after, an event occurred which removed 'Old Whitey' for ever from the political stage. His future career is involved in mystery. Whether he died under shelter, or upon the open common, or still lives, not one of his many thousands of sunshine friends have troubled themselves to enquire. Like other presidential appliances, he was employed as a means to the attainment of an end, and from the moment when that was achieved, or failed in the accomplishment of its purpose, his very existence was forgotten.*

* The incident referred to was subsequently brought before the United States Senate by Governor Foote, a senator from the State of Mississippi. No man in that distinguished body could make more of such material. His philippic against Mr. Seward for the part he bore in the transaction was of so overwhelming a character that both Senate and lobby, although convulsed with laughter, were almost inclined to compassionate the sufferings of the distinguished senator from New York All waited impatiently for Mr Seward's reply; but they waited in vain. He wisely preferred to adjust the affair in a more quiet way A few days after, Mr Seward met Governor Foote as they were promenading back and forth in a little space allotted for that purpose near the Senate Chamber, and, accosting him in a most friendly manner, said: 'Well, Governor, allow me to congratulate you on the cleverness and wit displayed in your speech the other day? Although suffering under the castigation, still I can do justice to the very effectual manner in which you administered it. Nevertheless, Governor, I don't think it was very kind or friendly to attack me so unmercifully.' 'Surely not, Mr Seward,' responded Governor Foote, 'I did not mean to be either kind or friendly; and I am glad you have not misunderstood me.' 'Yes, yes; I understand that,' replied Mr Seward, 'but I have a great favour to ask—a personal favour. Don't allow that part of your speech which referred to the silver curry-comb for "Old Whitey" to be published in the official register of the debates' All who are acquainted with the impulsive generosity of Governor Foote's nature know that he would respond as promptly to such an appeal in the spirit in which it was made, as he would to an invitation under a reverse state of circumstances to meet his adversary upon the field of honour. He at once complied with the request, and the speech referred to is not to be found in the official register of debates, but the recollection of the words he uttered upon the occasion, still lingers in the memory of the large audience who were present upon the occasion which elicited them

In the case of General Taylor, as in that of General Harrison, the change from previous habits and mode of life was too powerful a tax upon his mortal frame. Although he was the hero of a war, the greater part of his long life had been passed in the solitude of frontier fortresses in the distant back woods of the West, or in the quiet retiracy of his plantation home on the banks of the Mississippi. He had learned the duties, and had contracted the tastes, habits, and feelings of a soldier. He had never before mingled in party strife, and probably he imagined that party politicians cultivated the same sentiments and practised the same virtues, and were governed by the same lofty motives, which were taught in the school of honour in which he had imbibed his inspirations.

The office whose duties he had been called upon to perform had in a brief space whitened the dark locks and bent the stalwart frames of even the youngest of those who had preceded him as with the frosts and weight of many winters. How could he, whose hair was already white with age, hope to pass the ordeal unscathed? Many of those who had preceded (as well as those who followed after) him surrendered their dearly-bought honours, at the termination of their brief tenure of power, disappointed and broken-hearted—although their previous training and education had to a degree prepared them to buffet the waves and storms of parties and of factions. Is it wonderful that he, the upright old soldier and the inflexible gentleman, should have sickened and died under the ceaseless, relentless soul and body harrowing presence of such a load, bearing for ever and for ever upon his vitals?

In a year and a half from the date of his entrance into the executive mansion, as its master; to wit, on July 8, 1850, his body was borne away to rest in peace in a grave which was prepared for it upon the far away shores of the great Father of Waters.

'Rest in peace!' What a gush of bitter thoughts come rushing upon the mind when we reflect that even that peace has been disturbed by the impious footsteps of men calling themselves his countrymen; and who have done the sacrilegious deed by command of one who in an evil day has succeeded to the gallant dead as the elected occupant of the White House.

'Rest in peace!' Even the very worst of the political beggars who were turned away indignant and disgusted, hungry and disappointed, from the threshold of the executive mansion, might have been expected to give utterance to those words in the sincerity of their hearts, and to have prayed for their fulfillment. It may be that the utterance of the thought is vain; for, after all, what reck the unconscious dead—who, after life's fitful feverish dream, have sunk to that deep sleep which knows no waking—how many a wild beast prowls over the little space of earth where they lie buried? Yet the thought which springing to the lips finds utterance in the ejaculation—'Rest in peace!'—is a spontaneous outburst emanating from one of the softer traits of man's wayward nature, and we cherish the sentiment as something holy, something to prove that even the darkest passions find an end.

But a very few years before, the chieftain who had led the armies of his country to battle and to victory is borne to the Capitol, amidst the enthusiastic acclamations of his fellow-citizens, as their elected king. It is not for long he bears the grievous weight of his high honours. The crown of steel which they have placed upon his unaccustomed brow presses too heavily upon his brain, and, bearing with him the respect and the love of his countrymen, he dies and is buried. To-day that crown encircles the head of another, who sends off his armies to lay waste the fields, to make desolate the home, and to violate its most sacred mysteries—to steal the golden medals which a grateful country had bestowed as a reward for gallant deeds—to carry off the now rusty sword, which had never been drawn or sheathed except in obedience to the call of duty and patriotism —to rob of their last farthing, and to drive away, as penniless fugitives, the surviving members of the family of him who had served with honour as President of the great American Confederacy, and who had died without leaving a stain upon his reputation.

Such have been the scenes which within the past few months have been enacted at the family home of the late President Taylor. And—strangest of all the strange incidents in this episode of the war now raging around the home of Washington—the ruling spirit in this dark deed—he who occupies the post of principal Minister of State and chief adviser of the present President, is the same party leader, the influence of whose insidious flatteries and wily counsels were more feared and dreaded by the real friends of the soldier President than all the other appliances which were employed to corrupt his honest nature during his brief tenure of power. Even though it were a war as holy as it is wicked and unnatural, it might have been supposed that they would have respected *that* grave. Even though it were as just as it was cruel to desolate with fire and sword the Southern hearths, yet it was not unreasonable to hope that they would have saved *that* home! Even though they might find it in their nature to take away, as the legitimate spoils of war, the cherished family records of the offending Southerners, surely it might not have been regarded as too great a stretch of uncalculating generosity to have left untouched *those* mementoes of a country's gratitude and the rusty relics of a soldier's services! Even though it had been as right as it was wrong to despoil the sons and daughters of the South of their goods, and force them to flee to some other asylum which might offer them security against oppression and violence—surely it might have been thought that in very shame they would have spared the household and protected the family of him who had been their President! *

Returning from this digression, I will resume the thread of events connected with the history of presidential elections. Mr. Fillmore having, as Vice-President, fallen heir to the office made vacant by the death of General Taylor, served out the unexpired term. During this period the Free Soil party made desperate, but as yet ineffectual efforts, to take the lead as one of the two great parties to contest the prize of the presidency. They had almost succeeded, when the ever-generous heart of Mr. Clay

* A full account of the sacking of ex-President Taylor's mansion, and the robbery of the premises by the Federals, has been published by the New York press.

prompted him to seek a solution of the sectional issues which had been pressed by Northern politicians upon Congress by another 'compromise.'

Fatal word for the Southern States, for their compromises have always been concessions which, while weakening themselves, have strengthened without conciliating or appeasing their insatiable adversaries. Fatal word for those who are now suffering the horrors of a ruthless invasion, for if they had not postponed, by these hollow truces, the inevitable issue which sooner or later the presidential elections were bound to make, they would have been relatively stronger and more able to meet the shock of arms with their ever accumulating foes, even if a firmer policy would not have wholly averted the sanguinary scenes which are now being enacted. Fatal word for the perpetuity of the Union, for if the South had never made a concession of their rights, the North might not have pressed the South to the wall under the delusive hope that having surrendered a part they would yield up all their liberties without a struggle.

Mr. Clay's influence achieved to a certain point the purpose he sought to accomplish. A 'compromise' was pushed through Congress—that is, the South yielded some of her rights in return for new guarantees for the remainder—and the discomfited leaders of the proposed sectional movement were obliged to postpone to a more auspicious day the consummation of their plans. The dying Whig party had another short lease of life, only, however, to disappear for ever ere the close of another presidential term.

Canvass of 1852.

Candidates, Mr. Pearce (Democrat) and General Scott (Whig)—Mr. Pearce elected President.

The Democratic party, which had been displaced during the preceding four years by the election of General Taylor, nominated for the ensuing canvass Franklin Pearce, of New Hampshire. The Whigs—now the Government party—fell back upon the material which had served their turn so well four years before—namely, the 'heroes' of the Mexican war. They nominated General Winfield Scott, who had served with distinction through two wars, and was at that time the ranking general in the United States service. He was a Virginian by birth, and a New Yorker by adoption, with an official residence at Washington. He certainly entered into the contest with a greater military reputation than any or all of those who had previously found the way to the White House through such an instrumentality. In the field he had always been victorious, or had, at least, come out of all his conflicts with increasing reputation; but with the pen as his weapon he had been as uniformly unfortunate. It was even a matter of boast with his friends—transposing the same words employed to designate the character of a British Sovereign—that 'he never said a wise thing, and never did a foolish one.' I am not prepared to decide that either affirmation was wholly true or wholly false. On the contrary, he has said many sensible things, and while he has done much which would justify his claim to the possession of a high order of military talent, and but little which would lead to a reverse conclusion, it is certainly in evidence that he has committed more than one egregious blunder.

True it is, however, that whatever may have been his merits as a military commander, he was almost universally regarded by his fellow-countrymen as not inferior in military capacity to any other captain of the age. When he descended from the lofty platform on which it was his pride and boast always to stand, and attempted to practice even the rudimentary arts of the demagogue, he always made a failure; but on such occasions the people laughed at and forgave him. The stump speech he delivered in presence of a mixed assemblage after his nomination, in which he spoke of the joy which it always gave him to listen to the '*rich German accent*' and the '*broad Irish brogue*,' was one of the descents referred to; but it proved also the growing power of that foreign element which afterwards, under a more perfect organisation, may be said to have turned the scale in favour of the Republicans in the last civic struggle of the South for the maintenance and preservation of her constitutional rights.

Military fame had been hitherto employed in presidential elections, and had always and under all circumstances secured success for the party which had the good fortune to possess such material. Now the greatest captain of them all in the estimation of friends and foes came forward to solicit the suffrages of the people, and yet strange to say, when considered in connection with past results, he was not only defeated, but overwhelmingly defeated.

He received the votes of only four States, namely, Vermont and Massachusetts in the North, and by the meagrest possible majority of Tennessee and Kentucky in the South-west. North, South, and West, may be said to have voted almost as a unit for Franklin Pearce—a change of a few thousand votes in four States would have given him *the unanimous electoral vote of every State in the Union.* Never before or since, in the whole history of the American Government, did any citizen ever receive so large a number of votes in the Electoral College.

This was in the year 1853. When we look to the then unblemished name and renown, and popularity as a military chieftain, of General Scott—when we look back to the events bearing upon the contest which preceded this canvass, and then to those by which they were swiftly followed, we are lost in amazement. There was but one brief four years intervening between the one term of Franklin Pearce and the advent of Abraham Lincoln. It was as though a family of brothers had lain down at night to peaceful slumbers, and had awoke in the morning dagger in hand to engage in deadly strife. But our marvel increases when we consider that but for the merest chance, to which I will hereafter refer, the catastrophe which happened upon the election of Lincoln would have occurred four years earlier! But for a single circumstance, utterly trifling and unimportant in itself, the contest which ended in the election of Franklin Pearce by the almost unanimous voice of the entire Confederation would have been followed by another which would have inaugurated the same terrible tragedy that followed swiftly upon the induction of the present President to power!

Was this revulsion produced by any external pressure? No: the country was at peace with all the world, and with the exception of a somewhat bolder and more active interference of foreign political Abolitionists, the influences directed from abroad were but slightly augmented in force. Was it in consequence of the further acquisition of territory breeding dissensions amongst the squatters which had not previously existed? No: for although the troubles in Kansas had been brought about, bought and paid for by the Republican leaders in order to make political capital for the next campaign, the same sources of discord had always existed, and the same species of party trickery had been often previously resorted to. Even though we may be disposed to give to the Kansas squabble an undue importance, still the controversy had been virtually settled, and to the entire satisfaction of the North, long before Mr. Lincoln had been even thought of as a candidate for the presidency. What, then, was the moving cause of this most wonderful and unprecedented revulsion in the public sentiment of the American people. Those who will take the pains to consider the condition of parties at this particular moment will not fail to discover a solution of the apparent enigma. It was at an epoch when all previously existing parties which had contested for the prize of the presidency, except one, had been dissolved. The Democratic party stood, the only political organisation which could lay claim to any other title than that of faction. The Whig party had perished never again to be revived. The atoms of matter out of which to construct another party, although discordant, were abundant. All that was necessary to make them formidable was a skilful combination of the whole into one compact mass, which could be held together upon a single point. Let us investigate the facts bearing upon the subject somewhat in detail, for to understand thoroughly the merits of the existing war between the sections, it is necessary to know why, and under what circumstances, and for what avowed purposes the Republican party was created.

Last Appearance of the Whig Party—Year 1853.

The 'ship of the Whig party' had been for some years in a sinking condition; and the fatal truth became more and more manifest that it could not be kept afloat for many days longer. Upon the defeat of General Scott the last of its crew deserted its now rudderless, sailless, pilotless hulk, and it sank beneath the calm waters into which it had drifted. It was the creation of the genius of the great architect Clay. Constructed amidst the political convulsions which agitated the great Republic, it was launched upon the angry waves in the midst of an ever-increasing tempest. Its life was spent in buffeting the billows. Its fate was most wayward, for although it was often in view of the harbour for which it was destined, yet ever, even when the skies seemed brightest, a storm would arise, and never, when its great captain was at the helm, could he do more than carry it safely out from the breakers into deep water. But always it carried itself most gallantly, and even in the instant of disaster flaunted its flag in the very face of its victorious enemy, and defied him again to combat. Its great constructor and commander at length died—its crew deserted—and it was left to float out and perish in a sea as remarkable for its unruffled smoothness, as was the troubled ocean on which it was first launched, or that which followed its dissolution, for its tempestuous fury.

The disappearance of the Whig party was a harbinger of the most disastrous event which could have befallen the country, in so far as its interests were involved in a prolongation of the Union. As long as it existed as the rival of the Democratic party, it was impossible for the Free Soilers, or Abolitionists, to create a sectional party sufficiently formidable to disturb fatally the harmony of the Republic. But its hour had come, and there was no human agency that could save it. It could not in its nature survive for a single day the triumph of sectionalism in the hearts of a controlling moiety of its Northern supporters.

It will be remarked that at the point of time we are considering, as upon a former occasion in its history, the apparently overtowering strength of the Democratic party constituted its chief element of weakness. Its highest interest, and what was of vastly more consequence, the true welfare of the country, would have been much more effectively subserved if it had defeated without crushing the Whig party—gained the battles without routing the enemy—leaving him always a sufficient number of the honourable trophies of war to keep up his spirits and induce him at another time to return to the conflict. The interests involved and the policy to be pursued in political contests reverse many of the great principles of war. In the latter you destroy your enemy and the conflict is at an end. In the former the struggle never ceases, for if you crush him he disappears only to return again as your enemy under another flag; or to mingle himself up with the victors, where he cannot be distinguished from the rest, and must of course be fed and clothed, and treated as a friend, until he may again enlist under some other banner.

It does not come within the scope of my design to trace the history of parties or factions from their commencement. I merely propose to consider them after they have been sufficiently developed to take their rank as leading contestants for the prize of the presidency. In the conjuncture at which we have now arrived it became necessary to construct a party to take the place of the late Whig party, in opposition to the Democrats. It was, indeed, a motley crowd which claimed the right to officiate at the christening. The controlling spirits of the Conventions which were called for that purpose were of course the active intelligent professional politicians. They were bound indissolubly together by only one common interest: they were out of power and would be in. Politics was their trade: the offices, that is the spoils, were their rewards, their pay, their rightful plunder. They had only the same interest in sustaining a good cause, that a lawyer has who engages with his client for a fee conditional—no more, no less. As the lawyer is not often squeamish in regard to the merits of the case he thus espouses, provided it contains the elements of success, so it was with

and even in te inst
in the very fae of i
him again to cmbat.
mander at lengh died—
left to float o and peri
its unruffled smoothness,
which it was rst launch
its dissolution for its temp

The disapperance of th
binger of the ost disastrou
befallen the cuntry, in so f
involved in a prolongation o
as it existed a the rival of th
was impossibl for the Free So
to create a secional party suffi
disturb fatally the harmony of
its hour had cme, and there wa
that could say it. It could not
vive for a singe day the triumph
the hearts of a controlling moiety
supporters.

It will be remarked that at the poi
considering, a upon a
the apparently
eratic part
Its high
seque
have
defe
the
a

the politicians referred to. Hence it constituted no part of their business to mould parties in conformity with established principles, but rather to fit their principles to the parties. The question to be decided was not what was right, but what would achieve success. They were out of power, out of place, often out of money, and sometimes out at the elbows; and they assembled in solemn conclave to decide upon the surest and readiest means of getting in. Let me not be misunderstood here or elsewhere when I may seem to cast censure upon all who were engaged in public affairs. I believe truly that those who sought primarily to do good for the country were equal in number to the large class referred to above; but they mingled less actively in the management of party affairs. The professional president-makers always managed to get the power into their own hands, and they shaped the policy of the parties in such manner as suited their own private interests.

There are no pages in the history of American parties more instructive than those which record the circumstances connected with the creation of a new political organisation to take the place of the Whig party. Let us glance at the elements which were spread out before the constructors. One of the most formidable of these was

The 'Know-nothing,' or American Party.

This party originated in a very natural feeling of opposition on the part of native citizens to the naturalisation laws, and to the great power exercised by foreign-born citizens in controlling the elections. So long as this latter class constituted only thousands of voters they excited but little attention or opposition. They were, in fact, courted by all parties; but when they numbered hundreds of thousands, and commenced to organise themselves into an element of political power, distinct from the native-born citizens, for the avowed purpose of introducing European radicalism into American institutions, and leading the Republic into a war of aggression against all monarchical Governments whose subjects might claim their aid, it was not unnatural that those who were native-born should begin to entertain doubts about the propriety of conferring upon strangers, almost at the moment of their arrival in the country, the political rights which were enjoyed by themselves.

Unfortunately, the American party, instead of advocating a change of policy by extending the legal term of residence necessary before naturalisation, organised an opposition to all persons of foreign birth who were already citizens. They pledged themselves by solemn obligations, and at first even by oaths, to refuse to affiliate or have any political association with foreign-born citizens or Roman Catholics.

This party first made its appearance in the Free States, and swept over the country like a whirlwind, carrying everything before it. There was a mystery about it, both in regard to its origin and the manner in which its influence was brought to bear upon elections, which at first attracted the multitude, who are always pleased with that which is new and which captivates the imagination. A large majority of those who are now the most conspicuous leaders of the Republican party, deceived by its ephemeral popularity, plunged into the current which for the moment seemed destined to sweep down all opposition. The Democratic party in the North was prostrated as if by a stroke of lightning, and 'Know-nothingism' for a season reigned almost without a rival. At length it came to try its strength in the South. It was heralded by the splendour of its triumphs in the North, and there is no doubt but that even in the South it would have met with a great measure of favour if it had proposed only a reform in the future, instead of attempting to interfere with rights which were already established. The Southern Democrats, as a body, together with a large number of the old Whigs, combined in opposition to the new party, and it was overwhelmingly defeated in every Southern and Slave State. This result proved disastrous to the fortunes of the American party. Its time-serving supporters in the North hastened to retrieve their error by deserting its standard and passing into the service of other parties. The 'Know-nothings' from that moment ceased to be the terror of foreign-born citizens and Catholics.

Verily, the South is to-day reaping its reward for thus coming to the rescue of foreign-born citizens in the days of their peril. These same foreigners and these same Northern 'Know-nothings' have now joined their forces in the war of subjugation against the South. The generals, the colonels, the soldiers of the Northern army are made up indiscriminately of these two powerful ingredients. The foreign-born general, at the head of his hosts, pressing to the side of General Banks, draws his sword to slay the people who, in despite of Banks and his followers, defended them successfully against the assaults of the 'Know-nothing' party! Verily, the South is to-day reaping its reward!

The Northern 'Isms,' and their Political Uses.

In almost every State and county in the North and West there were special associations, established chiefly under the auspices of New England philanthropists and clergymen, for the promotion of certain designated political, moral, or social objects. The prime movers or adherents of these were not always politicians in the ordinary acceptation of the term. They were not all playing a game to secure the spoils of office, for the sake of the spoils alone; but president-making had invested them with rights of sovereignty, and being sovereigns, they did not like to be witnesses of what they chose to consider the political or moral destitution of their subjects without making an effort to ameliorate their unhappy condition. Many of these were in their inception worthy of respect. They aimed at the establishment of reforms, or the incorporation of new principles in the social system, which might under ordinary circumstances have been developed into real blessings. But under the ever active stimulant of the presidential elections, they became the mere hot-beds of a crazy fanaticism. The names of these various associations were expressive of the leading idea of each. Collectively they were known under the general designation of 'Isms.'

First and most important was 'Abolitionism,' with its more plausible but more insidious offshoot, 'Free Soilism.' Then followed 'Atheism,' 'Agrarianism,' 'Woman's-rightsism,' 'Free Loveism,' 'Fourierism,' and many others of less note. I have only named those which were considered as of sufficient importance to be courted in one way or another by political party leaders.

In the next class, and second only to the combined influence of those above named, were the naturalised foreigners, who at this epoch had in a great measure constituted themselves into a unit of power.

Added to these were the life-time opponents of the Democratic party, who still desired to maintain that attitude.

These were the elements out of which it became necessary to construct an 'Opposition,' to take the place of the defunct Whig party! Behold the political 'outs' assembled in solemn conclave, with all these materials spread out before them. The Southern Know-nothings were there, but what had they to offer? They had failed to carry a single State. Besides, this was a strictly national party: that is, its arguments were addressed to one State as much as to another. It sought to unite in one party all native-born-citizens; and was as much opposed to sectionalism as its predecessor, the Whig party, had been. Why should the constructors of the new party abandon such splendid and abundant material as in the North lay idly awaiting the skilful hand of the political architects to combine into one compact mass, in deference to the opinions, or interests, or prejudices of those who could not bring them a single electoral vote?

What a very perplexing question these out-of-place and out-at-the-elbow politicians were called upon to settle; and how very coolly they canvassed its merits! Should they ask the South to unite with them in waging an exterminating political war against foreign-born citizens and Catholics; or, on the other hand, should they invite the foreigners to unite with them in making war upon the South? That was the issue to be settled; and hence, from the stand point occupied by the president-makers, there was much significance in the enquiry they addressed to the Southern Know-nothings: 'How many electoral votes can you bring to our aid if we adopt your national American platform?' 'Alas! not certainly one,' was the response.

On the other hand, by a skilful combination, all the other materials above referred to might be brought to bear against the South. The party which could succeed in carrying a majority in each of the Northern States would of course carry the presidential election. The South did not furnish a single proselyte or advocate of the 'Isms,' and contained comparatively but few naturalised citizens. Even these were for the most part of the better class, who, upon assuming the duties of citizens, had quietly and modestly merged themselves into the general mass, and acted indifferently with one or another political party, as their interests or inclinations may have suggested.

The result might have been and was foreseen. All the efforts of the Whigs of the North and South to reconstruct another party upon a national basis proved abortive. They met in convention at Philadelphia—that is the 'Know-nothing' or American offshoot of the old party, which was for a brief season the successor of the Whig party—discussed the conflicting propositions just referred to—quarrelled, of course, and separated for ever. The last bond of union between them was severed, because the Whigs of the South could not carry their States for what was believed to be a violation of the constitutional rights of foreign-born citizens. In looking back to that exciting period, when the violence of the storm against foreigners and Catholics still swept almost unresistingly over the North, I find nothing to regret in the attitude occupied by the South. She stood forth in defence of the Constitution and the laws of the country, and though she was defending those who are now attempting to deprive her of all her rights, and to lay waste her lands and to murder her citizens, still she was right. On the other hand, I can well understand how a portion of the Southern people should at first have joined the North in their crusade against foreigners. They probably never intended to accomplish any other political result than to arouse an American feeling sufficiently strong to prevent the foreign-born citizens from becoming a controlling element in the management of the Government.

There were other patriotic citizens who sought earnestly to place the new party upon a platform which might embrace alike every State in the Union. Their great desire was to preserve the national features of the old Whig party, and if that could be achieved, they were willing to make any reasonable concessions which might be demanded.

But the weight of the argument—that is, the weight of votes—was in favour of a combination of the Northern elements into a sectional opposition to the South. The result was *the establishment of the Republican party upon a purely sectional basis.*

From the moment this deed was accomplished, nothing short of a direct 'interposition of Providence' (as unanticipated succour in the hour of need is often denominated) could have saved the fabric of the Union. Such a combination of radicalism, madness, and fanaticism, embracing materials so utterly discordant, never before existed in a political party.*

I will now refer to some of the means which were immediately set on foot by the new party to widen the breach between the North and the South to an impassable gulf.

Missouri Compromise.

This will take me back once more to the excitement of 1820, which was produced by the application of Missouri for admission as a State of the Union with a slavery constitution. The wild fury of the storm which swept over the North upon that occasion was not more remarkable for the suddenness with which it sprang into existence, than for the absence of any new cause which might have been supposed was sufficient to produce it. The entire North was in a blaze of excitement, which creating a counter excitement in the Southern States, seemed ready, even at that early day, to sever the Union. It adds one more to the long series of striking events recorded in the brief history of the Republic, which cannot be accounted for by any rational rule of interpretation, if we reject the hypothesis that it was one of the consequences flowing from the madness

* *Mr Bates*, of Missouri, made a speech in St Louis, August 10, 1856, from which I make the following extract. He was *then* a Whig fossil he is *now a member of Mr Lincoln's Cabinet'*

'The Republican party,' said Mr Bates, 'is not a mere array of men. it is a hasty agglomeration, *made up of the odds and ends of every party that ever existed in the North'* . . . Mr Seward *was* that distinguished Whig—he *is* that distinguished Republican At the North *whole States of the American party* have united with the new organisation. . . . In proportion to its ardour will be the shortness of its life' produced by presidential elections. The Abolitionist might say that it was the result of a prevailing sentiment existing in the Northern mind against the Institution of Slavery, which God in His infinite wisdom had suddenly called into existence, and this solution might be accepted by many in the absence of any proof to refute such an assumption. But specific evidence is not wanting to prove that the event referred to could not have resulted from this cause. Other Slave States were admitted into the Union before and even after the application of Missouri, without exciting a single murmur of disapprobation founded on the slavery question. The student of American party history will find that the degree of sectional or anti-slavery excitements depended entirely upon the uses to which they might be applied in presidential elections. In the controversy growing out of the application of Arkansas for admission into the Union in 1836, the North, as we have seen, repudiated the so-called Missouri Compromise, and opposed the measure by an almost strictly sectional vote—a portion of the Democratic party of the North voting for the admission. But when, ten years later (1846), Florida applied for admission as a Slave State, she was admitted without excitement or serious opposition by the large majority of 36 'yeas' to 9 'nays' in the Senate, and by 144 'yeas' to 48 'nays' in the House of Representatives. At the time the territory of Tennessee was ceded to the United States Government by North Carolina, one of the conditions agreed to was that Congress should never do anything which would *tend* to the emancipation of slaves. The language was significant. It was not necessary to announce that they would not interfere directly with slavery, for that was provided against in the Constitution; but there might be unfriendly legislation. Hence the Congress agreed for itself, and as far as it could, bound its successors, never to do anything which might even 'tend' to the emancipation of slaves. Upon these conditions Tennessee was afterwards admitted into the Union without any opposition from any quarter.

In the Missouri difficulty, Mr. Clay, the 'great pacificator,' came forward with a proposition for a compromise. As this measure, a full generation later, acquired great prominence in the sectional contests of that period, I will give to it more attention than its intrinsic merits might seem to justify. This is the more necessary in consequence of the erroneous opinions which are entertained in regard to it, not only at home, but abroad.

It was in the session of 1819–20 that Mr. Clay proposed that Missouri should be admitted as a State into the Union, and that thereafter no State with a slavery constitution should enter the Union north of the parallel of 36° 30′. This proposed compromise swept away from the South a large portion of the territory of Louisiana, and in fact gave up to the Free States the greater portion of the most valuable territory belonging to the South. This line was the prolongation of the Southern boundary line of Virginia and Kentucky. The restrictive clause, however, was adopted and voted for by a large majority of the Northern representatives in opposition to the wishes of the great body of Southern representatives, upon the express condition and understanding that Missouri should be admitted without farther hesitation or restriction, and the belief has been entertained by many that under this compromise that State was forthwith admitted into the Union. But this is not only not true, but in the very next session of Congress—that is, in 1820–21—when Missouri applied again for admission, her application was rejected by an almost strictly sectional vote of 83 'nays' against 79 'yeas.' This was in the House of Representatives. In the Senate the application shared the same fate. Finally, however, a Bill for admission passed the Senate, but was rejected in the House. Again, another Bill passed the Senate, which was again rejected by the House. At last, it was proposed that the State should be admitted upon the condition that her Legislature should first declare that the clause in her Constitution relative to the immigration of free negroes into the State should never be construed to authorise the passage of any Act by which any citizen of either of the States of the Union should be excluded from the enjoyment of any privilege to which he might be entitled under the Constitution of the United States. Missouri having assented thus to amend her Constitution was admitted as a member of the Union, according to the terms of the Bill, by proclamation of the President.

It will thus be perceived that Missouri was not received into the Union under the so-called compromise, but that *nearly twelve months thereafter she was still fruitlessly struggling for admission.* The proposition of Mr. Clay, however, passed into history as the 'Missouri Compromise;' and, after the lapse of many years, the line of division thus marked out was held by many to be a proper settlement of the question of boundary. It is true that a majority of the South voted against this restriction; yet it is also true that at any period thereafter the Southern States would have been willing to have adopted this as the dividing line between the North and the South for the sake of peace. But a majority of the Northern representatives and senators in Congress have, from that day to this, constantly denied that they were under any obligations to recognise the Act as binding. Upon every occasion when the subject afterwards came up for consideration they *repudiated the Act as null and void.* In 1836, when Congress was considering the application of Arkansas for admission, Mr. Cushing, of Massachusetts, spoke the general sentiments of the Northern sectional party when he said, in a speech in the House of Representatives:—

'It is demanded of us—Do you seek to impose restrictions on Arkansas, in violation of the compromise under which Missouri entered the Union? I content myself with replying, that *Massachusetts was not a party to that compromise: she never either directly or indirectly assented to it.* Most of her representatives in Congress voted against it. Those of them who voted for it were disavowed and denounced at home.'

Thus spoke a representative of Massachusetts in 1836; and, in accordance with these views, a large majority of his colleagues of the North voted upon that occasion. They acted almost as a unit in opposition to the admission of Arkansas, in entire contempt of the so-called Missouri compromise, and with a distinct disclaimer of any obligation upon their part to be bound thereby.*

Again, in 1847, after the acquisition of additional territory by purchase from Mexico, the South proposed that the same line of 36° 30′ should be extended through all the possessions of the American Union; but again the North, under the lead of Mr. Wilmot of Pennsylvania, refused, and voted almost unanimously that citizens of the Southern States should not be permitted to enter with their property upon any part of the territory *upon either side* of the Missouri Compromise Line.

Once more, in 1848, the South made another united effort to induce the North to commit itself to the principle of the Missouri Compromise. The Bill for the establishment of a territorial Government for Oregon was before the Senate. On the motion of Mr. Hale, of New Hampshire, the anti-slavery clause of the ordinance of 1787 was added to the Bill. Mr. Douglas, of Illinois, then moved to amend the Bill as follows:—

> That the line of 36° 30′ of north latitude, known as the Missouri Compromise Line, be, and the same is, hereby declared to extend to the Pacific Ocean; and the eighth section (of the Bill for the admission of Missouri), together with the compromise therein effected, is hereby revived and declared to be in full force and binding for the future organisation of the territories of the United States, in the same sense and with the same understanding with which it was originally adopted.

At the time this proposition was made by Mr. Douglas there were fifteen Northern or Free States.

* See Report of Congressional Proceedings for the year 1836-7.

All the senators representing ten of these voted against the amendment: viz. Maine, New Hampshire, Vermont, Massachusetts, Rhode Island, Connecticut, New Jersy, Ohio, Iowa, and Wisconsin. Three were equally divided: viz. New York, Illinois, and Michigan. While only two, Pennsylvania and Indiana, voted in favour of the proposition. Thus there were twenty-three Northern senators voted against the application of the Missouri compromise, while only seven voted in its favour.

Finally, in 1850, the South made a last effort, but in vain, to induce the North to agree to abide by the so-called Missouri Compromise, upon the occasion of the application of California to be admitted as a State into the Union. The proposition was then made in due form by a suggested amendment of Mr. Turney, of Tennessee, to extend the Missouri Compromise Line to the Pacific Ocean, and thus settle, as far as could be done by Act of Congress, the line which should divide the territory of the North from that of the South.

It was upon the discussion of this Bill in the Senate that Mr. Calhoun made his last speech. The hand of death was then upon him. His gigantic mind could grasp the whole subject; but his vital powers were too feeble to enable him to give utterance to his thoughts. The speech was read for him by his friend, Mr. Mason, of Virginia. They were the last words of the great Carolinian. It was as the voice of one speaking from the tomb; but his prophetic words fell unheeded upon the ears of those who were risking liberty, Union, everything for the sake of winning the prize of the presidency.

Extract from Mr. Calhoun's last Speech in the Senate—Year 1850.

I have believed from the first, senators, that the agitation of the subject of slavery would, if not prevented by some timely and effective measure, end in disunion. Entertaining this opinion I have, on all proper occasions, endeavoured to call the attention of each of the two great parties which divide the country to adopt some measure to prevent so great a disaster, but without success. The agitation has been permitted to proceed with almost no attempt to resist it until it has reached a period when it can no longer be disguised or denied that the Union is in danger. . . . It is a great mistake to suppose that disunion can be effected by a single blow. The cords which bind the States together in one common Union are far too numerous and powerful for that. Disunion must be the work of time. It is only through a long process and successively that the cords can be snapped, until the whole fabric falls asunder. . . . The cords which bind the States together are not only many but various in character—some are spiritual or ecclesiastical—some political—others social. The strongest of those of a spiritual and ecclesiastical character consisted in the unity of the great religious denominations, all of which originally embraced the whole Union . . . The first of these cords which snapped under its explosive force was that of the powerful Methodist Episcopal Church. The numerous and strong ties which held it together are all broken, and its unity gone. They now form separate churches The next cord that snapped was that of the Baptists, one of the largest and most respectable of the denominations. That of the Presbyterian is not entirely snapped, but some of its strands have given way. That of the Episcopal Church is the only one of the four great Protestant denominations which remains unbroken and entire.

The strongest cord of a political character consists of the many and strong ties that have held together the two great parties which have with some modifications existed from the beginning of the Government. They both extended to every portion of the Union, and strongly contributed to hold all its parts together. But this powerful cord has fared no better than the spiritual. It resisted for a long time the explosive tendency of the agitation, but has finally snapped under its force—if not entirely in a great measure. Nor is there one of the remaining cords which have not been greatly weakened. If the agitation goes on, the same force acting with increased intensity, as has been shown, will finally snap every cord, when nothing will be left to hold the States together except force. But surely that cannot with any propriety of language be called a Union, when the only means by which the weaker is held connected with the stronger portion is *force*. It may, indeed, keep them connected; but the connection will partake much more of the character of subjugation on the part of the weaker to the stronger than the union of free, independent, and sovereign States in one confederation, as they stood in the early stages of the Government, and which only is worthy of the sacred name of union. . . .

It is time, senators, that there should be an open and manly avowal on all sides as to what is intended to be done. If the question is not now settled, it is uncertain whether it ever can be hereafter; and we, as the representatives of the States of this Union, should come to a distinct understanding as to our respective views, in order to ascertain whether the great questions at issue can be settled or not. If you who represent the stronger portion cannot agree to settle them on the broad principles of justice and duty, say so; and let the States we both represent agree to separate and part in peace. If you are unwilling that we should part in peace, tell us so, and we shall know what to do when you reduce the question to submission or resistance. If you remain silent, you will compel us to infer by your acts what you intend. In that case California will become the test question. If you admit her under all the difficulties that oppose her admission you compel us to infer that you intend to exclude us from the whole of the territories, with the intention of destroying irretrievably the equilibrium between the two sections. We would be blind not to perceive in that case that your real objects are power and aggrandisement, and we would be infatuated not to act accordingly.

These were the last words of the great Carolinian in the Senate Chamber of the United States. He died before the Bill for the admission of California passed. Mr. Turney's amendment was rejected by a strictly sectional vote, that is, every senator from every Northern State voted against it; and thus, for the last time, the South proposed, and the North unanimously refused, to abide by the Missouri Compromise. Upon the other hand, when the Bill for the organisation of the territorial Governments of Utah and New Mexico was before the Senate, Mr. Seward, of New York, offered an amendment in the following words:—

> Neither slavery nor involuntary servitude, otherwise than by conviction for crime, shall ever be allowed in either of said territories.

Upon this proposition, which was intended as a positive and direct repudiation of the Missouri Compromise, the senators from but one Northern State, Iowa, voted against it. The senators from New York, Pennsylvania, and Michigan were divided equally; while all the senators from the eleven remaining Free States voted in favour of the amendment: namely, Maine, New Hampshire, Massachusetts, Rhode Island, Connecticut, Vermont, New Jersey, Ohio, Indiana, Illinois, and Wisconsin. The vote in the entire North stood—for the proposition, twenty-five senators; against it, five senators. Thenceforth it would have been absurd to have continued the so-called Missouri Compromise upon the statute books. Although the proposed division line between the North and the South gave up by far the most valuable territory to the North, yet the South was willing to adopt almost any line which would bring peace, and which would have had the effect of removing this sectional issue from the presidential contests. But all was of no avail. Numbers were upon the side of the North—numbers could control presidential elections—and the president-makers of the North would consent to no scheme which might diminish their chances of getting possession of the Government. Upon the passage of the California Bill, many of the Southern senators were convinced that the North intended to employ the mere power of a majority to subvert the Constitution; and they gave utterance to their feelings upon the occasion by the following

Protest, signed by Messrs. Mason and Hunter, Senators from Virginia; Butler and Barnwell, from South Carolina, Soulé, from Louisiana; Turney, from Tennessee; Atchison, from Missouri; Morton and Yulu, from Florida; and Jefferson Davis, from Mississippi—Year 1850.

We, the undersigned senators, deeply impressed with the importance of the occasion and with a solemn sense of the responsibility under which we are acting, respectfully submit the following protest against the Bill admitting California as a State into the Union, and request that it may be entered upon the journal of the Senate. We feel that it is not enough to have resisted in debateal one a Bill so fraught with mischief to the Union and the States which we represent with all the resources of argument which we possessed; but that it is also due to ourselves, the people whose interests have been entrusted to our care, and to posterity—which, even in its most distant generations, may feel its consequences—to leave, in whatever form may be most solemn and enduring, a memorial of the opposition which we have made to this measure, and of the reasons by which we have been governed, upon the pages of a journal which the Constitution requires to be kept so long as the Senate may have an existence.

We have dissented from this Bill because it gives the sanction of law, and thus imparts validity to the unauthorised action of a portion of the inhabitants of California, by which an odious discrimination is made against the property of the fifteen slaveholding States of the Union, who are thus deprived of that position of equality which the Constitution so manifestly designs, and which constitutes the only sure and stable foundation on which the Union can repose.

Because the right of the slave-holding States to a common and equal enjoyment of the territory of the Union has been defeated by a system of measures which, without the authority of precedent, of law, or of the Constitution, were manifestly contrived for that purpose, and which Congress must sanction and adopt should this Bill become a law.

Because to vote for a Bill passed under such circumstances would be to agree to a principle which may exclude for ever hereafter, as it does now, the States which we represent from all enjoyment of the common territory of the Union—a principle which destroys the equal rights of their constituents, the equality of the Southern States in the Confederacy, the equal dignity of those whom they represent as men and as citizens in the eye of the law, and their equal title to the protection of the Government and the Constitution.

Because all the propositions have been rejected which have been made to obtain either a recognition of the rights of the slave-holding States to a common enjoyment of all the territory of the United States, or to a fair division of that territory between the slave-holding and non-slaveholding States of the Union.

But, lastly, we dissent from this Bill, and solemnly protest against its passage, because in sanctioning measures so contrary to former precedent, to obvious policy, to the spirit and intent of the Constitution of the United States, for the purpose of excluding the Southern States from the territory thus erected into a State, the Government in effect declares that this exclusion is an object so high and important as to justify a disregard, not only of all the principles of sound policy, but also of the Constitution itself. Against this conclusion we must now and for ever protest, as it is destructive of the safety and liberties of those whose rights have been submitted to our care—fatal to the peace and equality of the States which we represent—and must lead to the dissolution of that Confederacy in which the slave-holding States have never sought more than equality, and in which they will not be content to remain with less.

To return again to the subject of the repeal of the Missouri Compromise. It was true, as stated by the representative of Massachusetts, and as declared by the Northern representatives generally, that Congress possessed no *legal* power to decide upon any territorial division line between the North and the South. Certainly one Congress had no right to bind its successors not to repeal their acts. A law enacted by a legislative body can only be binding so long as it remains unrepealed, and such Act is always repealable unless the Constitution itself specifically provides for its perpetuation, as in the case of the creation of corporate bodies, where a contract is made and rights are vested for a limited time in individuals. It would be absurd to declare that Congress could withdraw a subject from all future legislation.

But there were other and more powerful reasons why the Missouri restriction should never have been adopted; or, having been adopted, that it should have been repealed as soon as the excitement of the occasion which produced it had passed away. It was not only unconstitutional, but was a palpable and direct violation of treaty obligations, involving an act of bad faith towards France. The territory which was embraced within the restriction was obtained by purchase from the Emperor Napoleon, with the express stipulation in favour of the French subjects thus transferred, that their rights of person and property, which included slaves, should be respected; and that they should be invested with all the rights of the other States of the American Union. The Missouri compromise repealed this treaty obligation, and took away from French subjects the rights which the United States Government had bound itself to respect. The following is the text of the stipulation in the treaty between France and the United States here referred to:—"The inhabitants of the ceded territory *shall be* incorporated into the Union of the United States, and admitted as soon as possible, according to the principles of the Federal Constitution, to the enjoyment of all the rights, advantages, and immunities of citizens of the United States, *and in the meantime shall be maintained and protected* in the free enjoyment of their liberty, property, and the religion they profess.' By the law of nations this act of bad faith would have authorised France, if she had possessed the power and the will, to reclaim the territory she had ceded. Whether or not she might choose to exercise this right, the violation of the compact was unconstitutional, because it was in derogation of treaty stipulation and vested rights.

Upon this point I am able to quote an authority which of all others the Abolitionists or Republicans will be least disposed to question. John Quincy Adams, of Massachusetts, the most respectable and the most distinguished statesman of the anti-slavery school in modern times, was emphatic and decided. His prejudices were in favour of the restriction; but his judgment pronounced it to be unconstitutional. He was a partisan of the North in the broadest sense, but he was not disposed to gratify his sectional prejudices at the expense of good faith and by a violation of the fundamental law of the land. He held that the obligations of a solemn compact with France, and with those who had been her subjects, constituted *a higher law* than his own mere personal inclination—a more imperative obligation than the aggrandisement of his own section, or the deprivation of the South of its lawful rights—a fountain whose source was higher than the 'God-like voice of the people of the North.' How different were the operations of '*conscience*' in the case of Mr. Adams and the politicians who at the present day claim to be following in his footsteps! His conscience impelled him to regard his oath and his duty to the Constitution as the guides of his actions. They claim that their 'virtuous impulses' justify them in violating the obligations of both.

The speech of Mr. Adams to which I refer was delivered in the House of Representatives in the year 1836, upon the application of Arkansas for admission as a State into the Union. It is well worthy of the calm consideration of the leaders of the Republican party, who have forced the South into secession from the Union, in defence of what even Mr. Adams maintains were their constitutional rights.

Extract from the Speech of Mr. Adams, showing the Unconstitutionality of any Congressional restriction upon Slavery in the Territories.

I cannot, consistently with my sense of my obligations as a citizen of the United States, and bound by oath to support the Constitution—I cannot object to the admission of Arkansas into the Union as a Slave State. I cannot propose or agree to make a condition of her admission, that a convention of her people shall expunge this article from her Constitution. She is entitled to admission as a Slave State—as Louisiana, and Mississippi, and Alabama, and Missouri have been admitted—*by virtue of that article in the treaty for the acquisition of Louisiana which secures to the inhabitants of the ceded territory all the rights, privileges, and immunities of the original citizens of the United States; and which stipulates for their admission into the Union conformably to that principle.* Louisiana was purchased as a country wherein slavery was the established law of the land As Congress has not the power, in peace, to abolish slavery in the original States of the Union, *they are equally destitute of the power in those parts of the territory ceded by France to the United States.* Slavery is in the Union, the subject of internal legislation in the States; and in peace is only cognisable by Congress, *as it is tacitly* tolerated and protected where it exists by the Constitution of the United States; and as it mingles in their intercourse with other nations. Arkansas, therefore, comes, and has the right to come, into the Union with her slaves and her slave laws.

Without, however, considering the constitutional objections or treaty stipulation opposed to the Missouri restriction, it was a great blunder on the part of the South to have consented, even by a silent acquiescence, to such an odious discrimination against her; but when—as is clearly established by the foregoing reference to facts—the Northern party utterly disclaimed any obligation upon their part to consider themselves bound by the miscalled compromise—when, as is well known, the Abolition or Republican party claimed the whole of the territory on both sides of the compromise line as their exclusive property, can any assumption be more absurd and unjust than that there was an obligation on the part of the South to regard the compromise as binding? If it was obligatory on one party, it was equally so upon the other; but the truth was that it was not, and could not have been legally binding upon either. It was at best only one of those desperate expedients which are sometimes resorted to in order to establish a temporary truce between irritated adversaries. Hence, when it was repudiated by the North, as was the case at all times, it was—if for no other reason than this—very properly repealed.

If this enactment had been stricken from the

statute-books in ordinary times, it would not probably have awakened a single violent emotion: it had remained inoperative from the day of its adoption, and would have continued so for all time to come. It was of a character with the Act before referred to, in which the Congress agreed that nothing should ever be done which would 'tend' to emancipate slaves—except that in the latter, future Congresses were enjoined to comply with their constitutional obligations, while in the former, they were commanded to violate them.

As matters then stood, however, the repeal came just in time to suit the purposes of the politicians of the North, who had been thrown out of employment by the downfall of the Whig party. Massachusetts, Vermont, and other Free-soil States, took the lead in denouncing the repeal as a violation of good faith on the part of the South, which left them free thereafter to pursue their aims against the Southern States, without being restrained by compromises or constitutions. And yet these States always strenuously denied that they had been in any way whatever committed to this compromise. On the contrary, they derided and repudiated it in every manner possible, whenever an occasion offered itself. They wept over the repeal as a parent might weep over the demise of his last child; and yet during its entire life it was spurned and disowned.

Shortly thereafter the territories of Kansas and Nebraska were opened for settlement, and thus a field presented itself wherein a practical turn might be given to the question which had been raised. Never was there exhibited a greater amount of skill in bringing up the excitement of the Northern mind to the presidential fever-heat than was shown by the wire-workers of the Republican party in their management of this new issue. The leading Republican journals despatched correspondents to Kansas, whose duty it was to send back a tale of daily horrors for the edification of their readers. 'Kansas Aid Societies' were formed throughout the Free States, and large sums of money were subscribed for the purpose of encouraging fighting emigrants to go to Kansas. The churches were in many places employed to minister to the passions of the multitude, and the clergymen took up subscriptions of rifles from their congregations to forward the pious work 'of shooting the Gospel to all Southerners.' The lowest and the vilest rabble of the cities were armed, equipped, and forwarded to the field of action. Such a concentration of thieves and blackguards were never before congregated in the back-woods, as constituted the bulk of the army of mercenary cut-throats employed and sent out from the North to that unhappy territory.

Of course, upon the appearance of this rabble, law and order were at an end. They at once engaged in the work for which they had been employed, and very soon produced those disorders which they were paid to create.

It was in this manner that the Kansas troubles originated; and, although there are doubtless many Northern citizens who even now believe the stories which were set afloat by their party leaders, yet, when time shall have cooled the passions of the more sober and reflecting portion of the Northern people, they will see and acknowledge the errors into which they were led by designing and corrupt men.

Disinterested persons, who desire to arrive at just conclusions, need only consider the time when and the circumstances under which these scenes were enacted. They occurred, as we have seen, upon the downfall of one party and at the uprising of another upon its ruins. All who have been close observers of the manner in which excitements have been gotten up to assist in president-making—all who are familiar with the characteristics of professional president-makers, and of the appliances they employ to subserve their purposes—all who know the character of the Northern sensation press, and its entire unreliability as a vehicle for the communication of truth—all who will consider of the party advantages which would ensue to the promoters of these troubles, if they could succeed in arousing the pride, and thus combining the entire North into a unit of political power—and last, though not least, all who will consider that the South had very much to lose and nothing to gain by raising such an issue at such a time, must conclude that the whole affair in its inception and consummation was simply a party movement of the Northern politicians, seconded by the ferocious fanaticism of the Abolitionists.

I do not believe that the great body of Northern citizens who participated in the excitement were aware of the special object for the accomplishment of which it was produced; but they were deceived, and acted upon a false impression and under a strong delusion. On the other hand, I do not pretend to say that the Southern people did not in turn become exasperated, and meet their assailants half way in the contest which ensued.

The candid enquirer who desires to arrive at just conclusions in regard to this Kansas trouble, and finds it difficult to decide where there exists such a conflict of testimony in regard to the facts, should consider the relative positions occupied by the North and the South in regard to the settlement of territories. The South had no redundancy of population, and no access to foreign countries for a supply, as the North had—they had no immigrant foreigners—they were not ready to take Kansas, if it had been offered to them as a free gift: the climate and soil were so much less adapted to slave labour than the neighbouring territory, that only an insignificant number of slaves would have been taken there, and the State would in any event have been a Free State. The entire population of the South, whose condition would have been improved by emigration, would not have been sufficient to form a State. It seems to me that those who will give the Southern people credit for common sense could never suppose that they would have seriously attempted to compete with the Free States in sending emigrants to the frigid regions of Kansas and Nebraska.

But more than all this, the candid reader must give the Southern people credit for the possession of some of the qualities of a reasoning and an intelligent people. It is well known that neither the South—nor any State of the South, nor any party or citizen—ever claimed an exclusive right to any portion of the public domain. They only claimed that they were entitled to *equal privileges* with the

Northern people in the territories which were the common property of both. On the contrary, that party of the North whose conduct we are now considering, claimed as their own rightful possession and inheritance *all* the territories, and every foot of territory, belonging to the entire Confederacy. It was the great, the fundamental, the sole principle upon which they professed to enter upon the struggle for the presidency. Whatever may have been the ulterior purposes of their leaders, this was their only avowed measure, sedulously denuded of any side issue. The South believed that this was but the commencement of a series of usurpations. They knew that the plan of excluding the Southern people from the territories opened the way wide for their utter ruin. They knew that the power of numbers was against them, and that, although in battle one brave man may overcome two cowards, yet at the ballot-box a city burglar was more potent than the judge upon the bench. In view of all these facts, I will propound two interrogatories to the intelligent reader.

If the Northern party, as they notoriously did, utterly denied that there existed any obligation upon their part to regard the Missouri compromise as binding—if the Northern party claimed, as they did, all the territories of the Union for the Northern people—was it not absurd to hold the Southern people as bound by that 'compromise?'

If it be true that the Northerners or the Southerners went into Kansas with a view to drive the other out, and to take exclusive possession of the country, whom do reason, common sense, consistency, interest, and probability, one or all, indicate as the party which might be presumed to have been animated by such an intention?

If there had been no party interests to subserve, and no political aspirations to promote, and no hopes founded upon presidential elections to gratify, I cannot discover the shadow of a reason for believing that the settlement of Kansas would not have been accomplished under the operation of the same influences which had already, without enlisting a single angry passion or creating an unkind feeling, peopled the wilderness with prosperous States, both slave and free. Left to the operation of natural causes, which, if they had not been perverted by external force, would have led irresistibly to their legitimate conclusions, the laws of nature and of climate would, under the existing circumstances, have settled the imaginary question in a manner entirely in accordance with the sympathies of the Abolitionists. But, whether this assumption be true or false, the final issue would have been reached without violence and without excitement. The solitude of the forests of Kansas would never have been disturbed by night, except by the bark of the watch-dog; nor by day, save by the woodman's axe, preparing toilfully the way for the slowly but surely advancing tide of civilisation, as it marched on with resistless power to the accomplishment of its great mission.

I have not presented these views as the partisan of the South, nor as the adversary of the North. If incidentally they lead to the acquittal of the one or the condemnation of the other, it must be attributed to the facts which I have adduced to establish my accusation against the prime source and fountain of all our troubles. While I do not excuse the instruments whose ready obedience has produced this unutterable woe; yet, with all the earnestness of one who has drawn the inspiration of his thoughts from a life-time experience and observation, and whose convictions have been forced upon him in despite of his own will—in despite of his education and early training—in despite of his prejudices—I do condemn the presidential elections as the prime cause of the unnatural effort of the North to deprive the South of its rightful inheritance. This was the deadly upas growing and flourishing amidst our great wilderness of ever-blooming flowers, of every odour and of every hue, whose magnificent proportions attracted them to take shelter under its spreading branches, only to infuse its poison into their blood and madness into their brains by the inhalation of its pernicious odours.

If there be still those in America who believe that the devastating war which is now being waged by the North against the South is but the offspring of a sentiment of philanthropy, guided and directed by a spirit of Christianity—if there are any who believe that it is but the outpouring of a virtuous people residing upon one side of an imaginary line, who cross the border to punish the vices and sins of another portion of the same people residing upon the other side of that geographical division—though we may wonder at the perversity of their judgment, we must remember that the poison which has dethroned reason and sense, and the sentiment of humanity, is still coursing through their veins, and blinding their eyes, and hardening their hearts. Looming up in the future there are still other Presidents to elect—still other and richer spoils to distribute to the victors—still other ambitious aspirants for the honours and the trappings of power—still other plunderers who would riot in the enjoyment of the public treasure—and still an ever-increasing multitude, ready to be led to slaughter or be slaughtered, by leaders who only employ them as instruments for the accomplishment of their unholy purposes of avarice and ambition. The people do not yet perceive that they are living under a despotism to which the subjects of no living monarch would yield a tame obedience. They do not yet perceive that the privilege of electing a new king every four years, under the dictation of a few designing leaders, does not carry liberty in its train. They do not yet perceive, that though they may change their rulers according to their varying humours, they are still but the puppets and instruments of those on whom for the time being they may lavish their smiles. Ephraim is still joined to his idols.

I have dwelt thus at length upon the incidents connected with the final dissolution of the Whig party, and the organisation of the Republican party out of the loose elements which might be combined in opposition to the national Democratic party, in order to show that the sectional excitements which immediately followed were the result solely of party manœuvres, which were designed to affect the presidential elections. I do not believe that in the inception of these sectional issues the president-makers looked beyond the immediate party results which might be deduced, nor that the great body of the people who gave them their aid paused to consider the direction in which they were tending; but they were recklessly indifferent to any consequences which might follow, provided their immediate object was accomplished. The greed for presidential bounties silenced the conscience of the one; and the pride of sectional dominion, stimulated to unnatural fervour by presidential elections, closed the eyes and the ears of the other.

Presidential Contest of 1856.

Anti-Southern Mania—Election of Mr. Buchanan.

The old Conservative Democratic party which had existed almost from the foundation of the Government, and upon whose continued success as opposed to the Northern sectional party now rested the only hope of perpetuating the Union, nominated for the presidency James Buchanan, of Pennsylvania. The Radical, or Republican party, as they now called themselves, nominated John C. Fremont, a man who had never before been distinguished for any public service, except one or two successful voyages across the Rocky Mountains. The American party also put a candidate in nomination, ex-President Fillmore; but, as had been foreseen, the revolutionary doctrines of the Republican party occasioned so much alarm, that many old Whigs who would otherwise have supported Mr. Fillmore joined the Democratic ranks.

We may here note the broad differences which existed between the two leading parties now contesting for the presidency.

The Democratic party was founded upon the main leading idea of a strict and literal construction of the Constitution—that the States, as sovereign members of the league, should be left in the possession of every right of sovereignty which had not been specifically delegated to the general Government — that no majority, however large, of the people of the United States could divest the smallest of the States of its sovereign rights, and that the veto power vested by the Constitution in the President should remain entire, to protect the Government against hasty and inconsiderate legislation under a temporary excitement. In short, it was, in the literal acceptation of the term, a Conservative party.

The Republican party, on the other hand, was essentially radical. It announced as its leading idea that there was 'a higher law than the Constitution' or the statutory laws of the land—namely, the public conscience; that the voice of a majority of the people was the voice of God, and as such should be obeyed; and that 'constitutions and laws could not rise above the virtue of the people.'* It combined within itself all the revolutionary elements which existed amongst the people, and relied for success solely upon creating in the minds of a majority of the citizens of the North a feeling of hatred against the people of the South.

None but the blindest partisan of the North could fail to foresee that the success of the Republican party would force the Southern States as an alternative against

* Wm H Seward's exposition of the principles of the Republican party.

utter ruin to withdraw from the Union. The excitement created by the contest was probably less demonstrative than upon many similar occasions before, but it was deeper and more intense. Still the doctrine of State sovereignty was so generally entertained, that there were perhaps few who believed that a war between the sections would be a necessary consequence of secession; and many still hoped, that even if the Republicans should succeed in placing themselves in power, they would be content with the enjoyment of the loaves and fishes, and would agree to abandon their suggested unconstitutional encroachments upon the rights of the South.

The personal popularity of Mr. Buchanan in some of the Free States, and especially in the great State of Pennsylvania, of which he was a citizen, gave the victory once more and for the last time to the Democracy. The Republicans charged their adversaries with having secured the vote of Pennsylvania by promising a highly-protective tariff upon iron, one of the principal manufacturing interests of that State. It is possible this may be true, for it was believed that the vote of Pennyslvania, and that alone, would insure the success of the Democrats, and consequently another four years' guarantee for the preservation of the Union. Mr. Buchanan was elected; but he received only sixty-two electoral votes in the North, while his Republican competitor did not obtain a single vote in the South. The result of this contest proved conclusively that the North could in a subsequent election be combined against the South. Such a combination would leave the fifteen Southern States at the mercy of an unbridled majority of a people who entertained against them the bitterest prejudices. Under the rule of a single monarch, no matter how despotic, there is a limit to his demands upon his subjects. His pride or his avarice may be satiated by a comparatively light burthen imposed upon each. But what hope had the Southern States with many millions of Northern masters to rule over them? Will it be said that the South might trust itself to the magnanimity or the generosity of the people of the North? It may be replied to this, that the people of the North were led astray by wicked leaders, who used them merely as instruments to the accomplishment of their own ambitious schemes. The right to elect Presidents had already been virtually arrogated to themselves by the most unscrupulous section of the party politicians, and all the efforts of these were employed to inflame the passions of the people against the South. But almost as potent as the influence of the politicians was that exercised by an intolerant political clergy. Not the entire clergy—perhaps not the greatest number; but the most fanatical, the most active, the most influential—and, I may add, the most bloodthirsty. It was the influence of these which gave to the sectional contest its ferocious features. The mere politicians might have been satisfied by the attainment of the objects of their ambition. The manufacturer would have been content if he had been permitted by means of protective duties to grasp the wealth of the South and transfer it into his own strong box. But the religious branch of this sectional organisation had elevated the slave to the position of an idol. He was literally and truly worshipped as something holy, and they sought to crush the Southern white men by forcing them in effect to change places with the African. Fanaticism, stimulated to madness by the presidential elections, seemed to have bereft them of all reason. Southerners were regarded by them as fit subjects for the dagger of the assassin; and the assassin was elevated to the rank of a saint.

The four years of Mr. Buchanan's administration of the Government were employed by the two great parties in preparing for the final struggle, which was to decide the fate of the Union. The Democratic party of the North was evidently giving way before the all-engrossing tide of sectionalism. Firmness on their part might have given another success to the national party; but many of the leaders faltered, prevaricated, and tried to steer a middle course between right and wrong. The storm seemed ready to engulph them, and they sought safety in flight: they virtually abandoned the old States-rights doctrine at the moment of its greatest peril, and all was lost. Perhaps they believed that this was the better policy. It may be that they felt themselves unable any longer to stem the tide of sectionalism, which they had so long successfully resisted, and that they fell into the current in order to direct it when the storm should have abated. If so, most grievously have they miscalculated both their courage and capacity.

It may not be inopportune in this connection to note one of the demoralising influences of the popular elections for the Presidency, which constituted certainly not the least objectionable feature of the system. This influence was even more observable amongst the enlightened class of citizens than among the uneducated. While mere physical courage may have been augmented by the contact of classes and masses, the principle of moral courage was almost annihilated. They could confront and combat an enemy in a personal encounter, or upon the field of battle, with unquailing spirit, but they cowered and trembled, and submitted without an audible murmur, to the most iniquitous exactions, if for the moment they seemed to have the sanction of the popular will. The multitude might to-day clamour for the immediate enfranchisement of all slaves, and to-morrow hang every African upon whom they could lay hands, to the lamp-posts of their cities, and still they would exclaim, with submissive accent and reverential deference—Vox populi, vox Dei!

The influence of these sentiments makes the citizens of the United States to-day the veriest cowards, and flatterers, and sycophants that ever kissed the earth in token of abject submission to a despotic ruler. Liberty is held in subordination to loyalty, while loyalty is interpreted to signify a blind obedience to the behests of their masters.

But for the constantly accumulating evidence of the existence of such sentiments amongst even the better class of citizens, one could scarcely credit the fact, that these are the inheritors of the land of Washington and his compeers, and the descendants of liberty-loving sires, who, after establishing by their valour the independence of their country, bequeathed to their posterity the rights and the privileges of free men. Surely no evil of less magnitude than that we have been considering could have produced so marked a change from sire to son.

Anti-Southern Mania.

Sectionalism triumphant—Lincoln elected President—Year 1860.

It became manifest, long before the conventions assembled to nominate candidates, that the unity of the Democratic party had been broken upon the dividing line which separated the North from the South. The overwhelming force of Northern votes, directed by a spirit of sectionalism, was clearly bearing down all opposition. A considerable portion of the Democratic party north still manfully breasted the storm, and proclaimed their determination to uphold and maintain the equal rights of the States, regardless of the consequences to themselves. The great body, however, gave way before a power which they felt themselves unable to resist. Some of them proposed, in effect, that the South should abandon all claim to any participation in the Territories; whilst others suggested that the manufacturing States should be appeased by the offer of highly-protective duties. But, even if this had been the better policy at first, it was now too late. The president-makers of the North saw that the game was at last in their own hands. The popular mind had been excited to the proper pitch, and no human power could withhold from them a victory which was to be decided by mere numbers. The geographical line which divided the nation into two parts, called respectively the North and the South, was at last the sole dividing line between the political parties. Upon many occasions before, the sectional feelings of the North had made itself felt in the contests of parties, but, except upon transient occasions, it had never been supreme. Both the great parties resisted its pretensions for a long series of years. Before it could conquer the country, it was necessary that it should overcome, or rather take the place of one of these.

Mr. Clay and Mr. Webster, who were the leaders of the Whig party while it had an existence, were both opposed to slavery in the abstract. Mr. Clay, although a citizen of a slave-holding State, was nevertheless desirous of witnessing the abolition of slavery in his State, by the same process which had enabled the Northern States to rid themselves of the African population. But the Abolition party proper of the North had not a more determined adversary than he proved himself to be, whenever an effort was made to identify the principles of that party with the one to which he belonged. The leaders of the Abolition party often sought to get control of the machinery of the Whig party, but as often were they foiled by the determined resistance of the great Kentuckian. It may be instructive to quote some paragraphs from one of Mr. Clay's speeches upon this subject. The reader will discover that even at an early day it required all Mr. Clay's eloquence and popularity to repress the efforts of the Northern party to decide presidential elections by geographical lines.

As we glance over this speech, uttered more in sorrow than in anger, twenty-two years before the final consummation of the event he so much dreaded, we cannot fail to discover, in the earnest and emphatic condemnation uttered by Mr. Clay against his own friends and supporters, the danger which for long years menaced the liberties of the Southern States. Even then, in the opinion of this great party leader, the sword hung suspended over the South only by a single thread; and, in the solemn language of admonition, he warned his political associates and followers in the North against advancing another step in the direction they were tending.

Extract from Mr. Clay's Speech in the Senate, 1838.

There are three classes of persons opposed, or apparently opposed, to the continued existence of slavery in the United States. The first are those who, from sentiments of philanthropy and humanity, are conscientiously opposed to the existence of slavery, but who are at the same time no less opposed to any disturbance of the peace and tranquillity of the Union, or an infringement on the powers of the States composing the confederacy. The next class consists of apparent Abolitionists, that is, those who, having been persuaded that the right of petition has been violated by Congress, cooperate with the Abolitionists for the sole purpose of asserting and vindicating that right.* And the third class are the real ultra-abolitionists, who are resolved to

* Mr. Clay here refers to the memorable rule adopted by the House of Representatives the same year, in regard to the disposition to be made of petitions for the abolition of slavery. This rule originated in a motion made by Mr. William Slade, of Vermont, a member of the House of Representatives, upon presenting a number of abolition petitions, to refer them to a select committee, with instructions *to report a bill in conformity to their prayer*. Mr. Slade advocated the adoption of his motion in a speech distinguished by great bitterness against the Southern States, which in its progress gave rise to the most intense excitement throughout the House. At length the exasperation ran so high, that the Southern delegates withdrew in a body from the hall and organised a meeting, the object of which was to adopt some means by which they might be protected in the Union, or prepare for leaving it. On the next day, Mr. Patton, of Virginia, offered the following resolution as an amendment to the rules of the House, which being adopted by a vote of 135 yeas to 60 nays, had the effect of healing for the moment the fearfully portentous breach: —

'*Resolved*, That all petitions, memorials, and papers touching the abolition of slavery, or the buying, selling, or transferring of slaves persevere in the pursuit of their object at all hazards, and without regard to any consequences, however calamitous they may be. With them the rights of property are nothing; the deficiency of the powers of the general Government is nothing; the acknowledged and incontestable powers of the States are nothing; civil war, a dissolution of the Union, and the overthrow of a Government, in which are concentrated all our fondest hopes, are nothing. A single idea has taken possession of their minds, and onwards they pursue it, overlooking all barriers, reckless and regardless of all consequences. With this class, the immediate abolition of slavery in the District of Columbia and in the Territory of Florida [*malgré* the Missouri Compromise], the prohibition of the removal of slaves from one slave State to another, and the refusal to admit *any new State*, comprising within its limits the institution of domestic slavery [again regardless of the Missouri Compromise], are but so many means conducing to the accomplishment of the ultimate but perilous end at which they avowedly and boldly aim; are but so many short stages in the long and bloody road to the distant goal at which they would finally arrive. Their object is no longer concealed by the thinnest veil, it is avowed and proclaimed. Utterly destitute of constitutional or other rightful power, living in totally distinct communities, as alien to the communities in which the subject on which they would operate resides, so far as concerns political power over that subject as though they lived in Africa or Asia, they nevertheless 'promulgate to the world their purpose to manumit forthwith, and without compensation, and without moral preparation, three millions of negro slaves, under jurisdictions altogether separated from those under which they live.'

I have said that immediate abolition of slavery in the District of Columbia and in the Territory of Florida, and the exclusion of new States, *were only means towards the attainment of a much more important end.* Unfortunately, they are not the only means. Another and much more lamentable one is that which this class is endeavouring to employ, *of arraying one portion against another portion of the Union.* With that view, in all their leading prints and publications the alleged horrors of slavery are depicted in the most glowing and exaggerated colours, to excite the imagination,

---

in any State, District, or Territory of the United States, be laid on the table without being debated, printed, read, or referred, and that no further action whatever shall be had thereon.'

and to stimulate the rage of the people of the Free States against the people in the Slave States. The slaveholder is held up and represented as the most atrocious of human beings, and they would hunt down and proscribe from the pale of civilised society the inhabitants of that entire section.

But the means to which I have already adverted are not the only ones which this third class of ultra-abolitionists are employing to effect their ultimate end. They began their operations by professing to employ only persuasive means, and by enlightening the understandings of the slave-holding portion of the Union. If there were some kindness in this avowed motive, it must be acknowledged that there was rather a presumptuous display also of an assumed superiority in intelligence and knowledge. For some time they continued to make their appeals to our duty and our interest, but, impatient at the slow influence of their logic upon our stupid minds, they recently resolved to change their system of action. To the agency of their powers of persuasion they now propose to substitute the powers of the ballot-box; *and he must be blind to what is passing before us, who does not perceive that the inevitable tendency of their proceedings is to invoke finally the more potent powers of the bayonet.*

Mr. President, it is at this alarming stage of the proceedings of the ultra-abolitionists that I would seriously invite every considerate man in the country solemnly to pause, and deliberately to reflect, not merely on our existing posture, but upon that dreadful precipice down which they would hurry us. It is because these ultra-abolitionists have ceased to employ the instruments of reason and persuasion, have made their cause political, and have appealed to the ballot-box, that I am induced upon this occasion to address you

There have been three epochs in the history of our country at which the spirit of abolitionism displayed itself. The first was immediately after the formation of the present Federal Government. When the Constitution was about going into operation, its powers were not well understood by the community at large, and remained to be accurately interpreted and defined At that period numerous abolition societies were formed, comprising not merely the Society of Friends, but many other good men The next period when the subject of slavery and abolition incidentally was brought into notice and discussion was on the memorable occasion of the admission of the State of Missouri into the Union. The third is that in which we now find ourselves, and to which various causes have contributed. The principal one, perhaps, is British emancipation in the islands adjacent to our Continent. Confounding the totally different cases of the powers of the British Parliament and those of our Congress, and the totally different conditions of the slaves in the British West India islands and the slaves in the sovereign and independent States of this Confederacy, superficial men have inferred, from the undecided British experiment, the practicability of the abolition of slaves in these States All these are different. The powers of the British Parliament are unlimited, and often described to be omnipotent. The powers of the American Congress, on the contrary, are few, cautiously limited, scrupulously excluding all that are not granted, and, above all, carefully and absolutely excluding all power over the existence or continuance of slavery in the several States. The slaves, too, upon which British legislation operated, were not in the bosom of the kingdom, but in remote and feeble colonies, having no voice in Parliament. The West India slaveholder was neither representative nor represented in that Parliament; and, while I most fervently wish complete success to the British experiment of the West India emancipation, I confess that I have fearful forebodings of a disastrous termination. Whatever it may be, I think it must be admitted that, if the British Parliament treated the West India slaves as freemen, it also treated the West India freemen as slaves. If, instead of these slaves being separated by a wide ocean from the parent country, three or four millions of African negro slaves had been dispersed over England, Scotland, Ireland, and Wales, and their owners had been members of the British Parliament—a case which would have presented some analogy to our own country—does anyone believe that it would have been expedient or practicable to have emancipated them, leaving them to remain, with all their embittered feelings, in the United Kingdom, boundless as are the powers of the British Government?

Other causes have conspired, also, to produce the existing excitement. I say it with profound regret, and with no intention to occasion irritation, here or elsewhere, that there are persons in both parts of the Union who have sought to mingle abolition with politics, and to array one portion of the Union against the other. It is the misfortune of free countries that, in times of great party excitement, a disposition too often prevails to seize hold of everything which can strengthen the one side or weaken the other. But it is not true—I rejoice that it is not true—that either of the two great parties (Democratic and Whig) in this country has any design or aim at abolition. I should deeply lament it, if it were true. I should consider, if it were true, that the danger to the stability of our Government would be infinitely greater than any which does, I hope, actually exist. Whilst neither party can be, I think, justly accused of any abolition tendency or purpose, both have profited, and both been injured, in particular localities, by the accession or abstraction of abolition support.

These remarks of the Kentucky senator, who during nearly half a century maintained his position as one of the foremost party leaders, and who for a quarter of a century was the acknowledged head of the Whig party, are worthy of more than a passing notice. One can almost imagine that even in 1838 Mr. Clay was looking forward to the consummation of the scheme which had for its end the creation of a Northern sectional party, destined by means of the 'ballot-box and the bayonet' to destroy the liberties of the South. It must be remembered that Mr. Clay was never a champion of the South. On the contrary, he was peculiarly the friend of the North. The North favoured, while the South opposed his advancement to the presidency. It was in the interest of the North that he so long employed his great influence to establish a permanently protective system of duties upon foreign imports. Of all the leading politicians of his day, his interests and his sympathies would have been most naturally enlisted in favour of the Abolitionists, if they had been content to have employed only legitimate means for the accomplishment of their purpose. But Mr. Clay had himself been a principal actor in presidential contests. He knew how deeply the nation could be excited in presidential struggles, and he saw that if ever the Northern sectional party should succeed in placing itself in power, the liberty of the people and the union of the States would disappear amid scenes of violence and blood: hence the earnestness with which he warned the North against yielding to sectional fanaticism. Notwithstanding Mr. Clay's leaning towards the policy and the prejudices of the Northern people, he was never sectional in his feelings. He was in favour of the general policy of protecting domestic manufactures against foreign competition, but he hoped that the system would eventually induce the South also to engage in manufacturing, and thus equalise the burthens of taxation upon the two sections. He was, to a certain extent, embued with Northern prejudices against the institution of slavery, and he hoped to witness its disappearance by the same process which had already banished it from half the Continent. It could only be under the influence of a deep conviction that he would thus expose the dangerous tendency in the Northern mind to decide presidential elections upon sectional issues.

The speech of Mr. Clay, however, is more important as an admission of the well-grounded apprehensions of the South in regard to the future of such an agitation. It is impossible to say what were the intentions of the Northern agitators, or to assign a common motive for their persistent interference in the domestic affairs of the Southern States.

No doubt the greater number were actuated solely by a desire to win the prize of the presidency and the spoils of victory. Others believed that it was their duty to charge themselves with the guardianship of the Southern people, and they designed to do nothing more than to correct the morals of their neighbours according to their own standard. But, whether justly or unjustly, the South believed that the end would be fatal to their constitutional rights, and to their liberties as citizens. This opinion had at least the merit of being in accordance with the teachings of history. The instances are rare, indeed, where a nation has been benefited by active intervention in its domestic affairs by another. Where the power exists, such intervention always ends by subjection, and when we cast our eyes over the present condition of the nations of the world, we find misery and degradation as the characteristic features of almost every country which is held subject to another.

The deep-seated apprehension which existed among the more thoughtful citizens of the South has found expression at almost every epoch of this sectional contest. Mr. Clay's speech was uttered as a warning to those whom he regarded as friends—to the North, which had supported him for the presidency. But there were others who spoke more plainly in regard to the well-grounded fears of the Southern people. In 1849 a great agitation existed at Washington. Old party lines were for the moment obliterated; and in the delirium of the hour the Northern members of Congress seemed almost united in their determination to press the sectional agitation to the bitter end. Southern members seemed to lose hope. They held nightly consultations for the purpose of devising means to avert the impending blow. At length they issued an address to the people of the South, which fully set forth the dangers by which they were menaced:—

Extracts from the Address of Southern Members of Congress to the People of the South. Year 1849.

We, whose names are hereunto annexed, address you, in discharge of what we believe to be a solemn duty, on the most important subject ever presented for your consideration. We allude to the conflict between the two great sections of the Union, growing out of a difference of feeling and opinion in reference to the relation existing between the two races, the European and African, which inhabit the Southern section, and the acts of aggression and encroachment to which it has led. The conflict commenced not long after the acknowledgement of our independence, and has gradually increased, until it has arrayed the great body of the North against the South on this most vital subject In the progress of this conflict, aggression has followed aggression, and encroachment encroachment, until they have reached a point when a regard for our peace and safety will not permit us to remain longer silent. The object of this address is to give you a clear, correct, but brief account of the whole series of aggressions and encroachments on your rights, with a statement of the dangers to which they expose you. . . . . .

To destroy the existing relation between the free and servile races at the South would lead to consequences unparalleled in history. They cannot now be separated, nor can they live together in peace and harmony, or to their mutual advantage, except in their present relation. Under any other, wretchedness and misery and desolation would overspread the whole South. The example of the British West Indies furnishes but a very faint picture of the calamities it would bring upon the South. The circumstances under which it would take place with us would be entirely different from those which took place with them, and would lead to far more disastrous results. Then the Government of England emancipated slaves in its colonial possessions—a Government rich and powerful, and actuated by views of policy rather than fanaticism. It was, besides, disposed to act justly towards the owners, even in the act of emancipating their slaves, and to protect and foster them afterwards. It accordingly appropriated nearly $100,000,000 as a compensation to them for their losses under the Act. Since the emancipation, it has kept up a sufficient military and naval force to keep the blacks in awe, and a number of magistrates and other civil officers to keep order in the towns and plantations, and enforce respect to their former owners. . . . But the reverse would be the case between the blacks of the South and the people of the North. Owing their emancipation to them, they would regard them as friends, guardians, and patrons, and would accordingly centre all their sympathies in them. The people of the North would not fail to reciprocate these feelings, and to favour them instead of the whites. Under the influence of such feelings, and impelled by fanaticism and love of power, they would not stop at emancipation. Another step would be taken They would raise the blacks to a political and social equality with their former owners, by giving them the right of voting and holding public offices under the Federal Government. But when once raised to an equality, they would become the fast political associates of the North, acting and voting with them on all questions, and by this political union between them holding the white race of the South in complete subjection. The blacks and the profligate whites who might unite with them, would become the principal recipients of Federal offices and patronage, and would, in consequence, be raised above the whites of the South. We would, in a word, change conditions with them—a degradation greater than has ever yet fallen to the lot of a free and enlightened people, and one from which we cannot escape, should emancipation take place, except by fleeing the homes of ourselves and our ancestors, and by abandoning our country to our former slaves, to become the permanent abode of disorder, anarchy, poverty, and misery. . . . .

With such a prospect before us, the gravest and most solemn question that ever claimed the attention of any people is presented for your consideration. . . If you become united, and prove yourselves in earnest, the North may be brought to a pause and a calculation of consequences, and that may lead to a change of measures. If it should not, nothing would remain for you but

the bitter end.
hope. They held
pose of devising
At length they
the South, which
they were menace:—
the two
a difference of
existing betwe
which inhabit the
encroachment

to stand up immovably in defence of rights involving your all—your property, prosperity, equality, liberty, and safety. As the assailed, you would stand justified by all laws, human and Divine, in repelling a blow so dangerous.

I have given this address at such length, from the leading representatives of the Southern States, in the senatorial and representative branches of the National Congress, because they not only express the almost unanimous sentiments of their compatriots, but for the reason that they impress upon the unbiassed reader a clear perception of the hostile attitude occupied by the North, as well as the magnitude of the dangers with which the South was menaced. The address was signed by a committee of nearly fifty members of Congress, amongst which are the names of Jefferson Davis, John C. Calhoun, James M. Mason, R. M. T. Hunter, and others, embracing the leading representatives of every Southern State.

These words of warning were uttered, as we have seen, in the year 1849. Eleven years before—that is, in the year 1838—Mr. Clay, the champion of Northern interests, the admitted head of the protective system, the earnest emancipationist, the favourite candidate of the North for the presidency during an entire generation, delivered in the Senate the remarks which precede the address of the Southern representatives. The consequences which would ensue if the Northern section should succeed in creating a triumphant presidential party, were as clearly portrayed as they could be to-day by the pen of the historian in presence of the accomplished fact.

Still eleven years later, and the triumph of the sectional party at the ballot-box was complete and entire. The South and the North were no longer component parts of the same nation. The right of choosing the Federal President of thirty-three sovereign States was usurped by a combination of eighteen. The fifteen States thus ostracised by their confederates, had no more authority or weight in selecting their chief ruler than they had in placing the imperial crown upon the brow of the Emperor Napoleon. The long-cherished plans and schemes of their enemies in the North were at last brought to a successful close, and in the very moment of their final triumph the Union ceased to be. The legal formalities of separation were not in due form accomplished, but the link which held together the discordant parts of the great Confederacy was severed by the first gun which announced that Abraham Lincoln was the elected President of the Federal Republic.

If, after a calm survey of the events to which we have referred, the intelligent reader finds occasion to be surprised, in regard to the final result of this never-ending, still-beginning struggle for power, in which all the people of a nation that at length included thirty millions of inhabitants were ceaselessly engaged, his marvel could only be, that the inevitable end was not sooner reached.

The important events which succeeded each other with such startling rapidity after the inauguration of Mr. Lincoln as President, are so fresh in the public mind, that it is only necessary very briefly to refer to them.

In every meditated or accomplished act of the dominant party may be discovered a prolongation of the same party tactics, the same selfish policy—shaped only with a view to the presidential succession—which had marked their previous career. I think that all enlightened men will sustain me in the declaration, that there was not one, from the presidential chief to the humblest subaltern, who could for an instant of time grasp the idea of the great national question of life and death which presented itself for solution. A nation of more than thirty millions of inhabitants was apparently in the agonies of dissolution, and amongst all those who had been raised to power upon the wave of popular passions, engendered by designing demagogues and bankrupt place-seekers, there was not one who seemed able to elevate his thoughts above the commonplace instincts of party hacks.

The one sole all-absorbing question to the 'Republican' politicians was their *party interest.* Their party had been organised, their presidential victory had been achieved, on the basis of a certain set of declarations or 'principles,' called the 'Chicago platform.' By means of that platform they had united with them the anti-slavery party of the North; not that the anti-slavery party proper was in the beginning a majority of the North—it was but a minority—but, as a balance-of-power party, it gave the electoral victory to the party with which it coalesced or amalgamated. This alliance abolitionised the anti-Democratic party, which had thus had recourse to that fatal means of achieving a temporary political success. To break off from it was to disband the party, to confess the mistake committed, to undo the election consummated, in all but the mere temporary possession of the offices. Though this separation might have been the salvation of the Union, it would have been the suicide of the party. Of that act of supreme patriotism its controlling men and minds were not capable. They had full warning of the imminent consequences. The consequences were, in fact, already upon them. Seven States had seceded. Without a compromise war alone could bring them back, or break them down. The Southern Border States already declared that they would join the seceded States, if the coercive policy should be attempted against them. It was a hard alternative for the Republican politicians from the stand-point of mere partisans. The question was, the party or their country. Many hesitated, trembled, faltered at the prospect before them, if they should yield to the counsels of the vehement, the ferocious, the fanatic among them, who urged all their means of influence and of coercive party power to keep them up to the line of 'the platform' and the will of the incoming President. But *party* carried the day, and the Union was at end. While the Union lived, they hated and reviled it as a league with Death and a covenant with Hell. When they succeeded in destroying it, it became at once the god of their idolatry.

The 'Chicago platform' was their law book, their constitution, their bible. 'Show to us,' said the more conciliatory element of the Republicans, 'how we may save the party upon the principles of the platform, and at the same time avert the conflict with the South, and we will listen to you;' but as that in its very nature was impossible, they clung to the platform. Compromise, kindness could alone ward off the impending blow. 'WE CAN WIN ON UNION, BUT WE CAN'T ON COMPROMISE,' was the unblushing announcement of the Republican leaders in the halls of Congress during the last convulsive struggles of the Government for a little longer lease of life. What a volume of meaning is encompassed within that brief sentence! What a world of light it sheds upon the overshadowing power of party, and of the debasing influence of presidential contests! Our party may obtain a renewal of its lease of power, if we go forth to battle with the inspiring war-cry of 'THE UNION,' but we cannot win if we save the Union by a compromise!*

* I will here introduce two striking illustrations of what has been said above The first is contained in a most able and lucid pamphlet, entitled, 'Union, Disunion, and Reunion,' from the pen of the Hon. J. S. O'Sullivan, late American Minister to Lisbon. This gentleman addressed a letter to a leading Republican senator at the moment when the Government was crumbling to pieces, urging him to employ the influence of his position in devising some means to avert the impending dissolution of the Union. Mr O'Sullivan justly remarks in his comments upon the response, that 'in it is heard a sorrowful sigh of the prisoner in the chains of the party system, which fettered the ability even of enlightened and well-disposed men to save their country in its hour of supreme need '—The following was the reply of the senator:

'I have come to despair of saving the Union One month ago it might have been done; I fear it is now too late. The only question is, how the seceded States shall be treated. Could the true policy be adopted, they might be brought back ultimately, but I apprehend that incredulity, obstinacy, and every form of utter and astonishing folly will complete the work of destruction which has been so thoroughly begun.'

Thus acted the conservative element of the party in power; they trembled upon the brink of the precipice, they saw the madness of their policy, they sighed, but dared not break the shackles of party and come up to the rescue of that Union which they now profess to love.

The other illustration to which I refer is contained in the following

One might have supposed that even the merest charlatans would have been elevated to a semblance of decorum and dignity by the very magnitude of the events in which they were called to act so conspicuous a part. Hundreds of thousands of lives were staked upon the issue, and yet they only revolved the matter in their minds, to decide upon the manner in which they might turn it to profitable account in future presidential contests. A nation of thirty millions of warlike inhabitants, separated into two parts by a geographical line, divided by feuds of a century's growth, their strongest passions

note, which I have received from the Hon. Mr. Barret of Missouri, who was a member of Congress during the memorable period of secession, and an ardent advocate of compromise and conciliation.

'London, October 20, 1863

'MY DEAR SIR,—I cheerfully comply with your request. The individual who made use of the expression, "We" (meaning the Republican party) "can win on Union, but we cannot win on compromise," was the Hon. Owen Lovejoy of Illinois. This indication of the determined policy of the dominant party was made at the moment when conservatives of all parties, in and out of Congress, were endeavouring to promote the passage of some measure of compromise which would heal the difficulties between the two sections, and preserve or restore the Union, for some Southern States had already seceded. Mr. Lovejoy, at the head of the Republican party in the Representative branch of Congress, had opposed, and by his controlling influence may be said to have prevented, the passage of any and every proposition looking to peace and union. Shortly afterwards, Republican leaders and partisans were crying aloud for the Union, which, up to that moment, they had termed "a covenant with Hell." I agree with you that the expression referred to, coming at the time, under the circumstances, and from so distinguished and influential a leader of the party in power, was full of meaning. It indicated the inauguration of a new policy. In fact, from that moment may be noted an apparently almost fanatical love of the Union from the very men who were its bitterest revilers so long as the Union existed.

'Very respectfully, &c.,

(Signed) 'J. K. BARRET.'

aroused almost to frenzy, stood confronting each other, ready on the slightest indiscretion on the one part or the other to plunge headlong into that terrible war, whose carnage and atrocities have sent a thrill of horror throughout the civilised world.

The friends of compromise, conciliation, and peace in the National Congress implored the party in power to consider calmly for a single moment upon the probable consequences of such a conflict. 'You have all the power and patronage of the Government in your own hands,' said they; 'the offices and spoils are all your own: be content with these, and give to the Southern States at least an assurance that you will not attempt to carry out in practice the unconstitutional measures which they believe you meditate.'

The response was, 'No! Never will we comply with your demand. We are the representatives of the will of the people; we have fairly defeated you at the election polls, and we are not going to cast away our chances of success in the future by abandoning the platform of our party at the very instant of our triumph. We are the majority; the Government is ours, and you must submit or take the consequences.'

The 'Peace Congress' then assembled. It was composed of representatives of all parties from all the Border States. They, too, prayed the National Assembly to agree by words at least to do no act which might infringe upon the equal rights of the Southern States. But all was unavailing. Their response in substance was—

Till thou canst rail the seal from off our bond
Thou but offend'st thy lungs to speak so loud:
The pound of flesh which we demand from them
Is dearly bought; 'tis ours, and we will have it!
. . . . By our souls we swear
There is no power in the tongue of man
To alter us: we stay here on our bond!

And how did the chosen chieftain of this great nation, upon whose single word or act hung suspended the alternative of peace or war, deport himself in presence of this awful responsibility? A ribald jest,—'*There's nobody hurt*!'—a vulgar anecdote to elicit a smile or raise a laugh—'Let 'em kick up their heels, they'll tire of it after awhile'—were characteristic of all the responses which the occasion elicited from the last elected President of the Model Republic.

Oh people of the land of Washington, the day of your humiliation had dawned! Oh enemies of the great Confederation of American Republics, your hour of triumph had come at last!

Presidential elections had accomplished their mission—had achieved their work of degradation. The highest post in the Model Republic was at last occupied by a man whose innate vulgarity would have excluded him from the private salons of even many whose votes had aided in elevating him to that high station, while the great body of his followers amongst the party leaders had no loftier ambition than to make themselves secure in power, that they might riot and fatten upon the plunder of the public treasure, and make merchandise of the blood of the people.

Even at that moment peace might have been preserved—at least, war might have been postponed, thus allowing a respite for reflection and sober thought —without surrendering either honour, honesty, or dignity. A word from the President and a single act of conciliation emanating from the body of his supporters in Congress, would have done it. A truce might have been patched up, which would have upheld still a little longer the fabric of the Union—at least until the wild passions evoked by a succeeding presidential contest should have broken asunder the feeble bond of party compact.

But a war involved large expenditures, with augmented chances for plunder. It involved the creation of many thousands of new offices—contracts for the supply of the army—ships to be built, and spoils and confiscated estates to be taken from the enemy. It was not in their nature to resist the temptation.

These incentives turned the scale against the advocates of peace. The President ordered his ships of war to reinforce the rash, mischievous, and weak-minded Anderson, in order that they might be able to turn the guns of the frowning fortresses which commanded the harbour upon the hated city of Charleston. This act of war closed the last avenue of peace, and from that hour the great American Union ceased to be.

Upon the 19th day of April 1775, the first gun fired upon the plains of Lexington, announced to the world the approaching birth of a great Confederacy of Free States—the Declaration of Independence on the 4th day of July 1776, heralded the Rise of the Model Republic—the booming artillery from the now crumbled walls of Fort Sumter, upon April 13, 1861, proclaimed its Fall.

CHAPTER XV.

A DISCUSSION OF THE QUESTIONS OF RIGHT AND WRONG, AND OF LIBERTY AND DESPOTISM, INVOLVED IN THE ISSUE BETWEEN THE NORTH AND THE SOUTH.

ALTHOUGH it may not be strictly in accordance with the object for which these pages have been written, the occasion is not altogether inopportune for referring briefly to the views entertained by certain parties in Europe as well as in America, in regard to the great contest—for conquest upon the one hand, and for independence upon the other—which is now in progress upon the American continent.

The sympathies of a majority of mankind in such a contest, even when uninfluenced by personal preferences or interests, are generally enlisted in reference rather to the object which it is hoped will be attained, than to the abstract merits of the questions which may have produced the conflict. Yet there are few who will be found to assent to the doctrine that it is right to do wrong that even good may follow. The maintenance of such a principle of action uproots the very foundations of justice, unsettles all the compromises upon which society rests, and converts the most sacred compacts between man and man into mere ropes of sand, to be broken by the first rude hand which chooses to tear them asunder.

The written language which is employed to perpetuate a contract between individuals or nations, is in many cases susceptible of false interpretations. Language is in its nature imperfect, and where the will exists to give to it a meaning differing from the intentions of those who employ it, it is not difficult of accomplishment. Let us, then, for the moment, dismiss the discussion of all points which may elicit controversy, and confine ourselves to a consideration of such provisions of the Constitution as by common consent admit of but a single interpretation.

First, then, by the compact of Union, the States each delegated to the general Government, and retained for themselves, the same powers. This being conceded, it follows that all are equal under the Constitution.

Second. To each State was guaranteed the right to the absolute control of its own domestic affairs. The United States Government was precluded from any interference whatever with the relations of one citizen towards another, either as regards their persons or their property.

Third. The existence of African slavery was not only fully recognised, but the United States Government bound itself in a perpetual bond to restore to their lawful owners such slaves as might escape from a Southern into a Northern State.

Fourth. Not only were the separate States sovereign in regard to their internal affairs, but the Constitution in words stipulates that no State shall be divided, and a part thereof admitted as a member of the Union, without the consent of said State.

These provisions of the Constitution are admitted alike in both North and South. No statesman of the North, no politician, no run-mad fanatic or social reformer, not even a single newspaper editor, has ever claimed that either the Northern States or the Government of the United States had the constitutional right either to divide a State against its will, or to abolish slavery in a State where it existed. Mr. Seward even was constrained to admit this undeniable truth, and only claimed the right to exercise dominion over the South by the unwritten law of conscience. Even after Mr. Lincoln was the President, he declared in the most emphatic language that he had no power whatever under the Constitution to interfere with the institution of slavery. Notwithstanding his oath of office, he has already not only repudiated that obligation by proclaiming all the slaves of ten States to be free men, but he has given his official sanction to a law which divides the State of Virginia into two States.

And who in Europe applauds these palpable undeniable violations of the Constitution of the United States? They are, in many cases, the very men who profess to be the champions of constitutional liberty. And why is it that in their view a Constitution in Europe is a thing so sacred, and in America is only made to be broken? How may they consistently claim that the nations of Europe have a right to live under a government of their own choice, and yet bestow the tribute of their sympathies upon the States of the North in their efforts to subjugate the Confederate States?

There are those, however, who perceive the inconsistency of assuming that constitutional rights are not to be held as sacred in America as in Europe; and these endeavour to excuse or palliate the crime against Liberty by the plea, that the unconstitutional acts of the United States Government are 'war measures!' And is this, in sober seriousness, what the advocates of Democratic Liberty understand by a Constitution? Do they mean to declare that the Constitutions which they seek so earnestly to establish are only binding upon rulers in times of peace?

If this be in reality the true significance of constitutional liberty, then, indeed, are those who seek to establish such delusive and transient safeguards to personal liberty devoting themselves to the creation of a useless pageant for the people, but an irresistible weapon of despotism in the hands of those who hold the powers of the purse and sword.

But admitting even the monstrous assumption that the rulers of a people are only to be restrained by constitutional checks in times of peace, still the United States Government is without excuse, unless we go further, and justify a violation of the axiom of law, that a man may not take advantage of his own wrong. The very apologists to whom I refer claim that the sole purpose for which the Republican party, of which Mr. Lincoln is the head, was established, was to accomplish the emancipation of the slaves of the Southern States. The only significance of the election of Mr. Lincoln to the presidency, in the estimation of these very men, and the only reason, as they declare, for their sympathy with him and his cause, was because it indicated a determination on the part of the Northern majority to release the slaves of the South from the dominion of their masters. It is upon this ground, and this alone, that the sympathies of the anti-slavery party of the world is invoked. This theme is the burden of the appeal for favour to the cause of the North. It is the point of climax in their oratorical displays. It constitutes the heavy artillery in all their assaults upon the South. They pledge themselves to the fact that the Northern people in combining a majority to overwhelm the South at the ballot-box meant *emancipation*; nothing less, nothing more.

Thus it is claimed as a merit that the North acquired the exclusive possession of the general Government of the Union, with the premeditated design, in a time of profound peace, to rob the Southern States of their constitutional rights. For this purpose they had taken the purse and sword of the whole nation under their own control. The citizens of fifteen States of the Confederation were rigidly excluded from all participation in the management of a Government of which they formed so important a part, and over whose heads hung suspended by a single thread the sword which was ready to immolate them.

If these declarations of the advocates of the North be true, then by the universally recognised law of nature, it was not only the privilege but the duty of the threatened South to adopt measures of defence against the meditated aggression upon her constitutional rights, her liberties, her very existence as a free people.

In furtherance of this boasted purpose, the people of the North, wielding the Government of the Union, make war upon the Southern States, annul the Constitution upon the ground of military necessity, and are then not only pardoned, but commended by the professed disciples of universal emancipation and constitutional liberty, upon the plea that the preconceived purpose was not enforced until the war, which its announcement produced, was actually begun.

One can scarcely credit the fact that reasoning men could dupe themselves or others by such transparent sophistry. It adds another to the long catalogue of proofs to show that those who make the loudest professions of devotion to the interests of the great family of man, and who seem to seek with the greatest zeal the establishment of freedom for all, are at least as little averse as those whom they seek to overthrow, to the employment of despotic means for the attainment of their purpose.

In the case we are considering, they first seek to win the sympathies of the extreme party of emancipationists, by declaring that the North, in the election of Mr. Lincoln, announced a settled and unchangeable purpose to violate the clearest provisions of the Constitution, and then they seek to satisfy the scruples of those who may by chance entertain the belief that constitutional compacts ought to be held sacred, upon the plea that this premeditated assault upon the Constitution of the Federal Union was only carried into effect after the attempt to do the wrong had been resisted.

If we assume as true the declarations of Mr. Adams, and Mr. Bright, and all the other political and religious partisans of the North in Europe, that the sole aim of the party which made Mr. Lincoln the chief of the nation was to extirpate slavery from the neighbouring States, could it be hoped that the cause of real liberty as taught by Washington, or of true religion as taught by Christ, would be promoted by such a palpable violation of the most solemn and sacred compacts?

Can the friends of civilisation and progress entertain even a glimmering hope that the true interests of these may be promoted by the consummation of such an act of treachery, to be followed by the extermination of eight millions of a free people, who in response to the accumulated slanders which have been heaped upon them, may proudly, and with the earnestness of truthful sincerity, exclaim, 'Whatever may be our destiny in the future, the world has only known us through the benefits we have conferred upon mankind.'

The superficial reasoner is sometimes carried away by the *ad captandum* argument that the South committed the first aggression against the North by firing the first gun in the harbour of Charleston. At most this is a point of no force, for the firing of a gun at an enemy only proves the presence of an enemy. Will it be said that when a man's house is surrounded by his enemies, arms in hand, with the avowed purpose of killing or taking him prisoner, that he must await the first volley before he fires upon his assailants, or be deemed in law or morals the aggressor? Thus was it with the South. There is not an intelligent friend of the North living who believes that the South desired war. The actual war commenced when the determination of the United States to subdue the South was formed and decided on; the conflict may even have been delayed for a longer period, but still the war existed from the instant the parties commenced to raise and equip and send forward their forces to the contemplated scene of action.

Even a menace which would clearly indicate a settled purpose on the part of a nation to make war upon another, or upon a part of itself, would of itself be an act which would justify the party to be assailed in at once assuming the offensive; nor could they be regarded as the first aggressors, though they might fall upon and destroy the forces of the other.

Some of the partisans of the North, while admitting that the intentions of the Federal Government could only have been effected by a palpable breach of the constitutional compact between the States, justify the aggression by the declaration, that the religious sentiment and public conscience of the North constituted a higher claim to their fealty than written constitutions or political compacts. While denying, as every true friend of liberty must deny, that constitutional guarantees, which are designed even more for the protection of the weak than the strong, are to be broken by the majority, or by the Government which represents them, upon such a pretext; yet even admitting the validity of such a plea in extenuation, have we any sufficient evidence to show that the Northern majority were guided by a sublime sentiment of love for the African? If such was the motive by which they were governed, were there not more inviting fields for its display than in the Southern States of the Union? Why did they not send their armies to benighted Africa to destroy the owners of slaves there, to be followed by their strong-minded maidens to educate the freed men in the ways of the Yankee? With a fiftieth part of the expense in blood and treasure it would cost to accomplish the same work in the South, they might have freed every slave, and colonised every populous district of the entire coast of South Africa, with enough soldiers to have held their protegés in due subjection. Or if they preferred to go to war with a civilised people, Cuba lay invitingly open to their attacks. The same cause invited their intervention in Brazil. But the truth is manifest, that if the North hated slavery, it was not the far more intolerant slavery of Africa, or that of Cuba, or of Brazil; but only that slavery which they had bound themselves by the most solemn guarantees, if not to defend, at least not to molest.

That the dominant political party in the North intended to employ the institution of slavery in the South, in a certain contingency, as a means for the accomplishment of the subjugation of the Southern States, I am willing to admit. That they intended to render the slaves discontented, and to bring about such a condition of things as would keep the whites in a constant state of apprehension, may not be doubted in presence of the facts of their past history. That they employed assassins to penetrate into the more quiet districts to stimulate the ignorant slaves to insurrection, they themselves boastingly furnish us with testimony. So far as these facts may prove the sincerity of their devotion to the black man, they are entitled to their benefit. But I cannot see in them sufficient evidence of a philanthropic purpose to entitle them to the confidence, or regard, or sympathy even of the most ardent negro-emancipationists.

But though it be admitted that the will of a majority should not be restrained by constitutional barriers, and that the Northern people in their crusade against the South were actuated alone by an exaggerated sentiment of affection for the black slave, still the heart imbued with generous or noble sentiments will find ample justification for the resistance of the South against the consummation of a purpose, which, if accomplished, would have left her white free men in a condition of abject dependence upon that nation of people who of all others cherished against them the most bitter prejudices. Europeans who have only witnessed the influence of political or religious partisanship in arousing the malignant passions of the people against each other, cannot comprehend from this the exaggerated feelings of animosity which are produced amongst a people who every four years elect a new king. All the appliances which hosts of interested and artful demagogues may employ are used to create and perpetuate these feuds. As long as parties were not bounded by geographical lines, there was an impediment to the accomplishment of this purpose, in the personal intercourse which resulted from proximity; but so soon as territorial boundaries marked also the lines which divided parties, it may readily be imagined that enmities once engendered could be easily perpetuated by those whose ambitious purposes might be subserved by arraying one section against another.

CHAPTER XVI.

A DISCUSSION OF THE SUBJECT OF PERSONAL AMBITION IN ITS RELATION TO THE SECESSION OF THE SOUTH.

THERE is no quality of the human understanding more inexplicable than its proneness to accept illogical, improbable, and even impossible solutions of a question of controversy when they coincide with the promptings of the heart or the personal inclinations of those to whom they are addressed. It is inexplicable because, however much may be gained by deceiving others, it is scarcely to be believed that the success of any good cause may be permanently promoted by an advocate who deludes himself. It is charged by the exponents of Northern policy and passions that the Southern secesssion originated and was consummated under the promptings of personal ambition, and their partisans throughout the world echo the words and doubtless give credit to the declaration.

In considering the truth or falsity of this allegation what are we taught by the logic of facts? In all history there is recorded no other movement of a similar character so thoroughly and entirely the work of the great body of the people. The impulse came from the people—from the whole people—including every class and condition of the people—and their leaders were bound to obey. Resistance to the dominion of the North was a spontaneous outburst of human feelings, which, in an instant of time and without preconcert or preparation, reconciled all previous party divisions and animosities, and caused every heart to thrill with the same emotions, the same passions, the same unalterable purpose.

I know that the erroneous opinion is entertained by some that the act of separation had been long meditated by the Southern people, and that they did not develope their intentions until after ample preparations had been made for the conflict. The truth is that there was not the slightest preparation made for the unanticipated contingency of a war. The South had none of the materials of war. They had neither guns nor ammunition, except such as were placed there by the United States Government; and, notwithstanding the silly stories set afloat in reference to the supply of arms furnished by the late Secretary Floyd, it has been conclusively established by an investigation instituted by the Congress of the United States in reference to this charge, that the South at the outbreak of the war had not even an approximation to her *pro rata* proportion of army supplies.

But there is another and a stronger argument to disprove such an allegation. In a democracy it is impossible for such a revolution to be provided for in advance. The crisis of popular opinion which brings about such a result is produced by the occurrence of a marked event which, thrilling the whole mass, prompts it to immediate action. If they hesitate, the occasion passes away, and they dismiss the subject from their minds. To assume that this seeming abandonment of a conceived and still meditated purpose is only designed to gain time, and make preparation for a conflict upon which they have determined, is to be totally ignorant of the manner in which democracies are moved to action.

That the passions of the Southern as well as of the Northern people had been stimulated by the respective advocates of disunion in both sections is true, but these influences were in their nature exercised openly and in the face of the nation. There was no concealment of their purposes or wishes, and there could not have been. The object of these was not to make preparations for the conflict at arms, but to direct the public sentiment, or so to prepare it as to lead them to act upon the occurrence of some contingency in the future. When a democracy enters upon such a career as that which the South is now following they must be content to commence the conflict unprepared by previous preparation.*

REV. MR BEECHER AT EXETER HALL.

* On Oct 20, 1863, the Rev Mr Beecher was received by a large audience of Englishmen, who came to hear what he had to say in favour of the restoration of the late American Union. He came to England as the representative of the strong Union sentiment of the North—as the advocate of a war of extermination rather than to witness the final overthrow of the beloved Union He was received by his English friends as the authorised expounder of that irresistible Union sentiment, which, he says, pervades all classes of his fellow-countrymen. He appeared at Exeter Hall, and if one may judge of the importance of the occasion, by the greatness of some of those who are said to have interposed to make his oratorical effort a great success, nothing so startling has occurred since the days when our Saviour wrought miracles in the Holy Land of the prophets In referring to this occasion a few days later, in presence of a numerous company assembled at a breakfast at Radley's Hotel,

Could an unworthy ambition have animated eight millions of people to rise up as one man, to avert the

upon the invitation of 'The Committee of Correspondence on American Affairs,' the reverend gentleman said —

'He felt he could speak with perfect freedom in that assembly as to what he believed to be the interposition of Providence in his behalf since his arrival in this country. When he came from the continent he had been for more than twenty weeks without speaking. He was afraid he would not be able to speak in Exeter Hall. When, however, he spoke *to himself* on Tuesday morning, *he found his voice as clear as a whistle!* Some might say that his recovery was owing to the remedies he adopted, but he was disposed to think *that in their use he had the direct interposition of the Almighty!*'

But to return to the Exeter Hall meeting. The chairman, in introducing him, gave him the credit of being a pioneer in the great cause which the reverend gentleman crossed the ocean to advocate before an English audience. This honour he modestly declined in the following words —

'I should be glad indeed if I could take all the credit your chairman has bestowed upon me, but I am not bold enough to have been a pioneer. When I think of such men as William Lloyd Garrison, Wendell Phillips [and others]—when I remember that I came afterwards, rather to build on their foundation—I cannot permit in this far country the honour to be put upon me.'

The strongest and probably the most formidable disunion party that existed in the late United States previous to the election of Mr. Lincoln was that which was led by the present leaders of the Republican party. I will extract a few sentences from the speeches and writings of some of the most famous of these, to show that there was not only a party in the North entertaining disunion opinions or intentions, but that this party finally triumphed in the election of Lincoln.

Mr. Beecher referred his audience to Mr. Wendell Phillips and Mr. Lloyd Garrison as his models. Let us see how they regarded the Union, when there was a Union which might have been preserved.

Mr. Wendell Phillips, in commending the organisation of the Republican party, said —

'No man has a right to be surprised at this state of things. It is just 'what we have attempted to bring about. It is the first sectional party 'ever organised in this country. It does not know its own face, and 'calls itself national; but it is not national—it is sectional. The Re'publican party is a party of the North pledged against the South.'

On another occasion he said —

doom of subjection to an arrogant foreign master, and to defend themselves, as the Southerners have

'The Constitution of our fathers was a mistake. Tear it in pieces and 'make a better. Do n't say the machine is out of order. It is in order. 'It does what its framers intended—protects slavery. Our claim is dis- 'union—breaking up of the States!'

Mr Lloyd Garrison said:—

'This Union is a lie! The American Union is an imposition—a covenant 'with death and an agreement with hell!

'I am for its overthrow! . . . Up with the flag of disunion, that we 'may have a free and glorious Republic of our own.

'No act of ours do we regard with more conscientious approval or 'higher satisfaction—none do we submit more confidently to the tribunal 'of Heaven and the moral verdict of mankind—than when, several years 'ago, on the 4th of July, in the presence of a great assembly, we com- 'mitted to the flames the Constitution of the United States.

'The Republican party is moulding public sentiment in the right 'direction for the specific work the Abolitionists are striving to accom- 'plish, viz. the dissolution of the Union and the abolition of slavery 'throughout the land.'

Any argument addressed to English people, or any others whose sympathies might be enlisted by such an advocate as Mr Beecher in favour of the North, would be of course futile. If men and women who know his antecedents, and those of the leaders in whose footsteps he professes to be only an humble follower, can really be made to believe that the God of Truth actually and specially interposed to enable this man to palm-off upon Englishmen, the transparent falsehood of which he stands self-convicted before them, there is no resource but to allow them to continue in their ignorance. If Mr Beecher is fighting alone for the emancipation of the slave, then is he wholly unjustified in law or morals, for none doubt but there are many millions of slaves in other lands, who might be released from their bonds at much less cost in treasure, and without involving the necessity of exterminating eight millions of an enlightened and Christian people. If he professes to be fighting for the restoration of the beloved Union, for the sake of the Union, then is he proven to be by his own past life a hypocrite, unworthy the confidence of a virtuous or an enlightened or a Christian people. The reader may well suppose that I would not have made any reference to this blasphemous advocate of the North, but for the importance which attaches to him, as the admitted representative in England of the great War party of the United States.

The present United States Minister at the Hague, *Mr. Pike*, said:—

'I have no doubt that the Free and Slave States ought to separate. The 'Union is not worth supporting in connection with the South.'

done, against the invading hosts of an enemy of more than double their numbers? Could an unholy or unworthy ambition have prompted all the inhabitants of the South to surrender all their earthly possessions, their present comfort, their very lives, in what they believed to be the cause of national freedom? Where are now the luxuries, the wealth, the superfluities, even the necessaries of life, which were possessed at the commencement of the war by many hundreds

The 'New York Tribune,' now the leading organ of the Republican party, became poetical in the fervour of its hate against the Union, and vented its indignation against even the striped calico which waved over their public edifices, after the following fashion:—

THE AMERICAN FLAG

Tear down the flaunting lie!
　Half-mast the starry flag!
Insult no sunny sky
　With hate's polluted rag!

Even as late as December 1860 the 'Tribune,' in a leading editorial, contended that—

'Whenever a portion of this Union, large enough to form an independent self-subsisting nation, shall see fit to say to the residue, "We "want to get away from you," we shall say—and we trust self-respect, if not regard for the principle of self-government, will constrain the residue of the American people to say—"Go!"'

The following resolutions were passed at a meeting of the American Anti-Slavery Society:—

Resolved, 'That secession from the United States Government is the duty of every Abolitionist, since no one can take office or deposit his vote under the Constitution without violating his anti-slavery principles, and rendering himself an abettor to the slave-holder in his sin.'

Resolved, 'That years of warfare against the slave power has convinced us that every act done in support of the American Union rivets the chain of the slave—that the only exodus of the slave to freedom, unless it be one of blood, must be over the remains of the present American Church and the grave of the present Union.'

Resolved, 'That the Abolitionists of this country should make it one of the primary objects of this agitation to dissolve the American Union.'

of thousands of Southern citizens? All gone! Surrendered without a sigh of vain regret, to aid their country in the hour of its agony and its great peril, or to satiate the rapacity of their invaders.

They have beheld the flames enkindled by the torch of the incendiary, which consumed their dwellings. They have witnessed the desolation of their homes, and the desecration of their hearthstones by a ruthless soldiery, whose worst crimes against decency and humanity constituted their chief claim to the approbation of their Government, and won for them the plaudits of their fellow-countrymen. They have seen the inheritances derived from their ancestors, or the accumulations of their own gains, swept away for ever into the same vortex. They have witnessed the sacking of their cities; and, where once were thriving towns and even capitals of States, they behold only smouldering masses of ruins to mark the sites where they stood. They have witnessed the opening of the dykes constructed upon the banks of the great Mississippi and its tributaries—in order to reclaim the wild swamps, that they might be made to contribute to the wants of man—and where once there were thriving and productive plantations covered with thousands of inhabitants, nothing may now be seen save a wild waste of waters, or a solitary African as he paddles his canoe over the submerged fields which he had once cultivated. The dagger and the brand have been placed in the hands of the slaves, and they have been told with the insidious smile which well betrayed their meaning: 'Your master is gone—your mistress is alone and unprotected: go forth and show that you are worthy of the freedom we bestow upon you!' They have seen the churches consecrated to the service of Christ, and even our holy religion itself, prostituted by a fanatical Protestant priesthood to the unworthy purposes of sectional ambition. Clergymen preach to their already maddened congregations, and urge them not to pause in the work of slaughter until eight millions of a Christian people are exterminated. Like the Aztec priests in the days of the Montezumas their cry is still for blood, while each new deed of wholesale slaughter seems but to whet their appetite for more. Their most popular clergymen proclaim unblushingly to admiring multitudes that their motto is—'*Greek-fire for the masses of the Southern people, and Hell-fire for the leaders.*'*

* During the Dark Ages the world was accustomed to listen to the atrocious teachings of a wicked, licentious, and blood-thirsty priesthood; but we can scarcely credit the evidence of our senses when we discover that in the present enlightened era the atrocities which are preached by the clergymen who have espoused the cause of the North are unsurpassed in any feature of horror by the priestly executors of the will of Philip of Spain and the Duke of Alva. The clergyman of the United States who proclaims his motto to be that which I have above quoted has acquired a wide-spread popularity throughout the North. He is a principal leader of the Cheever, and Beecher, and Stowe school of political parsons.

It is probable that some of my readers may recollect the brilliant reception which was recently accorded to him in many Northern cities, but especially in New York. The only public hall in the city sufficiently spacious to contain his admirers was the great Academy of Music (the Opera-house). The vast edifice was filled to over-flowing with the *élite* of New York society, while from the hands of hundreds of gentle maids and approving matrons were showered bouquets upon the head of the model political parson.

If presidential contests produced no other evil influence than thus to convert the teachers of religion into raging demons, and their congregations into approving listeners, it would be alone sufficient to condemn the system. For the text of the model address from which I have quoted, the reader is referred to the columns of the 'Times.' I will only extract a

But in the face of all these accumulated and accumulating horrors, who has ever heard a murmur of regret, or a word of repining, or a reproach uttered against themselves or others of their fellow-sufferers, or the intimation of a wish to reconsider their act of separation, or to turn back from the path they are pursuing?

Could an unholy ambition have animated the hearts of men to endure such sacrifices to the bitter end; or have implanted in their hearts the single sorrow that, in losing all, they had nothing left to consecrate to the cause which they had espoused—but their lives?

Yet the sacrifices which the terrible conflict has entailed upon the wealthy are as nothing compared to the aggregate of those which have been endured by the great body of the people. The inauguration of the war found these living in happy contentedness in their humble homes, surrounded by all those simple comforts which, though small in the estimation of many, were nevertheless sufficient to satisfy all their wants. The little circle of friends and family by which each was surrounded were probably only the more warmly cherished because they were few in number. The great body of the Southern people live, not in cities, but upon the rich and productive lands of a country so vast in extent that to the unaccustomed eye of the stranger it seems to

few lines, to show the spirit which animates the leading branch of the clergymen who have enlisted under the bloody banner of the 'stars and stripes:'—

'The mediation I advocate is that of the cannon and the sword; and 'let there be no armistice on sea or land until all the rebels, front and 'rear, North and South, are *subjugated or exterminated*. My motto is— '"*Greek-fire for the masses, and Hell-fire for the leaders!*"'

be even now one great and unappropriated forest. Their characters have never been debased by dependence for bread upon the charity of others; they dispense hospitality to all who claim it, be they friends or strangers, but they never solicit alms from their fellow-men. They have no great store of gold; but no hour of their daily toil, however light, is disturbed by any apprehensions that nature and their own stout arms will fail to supply their physical wants.

Let it not be believed, for it would be a grievous error to suppose that the sacrifices entailed by the war are less deeply felt by these than by the wealthier classes to whose losses we have just referred. It is of such material that the great body of the Southern army is composed, and not one has shouldered his musket and started out to meet the invaders of his country, filled with the stern resolve to drive them back or perish, who did not leave an aching void behind him in his humble log-cabin, intensified by the thought that he might never come back again to cheer by his presence the hearts which loved him. Could an unholy ambition have impelled him to surrender all the comforts which surround even the humblest home in the South, to mingle only as a single atom in the ranks of an army, where he could hope for nothing but privations, and expect no immediate reward save the consciousness of having well performed his duty to his country?

But unworthy ambition is aggressive. So far from bounding its operations by the limits which circumscribe its own possessions, it seeks to extend its dominion over the territory of others. It cannot be that he who only defends his own is governed by unworthy ambition. What else has ever been sought by the Southern people, than to protect and guard their own country from hostile invasion? Do they seek to subdue the North, or any portion thereof, for their own uses? The flag of the old Union does not to-day float over one foot of territory by the willing assent of its inhabitants, of which the South would accept the dominion were it offered as a free gift. It is *separation* and independence for which they are now struggling, and *against Union* and despotism. They *repel*, instead of inviting, their former confederates to come under their flag. Their acts speak in a language the purport of which none can fail to discover: 'Separation! perpetual separation, from our former confederates; not dominion over them! We ask for peace, not war!' Are these the legitimate fruits of an unholy ambition, such as that which is ascribed to the Southern people?

Turning from the consideration of the part enacted by the great body of the people of the South, both rich and poor, upon whom the hardships of the war have pressed so heavily, let us consider the attitude of those who have occupied the position of leaders—who filled stations of honour, and trust, and profit—the senators and the representatives in Congress, and those who filled diplomatic posts abroad. These had already attained to the highest places within the gift of the Republic; and all except the last—whose positions afforded them no opportunity if they had possessed the will to minister to the revolution—were unremovable, except by their own Southern constituents. They would have retained their positions under Lincoln as well as under Buchanan. What personal motive could these have had which would have urged them to bring about the separation? They already occupied the highest places under a Government embracing thirty-two millions of people and thirty-four States, and they could hold those places in despite of the North. Their highest aspirations in the event of separation could only have extended to securing similar positions by the favour of the same constituency under a Government claiming only thirteen millions of inhabitants, and embracing at most not more than fifteen States. They surrendered the certainty of present honours, and emoluments derived from the Government of 'the great Republic,' with the doubtful contingency, in remote prospective, of being placed in corresponding positions under that comparatively feeble confederation of States—upon the entire population of which, by the machinations of their enemies, rested the ban of the unthinking, giddy, fickle multitude, who direct and govern the public opinion of the world. In all the wild vagaries of personal ambition did it ever before manifest itself in such a shape, or direct the aspirations of its votaries into such a channel?

Was it that they might reach the goal of the presidency that Southern senators supported the policy of separation? The very first act of the new Government, performed with the unanimous approbation of the Southern people, was to diminish the chances of those who might have entertained such a wish by lengthening the term of tenure. Besides, I betray no secret which might tend to bring the late Government of the Union into discredit, when I say that the day had passed by when a prominent senator would consent of his own free will to *come down* to the presidency. The office he held was for a longer period, with the almost certain prospect, at least in the South, of a renewal of his lease at the expiration of his term. Even as a member of the lower branch of Congress, he could look forward with reasonable confidence to a long career, to be closed it might be in the Senate. The presidential post repelled this class of politicians. He who could attain to its high honours did at most only flourish for a day—live miserably through a dreary four years of mental torture—finally to retire for ever from the scene of his labours and his disappointed hopes, only too happy if the obscurity into which he sank was so profound that he would no longer hear the revilings to which he could not close his ears during his brief and joyless reign.

To suppose that those earnest and deeply impressive words which fell from the lips of the senators and representatives of the South, when they bade an eternal adieu to the halls of the Congress of the United States, announcing the stern necessity which impelled them to abandon for ever the high places which they held under the Government of the great Republic, that they might share the privations of their fellow-countrymen, and pass away into comparative obscurity if not total seclusion, were uttered and acted upon under the promptings of personal ambition, is to reverse all the rules by which the motives of mankind may be measured by their deeds. As well might it be assumed that the wealthy, cautious, plodding, and successful merchant would in his old age voluntarily embark all the earnings of a life of toil upon a weak and untried vessel, upon a tempestuous sea, and without even a hope of adding to his worldly stores, as that those Southerners who held conspicuous places under the Government of the United States embarked their all upon the stormy sea of secession under the influence of ambition.

No! No! The struggle of the South for separation and independence did not originate in such a cause. Let none who seek in sober seriousness a truthful solution deceive themselves with the belief that they have fathomed the depths of that great movement by assigning it in its inception or progress to the unworthy promptings of personal ambition.

CHAPTER XVII.

CONCLUDING SUMMARY OF THE DEFECTS AND MERITS OF THE CONSTITUTION AS ILLUSTRATED IN PRACTICE.

HOWEVER the politicians and statesmen of America may shrink from an exposure of the real source of the disasters which have befallen the late Union—however they may tremble at the thought of approaching their master to speak to him the unpalatable words of truth and soberness which their fears may lead them to believe will not be listened to with patience—however much and however justly and harshly they may condemn the willing and wicked agents and instruments who employed themselves in accelerating our great disaster, they cannot, if they would, conceal from themselves the truth that the harvest field of bloody fruits we are now reaping with the sword sprang from the seeds that were sown by presidential elections. The evils which have already befallen from this fruitful hotbed of Radicalism, with its ever attendant train of disaster, are greater than tongue can utter. The magnitude of those which are to follow we are in mercy denied to know. We cannot now avert the calamities of the past; but Americans would be blind indeed if they did not see the cause, and madmen if they did not profit by the bitter lesson it has taught them. The poignancy of our regret as American citizens is magnified by the reflection that but for the existence of that one fatal detail in the machinery of our Government, the wisest statesmen, with all the light of experience, would scarcely dare even now to say that it was practicable to have improved it in any other material feature. Leave out that single error, once a blemish now a crime, and considered in reference to the circumstances under which it was created, it stands one of the noblest monuments of human wisdom.

Let us, in conclusion, glance once more at those circumstances, and briefly survey the results that were deduced from them.

The framers of the Constitution had but a single class of citizens from whom to derive the different elements necessary to the accomplishment of their purpose. Fortunately the States as sovereignties might be employed in contradistinction to the people of the States as citizens, and with these two elements as a basis they created the necessary checks and balances of their Government. Upon each of these elements acting independently of the other they conferred equal legislative power. The assent of both was necessary to complete the act of either, but one could negative the act of the other. They constituted together the Congress. The Senate was composed of two members from each State, without reference to population, who were chosen for a term of six years by the Legislatures of the States respectively. The House of Representatives was chosen for a term of two years by direct vote of the people, divided into districts of equal population.

Thus each State was entitled to a number coinciding with its population.

After a Bill had passed through both branches of Congress it was submitted to the President for approval or rejection. If he disapproved, it was returned to the body in which it originated, and unless two-thirds of each House voted to re-enact the law over the President's veto it fell.

But these were not the only conservative checks which might be interposed to protect the weak against the exactions of the strong. The Constitution defined the limits of the powers of the President and the Legislature. The members of the Supreme Court of the United States were nominated by the President, confirmed by the Senate, and held their offices for life. If a law, passed by Congress and approved by the President, should be decided by the Supreme Court to be unconstitutional, it ceased from that moment to be operative, and no power existed to restore it. From that decision there was no appeal.

The authors of the Constitution intended that the people should be the primary source of power; but they never designed that such power should be arbitrarily exercised. They did not provide that the country should be governed by a majority of the whole people acting as a single community, but that the moiety of power directly confided to the people should be exercised by an aggregation of majorities represented by the delegates to the general Congress. The action of a majority of these constituted the only mode provided for obtaining the expression of the will of the whole.

The important practical distinction between the rule of a single majority and that of concurrent majorities, is just the difference between a good and a bad Government—between rational liberty and unbridled despotism. The framers of the American Constitution were at least free from the popular fallacy that the absolutism of a majority acting as a unit was any the less to be avoided in the creation of a free Government, than the unrestricted rule of a single tyrant. They wisely considered that unity of power, the dominance of a single will, constituted the essence of despotism.

It would have been almost impossible to have constructed a scheme of government which, in theory, could be better adapted to the wants and circumstances of the people for whose benefit it was formed; and none could have more effectually protected the liberties of the people as a whole, or of the individual as a member of the community. It was intended to be essentially conservative in all its features. It may, in fact, be said to have been more conservative than any of the constitutional monarchies of Europe. The sense in which I employ the term 'conservative' is, that it preserved the established order and condition of things as they existed, while interposing reasonable impediments to change. It created, or rather confirmed certain rights; instituted certain fundamental laws, founded upon general principles of justice; and circumscribed the powers of those to whom were intrusted the management of public affairs within such limits, and interposed so many checks to prevent the violation of these principles, that even a forward movement could only be accomplished by the harmonious action of all the interests represented in the Government.

It will be readily discovered by a comparison that the Constitution of the United States was in *theory* more conservative than that of Great Britain. In the latter, the agreement of the two Houses of Parliament is practically sufficient to the enactment of any law. It is true that the Crown has the legal right to negative an Act of Parliament, but this power is never, under any circumstances, employed. The agreement of the Senate and House of Representatives, as we have seen, does not necessarily convert their act into a law of the land. The negative power of the President is not a mere inoperative provision of the Constitution. The 'veto' of this functionary has often been employed to arrest the passage of a law enacted by Congress; while the Supreme Court has cancelled the act of both President and Congress, when its terms were in violation of the provisions of the Constitution.

The Constitution of the United States was, in fact, a gathering together of the materials of what is called the British Constitution—in so far as they could be adapted to the then existing circumstances—with the addition of such improvements as experience had suggested. But, although perfect in theory, it unfortunately assumed the existence of a greater degree of virtue, fidelity, and enlightenment among those to whose management it was confided than has ever yet been found to exist among mankind. Hence the Government was a failure, although theoretically it was, and practically it might have been made to be, under proper management, an improvement upon that which served as its model, and which still stands as firm as 'the fast anchored isle' over which it exercises its beneficent sway.

The Constitution of Great Britain differs from that of which it served as the model in this: that while the latter is written, and methodically arranged into chapters and sections, the former does not exist upon parchment. Except that it may be said to have its root in *Magna Charta*, it is in truth a very myth, invisible to the eye, impalpable to the touch; but it lives in the hearts of all the classes of which the nation is composed, and for that very reason it constitutes a bond for the rigid observance of its requirements infinitely stronger than any written compact. The estates of which this system is composed, and which give to it its vitality, are the Crown, the Lords, and the Commons.

A Government thus constituted may be great, but rarely generous, oftentimes unjust. Generous actions spring from an impulse of the heart, and they may be only promptly executed in obedience to the dictates of a single will. In a democracy, or any other form of despotism, where the will of the sovereign may be executed upon the instant that it is formed, without the necessity of consultation or cooperation with others, generous impulses may be developed into deeds at the moment of their conception. Under the British Government this may be said to be almost impossible, because the impulse which may animate one or even two of the three elements of power may not exist in the other, or its influence may be counteracted by stronger impulses leading in a different direction: the ambition of the one may be held in check by the prudence of the other. The desire of the one to perform a noble act, involving a sacrifice of merely selfish interests, may be restrained by the cautious calculation of probable results, or the cupidity of the other. The pride and the courage which would lead the one to resist an insult, or repel an aggression, may be overborne by a timid fear of consequences on the part of the other. It may sometimes shape its foreign policy in obedience to a pressure imposed by a strong power, even at the expense of an incidental injustice to the weak; but in its intercourse with those who have not the power to protect themselves, or to return blow for blow, it will be often dictatorial and overbearing. The cooperation of all may be readily had in the performance of an act which it is believed will redound to the greatness, or add to the prospesity of the nation, even though it may involve in its execution what disinterested observers might consider a disregard of the higher sentiments which animate honourable men in their intercourse with each other. The heart of the nation may be moved under extraordinary circumstances to the performance of a noble deed, uninfluenced by selfish considerations, and the Government may be brought to act upon the impulse thus given; but the occasions when the three elements of power can be brought into harmony in behalf of such a cause are so rare and exceptional that they only prove more conclusively that the adverse is the general rule of action. These are blemishes or faults, the developement of which depend in a greater or less degree upon those to whom the administration of the Government may for the time being be confided; but they may be said to be incidental to the system. They only operate, however, to the injury of those who have no right to claim its protection, and do not affect the personal rights of citizens.

Though a Government, organised upon such principles, may not accord to others that liberty which it claims for itself, it guarantees freedom for its own subjects; though it may be tyrannical abroad, the rights of the citizen are protected at home; though it may fail to excite in the breast of a foreigner a sentiment of love, it challenges his respect.

Taken all in all, with its admitted defects, the British Government, combining as it does the most perfect security for life, liberty, and property, with the minimum of exactions from the citizens which is compatible with the attainment of these results, approximates more nearly to the accomplishment of those great purposes for which Governments are created than any other which has ever been instituted and successfully administered by man.

If the descendants of the fathers of the American Republics had manifested half the zeal in sustaining and supporting their Constitution, which they have exhibited in assailing its only weak point, the world would not to-day be the witness of one of the most monstrous wars of which we have a record in the pages of history. It would almost seem as though a large and controlling body of the American people regarded the Constitution as an enemy, whom it was their duty to destroy. After a laborious search, they discovered its weak point, and never ceased to assail it, until they had succeeded in severing the confederacy of which it constituted the only bond of union.

There is no more striking illustration of the truth that constitutions cannot be so guarded as to prevent political parties from perverting their plain meaning, while obeying their letter, than is furnished by the election and career of the present President of the United States.

Legally, he is supposed to represent the will of the majority, and yet in the popular vote, by virtue of which he holds his office, he was in a minority, as we have seen, of more than a million of votes.

More than this, he is in the name of the people of the United States carrying on one of the most gigantic and destructive wars ever recorded in history; and yet I presume even his candid partisans will admit, that if the question had been submitted to a vote of the whole people, North and South, there has been no hour since his inauguration that he would not have been hurled from power by a majority greater far than that which opposed his election.

Thus, a minority President, who holds his station as the representative of a minority of the people, and in violation of the will of the majority, assumes to govern in the name of the people.

In a country so vast in extent as the late United States, with a constantly and rapidly augmenting population from all the civilised nations of the world, it may well be doubted whether any Government would constitute a perpetual guarantee of union. It is even more doubtful whether mankind would be the gainer by such a concentration of power in the hands of a single nation, thus wielding by a single will hundreds of millions of inhabitants. That such augmentation of the population will occur within a period amounting to scarcely a span in the life-time of a nation, if there should be no repelling causes, is fully foreshadowed by the rapid increase which has taken place during the present century.

When, therefore, I express the conviction that the Constitution and Government of the United States—if proper provision had been made for the manner of appointing the President—would have been a perpetual guarantee of liberty and union, I mean it to be understood, that no other form of Government, and no other modification of the present Government, so far as regards its great leading features, or the general principles upon which it was founded, would have more certainly achieved that result. When, if ever, the mass should have become too unwieldly to be held together by a common bond, and had separated to form new and smaller and more homogeneous nations, as they doubtless would have done under any form of Government, they might have done so without the fear of any disaster to liberty.

The present position of the Government and people of the United States does not at all confute the truth of this assumption. It is a fact that there is no liberty under the iron sway of the party now in power—true that citizens, even of those States called loyal, have been, and are now being daily arrested and consigned to dungeons, without being permitted to know the charges against them, or to confront their accusers; or by virtue of the once sacred right of *habeas corpus* to compel their oppressors to cast off their chains. True, the liberty of the press no longer exists; but all this power of mischief and wrong in the hands of the Government, and in a great measure the will to do the wrong, as well as the disposition to submit to the wrong, resulted alone from the presidential elections. The lust of power induced the adherents of the present President to secure his election by pledging themselves to an unconstitutional interference with the rights of the South. In breaking down the power of the States, they destroyed the equilibrium of the Government. The manner in which the President was chosen invited the aggression upon the Constitution—the possession of the presidency conferred the power to achieve it—the loss of liberty was the consequence.

The conservative element of the Government fell before the irresistible and radical element of mere numbers, and the whole fabric was in ruins before the first gun from the fortifications of Charleston announced the beginning of the conflict at arms.

On the other hand, look at the attitude which has been maintained in the Confederate States of the South. When threatened with the loss of their constitutional rights in the late Union, they adopted a constitutional remedy by withdrawing themselves from that Union. Amid all the terrible scenes through which they have since passed, with vast armies of brutal and mercenary soldiers ravaging and desolating their country, the liberty of the citizen has remained inviolate, subject only to those necessary restrictions which the presence of invading armies imperiously demand. The writ of *habeas corpus* has never been suspended. A citizen arrested for a political offence has at all times been granted a fair trial by a jury of his countrymen; and not a single attempt has ever been made by the Government to limit in the smallest degree the liberty of the press. This important function of a free people has remained as perfect, entire, and complete as it ever existed under the old Government in a time of profound peace.* The long and ceaseless struggle on the part of a formidable party in the North to bring the South into a state of subjection was but the developement of a principle which appears to be at least a prominent ingredient in the nature of man. The history of the world has illustrated the truth that power is ever seeking occasion to assert its dominion over weakness. The great Governments of the Old World, whether despotic or free, have in every age sought to dictate the terms upon which weaker nations might be permitted to exist. They have assumed, in virtue of their ships of war and their armies, to make that power felt in some way by all who were too weak to defend themselves. In America, this relative power was decided, not by ships of war and soldiers, but by the numbers of voters. The North knew her superiority at the ballot-box, and endeavoured to employ it, as other great nations have employed the sword—namely, in the subjection of those who were weaker than themselves.

It was, perhaps, a consideration of the aggressive disposition of power which induced the representa-

* An article published in the 'Revue des Deux Mondes,' of which the authorship is attributed to one of the Orleans princes, contains a statement that the Confederate States Government exercised a rigid censorship over the press. We may account for this and many other errors in the publication referred to, when we remember that the information of the author was derived from around the camp fires of the Northern army, or the even less reliable sensation newspapers of the North. However this may be, the statement is altogether without foundation.

tives of the States in the constitutional Convention to frame with so much caution the articles which delegated certain powers to the Federal Government, and to guard with so much vigilance the sovereignty and independence of the separate States which formed the league. If no presidential election had ever occurred to stimulate the passion for conquest, and to renew every four years the unprofitable conflict—to embitter and exasperate the feelings of the people of one section against another, and to drown the voice of reason in the wild delirium of passion, the once united free States of America might have presented to mankind a spectacle very different from that upon which we are now gazing.

Probably the most striking phenomenon which attended the presidential contests was the *madness*, amounting almost to insanity, which seemed to seize upon the nation during the paroxysm of the struggle. We wonder at the frivolous means which were often resorted to by the partisan leaders to stimulate the passions of the people ; we are surprised that in a great empire, questions of such utter insignificance on the one hand, or of such grave import upon the other, should be made the issues in presidential contests; but our astonishment increases when we discover that in either case the same vein of unreasoning insanity seems to have pervaded the whole mass.

It is necessary to remember, however, that the President-makers had so fed the people upon poisons, that there was created a morbid appetite upon each recurring election for still more virulent doses. If these had not been administered in constantly augmenting proportions, there would have been a danger that the public mind would have sunk into a lethargic indifference, or, what would have been more fatal still for the President-makers, that reason would have assumed its empire over men's minds.

During many years, as I have shown, presidential elections were decided in reference to the suggested improper motives which prompted Mr. Clay to vote for Mr. Adams in the election of 1825. This insignificant question, which kept the whole continent in a blaze of frenzied excitement, was a chief instrument in determining the result of several presidential contests. Upon this issue the fate of presidential parties turned from 1825 to 1840, besides having incidentally played a conspicuous part in several subsequent contests. Scarcely had these passions subsibed, before the country plunged headlong into the singing and laughing paroxysm of the 'log cabin and hard cider' campaign. It was the farce following the tragedy. After the interval of one presidential term, in which the principal issue was the annexation of Texas, and an incidental revival of the charge of 'Bargain and Intrigue' against Mr. Clay, the Whig candidate, came the military mania—the days of hero worship—when hair from 'Old Whitey's' tail and mane was sought for with as much zeal as distinguished the Crusaders in their search for the true cross in the well-pits of Jerusalem. Then came a brief season of portentous repose, when the nation seemed plunged into a profound and dreamless sleep, only to be aroused as it were in the twinkling of an eye to that final and great madness which, under the promptings of unrelenting fanaticism, of personal hate, and an ungovernable thirst for sectional dominion on the part of the Northern majority, after a prolonged struggle of five years blotted out the Government itself, to be followed soon after by scenes of violence and carnage.

From first to last, the presidential contests constituted a perpetually existing bribe to the party politicians to plunge the country into great excitements, and to create and foster sectional animosities. As the nation progressed in wealth and importance, the number of citizens who occupied themselves in the business of President-making was enlarged. From hundreds they increased to thousands, and from thousands to hundreds of thousands. The issues they presented to the popular mind were such as seemed likely to arouse, and did in effect develope, the most violent passions of the people. They cultivated and brought into action the sternest fanaticism of an intolerant priesthood, and turned to profitable account the wildest vagaries of the most crazy social reformers. The more these questions seemed fraught with danger to the internal tranquillity of the Republic, the more available they were in the accomplishment of the purpose for which they were employed. However much the great body of the people may have desired to dismiss such subjects from presidential contests and from the halls of Congress, they were as powerless as infants in the hands of the agitators. The president-makers made up the issues, and the people had no other resource than to withdraw themselves from all participation in the affairs of Government, or to plunge headlong into the mad current, with the dubious consolation afforded by the reflection, that 'where all are fools or madmen, 't were folly to be wise.' There could be but one result of such conflicts, and such conflicts were the inevitable consequences of presidential elections.

The history of the United States Government proves conclusively that in a confederacy of States which choose their Presidents either by a popular vote of the whole people, or by an Electoral College chosen for that purpose, the choice will, sooner or later, be decided in reference to geographical lines. It does not matter how homogeneous or how united they may be in interests, a class of professional president-makers will come into being, and sooner or later they will be able to combine a larger against a smaller section. Nothing is more easy than for even a few designing and ambitious men to stir up strife amongst neighbouring States, which, once thoroughly aroused and implanted in the bosoms of the people, may be readily employed to accomplish the purpose which the Republican party of 1860 achieved under the nominal leadership of President Lincoln. The more virtuous the people, the fitter subjects are they to be preyed upon by the human vultures who are attracted by presidential elections to seize upon the substance of the nation. They constitute an ever-augmenting army of revolutionists in the very heart of the Government, against whom no effective opposition may be interposed. Their clamours drown the voice of sober reason, until in the end they vanquish every adversary. The people, the honest people, at length find themselves divested of every real attribute of sovereignty by men who profess to act in their name, on their behalf, and in their interest. Passion mounts the throne which should be occupied by reason, and the majority finally submit to despotism in the very act of depriving the minority of their liberties. The termination of such struggles for power as follow in the train of presidential contests must be, that the division, or section, or community having the smallest number of voters will be finally driven to maintain their liberties by the sword, or submit to be in effect held and treated as a conquered people

Such an alternative will be presented at an earlier or a later day to the smaller section of any confederacy of States of diversified interests, and embracing a large extent of territory, which elect their chief ruler through the agency of a mere majority of the whole people. The Federal compact, which binds together distinct States, can never produce that unity of interests and sentiments among the inhabitants which would make the larger States safe custodians of the rights and liberties of the weaker.

In concluding this branch of the subject I have been considering, it is proper to add, that the great evil did not consist alone in the fact that *the people* were either nominally or really intrusted with the prerogative of naming the President. I think, as I have before said, that the same results would have followed sooner or later even if the election had been confided, in the spirit of the Constitution, to the Electoral College. And we have already been taught by experience that an election by States in the House of Representatives was, if possible, even more objectionable.

Each mode involved a convulsion of the whole country; bitter sectional divisions; constant irritation of the public mind, in view of the uncertainty of the succession; hosts of office-seekers; delusive hopes of reward for abandoning the useful pursuits of life to engage in party politics; corruption everywhere, accompanied by constant change; all hastening the country onward to the same inevitable end—dissolution—war—the destruction of liberty.

There was but one remedy. There should have been always a President, but never an election.

CHAPTER XVIII.

A PLAN SUGGESTED FOR PROVIDING A PRESIDENT WITHOUT AN ELECTION—CONCLUSION.

THE American citizen, in turning his thoughts from the terrible present to the memorials, written and unwritten, of the Confederation which has just passed away, may dwell with feelings, not unmixed with pride and satisfaction, upon those which record the history of the UNITED STATES SENATE. From the beginning of the Government to the last day of its existence, it was to that body the hopeful American looked for succour and relief in the hour of gloom, and danger, and despondency. Its history is also the history of many of the greatest statesmen and the purest patriots which the Republic has produced. It was not always what it should have been. There were times when unworthy men obtained position there by their superior skill in pandering to the sectional prejudices of their countrymen; but if we look into the probable causes which conspired to place them in a position so much beyond their deserts, we can trace them out as the consequences of excitements produced by presidential elections. But for the influence of this original first cause of mischief—introducing into the Senate, though upon rare occasions, the demagogue and the sectional partisan—the list of those who have been members of that distinguished body would furnish the names of but few who retained their seats for a series of years, who might not have served with fidelity, and a reasonable degree of ability as the executive chiefs of the nation. The few names which blur the brilliant catalogue of statesmen, patriots, and orators were but specks which even add to the lustre of those whose greatness will be remembered and whose deeds will be applauded by the latest of their posterity. If the duration of the presidential term had been fixed at eight or, what would have been better, ten years, and if the Constitution had provided that the senator who had served in that body for the greatest length of years should, upon the occurrence of a vacancy, have become the President, and the senator next below him the Vice-President, what a change would have been wrought in the destiny of that great people who are now engaged in deadly conflict with each other.

When we cast our eyes over the long array of brilliant names which have adorned the Senate—when we reflect that these might, under such auspices, have added lustre to the office of President and to the era in which they lived, by occupying that high station, our regret and mortification for what has been, is heightened by a contemplation of what might have been—what would have been.

Clay! Webster! Calhoun!—names which will be remembered and respected while their mother-tongue is spoken; whose countrymen have often for each pronounced that eulogy to which no other language could add force—'*He was too great to be President!*'—bitter commentary upon the system which could call forth such praise—these, and others of equal merit, might have been Presidents, and one of their successors would to-day have been the President of a united, a prosperous, and a happy people; ay, more than all this, of a free people, if the great charter of the Confederation had been subjected to that simple change.

It would seem almost a waste of words to contrast the two systems with a view to show the advantages which might have resulted from such a modification of the Constitution. They are self-evident—they spring spontaneously to the mind and to the lips. We would have witnessed the selection of a President from among his fellow-citizens to rule over the Union, under the operation of a system in harmony with the principles upon which the Confederacy was created. He would have succeeded to the office without having excited a single angry emotion, without tumult, and without trickery. The sovereignty of the States would have been respected, because the smallest would have had an equal chance with the largest to fill the office with one of its own citizens; the will of the people would have been respected, because by their voice he would have started out upon his career. Through the agency of their immediate representatives, he would have been chosen a senator, and by a prolongation of their confidence only, the provisions of the Constitution would have carried him into the presidency.

He would have entered upon the discharge of his responsible duties already a veteran in the public service, free and untrammelled. No crowd of expectant partisans and office-seekers would have hung upon his skirts, or filled his ante-chambers with their clamours. None could have said to him, 'It is I who have made you what you are.' He would have owed no political debts except to his country, and his highest ambition would most naturally have been to serve it faithfully.

The army of professional president-makers, finding their occupation gone, would have employed themselves in more useful pursuits, better and happier men than when they followed the delusive phantom of popular favour—ever hoping for success, but always doomed, even in the hour of triumph, to bitter disappointments.

The influence of such a system would have stimulated each State to choose its senators from amongst their most worthy and capable citizens, and to continue them in that position in the hope that it might one day furnish the Union with a President. Thus there would have been a perpetual guarantee that the statesmen of the nation would have been sought out and employed in the public service. The presidential office would have maintained the dignity of the nation, and the nation would have maintained the dignity of the presidential office; while every department of the Government would have risen in the public esteem. It would also have been a great amendment to the system if the term of the senators had been eight years, and of the Lower House four years.

If it be urged that the commencement of such a plan of appointing a President would have been attended with difficulties, I reply, that these would have been by no means insuperable. The relative rank of the senators might have been decided at first by lot. True, it would have required a certain length of time to have fully developed the system;

but a few years would have brought the better men into the front rank.

There were still other means which might have been employed to overcome the trifling drawbacks which would have attended the inauguration of the system. The almost unanimous voice of the nation pointed to WASHINGTON as the first President. His nomination by the Convention which framed the Constitution would have been but the anticipation of a certain event, and would have been hailed with enthusiasm by the great body of the people.

Wherein would have been the objection to making Washington President for life, to be followed afterwards in regular succession for a single term of eight or ten years by the oldest senator?

CONCLUSION.

I have now finished—however imperfectly—that which I set out to accomplish. Having restricted myself within certain prescribed limits, I may have unwisely devoted more space to the elucidation of some points, and less to others, than their respective importance may seem to have demanded. Yet, as a whole, and in all its parts, it is a faithful delineation of facts. Those whom it may concern will decide for themselves whether these facts justify my conclusions. As one, however, whose destiny for good or evil is, and ever will continue to be, identified with the nation most deeply interested in a happy solution of the great question at issue, I will say that the more I reflect upon the events connected with this subject, in the brief career of the United States, the more thoroughly am I convinced that true rational liberty is utterly incompatible with an elective presidency. The shortening of the presidential term to one year has been advised by some of our wisest statesmen. This might possibly mitigate the evil in one sense; but would, I apprehend, augment it in another. The suggestion has more probably sprung from despair of eradicating the cancer rather than with any confident hope that it could be efficacious. The paroxysms of madness which seize upon the inebriate who takes an enormous dose of alcohol every four hours may be less violent if the quantity be divided into four parts and administered hourly; but I can discover no reason for believing that the final result upon the system would not be the same in both.

The evil does not consist alone in the fact of universal suffrage. On the contrary, I am inclined to believe that this universality of franchise modifies some of the evils which are attendant upon a more circumscribed electoral body. Upon strikingly great occasions, when a single simple question is presented for solution, involving the destinies of a nation, it would be far safer to submit it to the great body of the people than to any mixed assemblage of patriots and demagogues whom they might elect as their representatives. An illustration presents itself at this hour in the United States. There is not the faintest glimmering of a close of the war, and but little hope that that end will ever be reached so long as the control of the Government remains with the mere political jobbers, agents of contractors, and blood-thirsty fanatics, who now sway the destinies of the country. If a new election for members of Congress were ordered to-day, the chances are that a sufficient number of these would be returned to oppose successfully any effectual movement in the direction of peace, so long as the contest might be made to yield such enormous profits as are now realised by those who have the disposal of the patronage flowing from the war. But suppose that the isolated question of peace, with its alternative of an indefinite prolongation of the war, should be presented to the entire body of the people, or even to those States which still adhere to the Government at Washington, can it be believed for a moment that the decision would not be for *peace?* Peace now! with or without union. PEACE! even upon the terms proposed by the South, that each nation should decide for itself whether for reunion or perpetual separation.

No! Let none delude themselves. The irremediable evil consisted in the *fact* of the election, and would have been an evil utterly antagonistical to the enjoyment of enlightened liberty, no matter where, or with whom, or to what tribunal the duty or privilege of appointment might have been confided. It is this great *fact* that the American people must eradicate from their system of government ere they can hope to enjoy and perpetuate the benign blessings of freedom. It was the operation of this inflexible *fact* which produced a result that I recorded upon the first page of this volume, and which I now repeat at its close:

The American Union as it existed in the days of Washington is no more and will never be again.

LONDON
PRINTED BY SPOTTISWOODE AND CO
NEW-STREET SQUARE

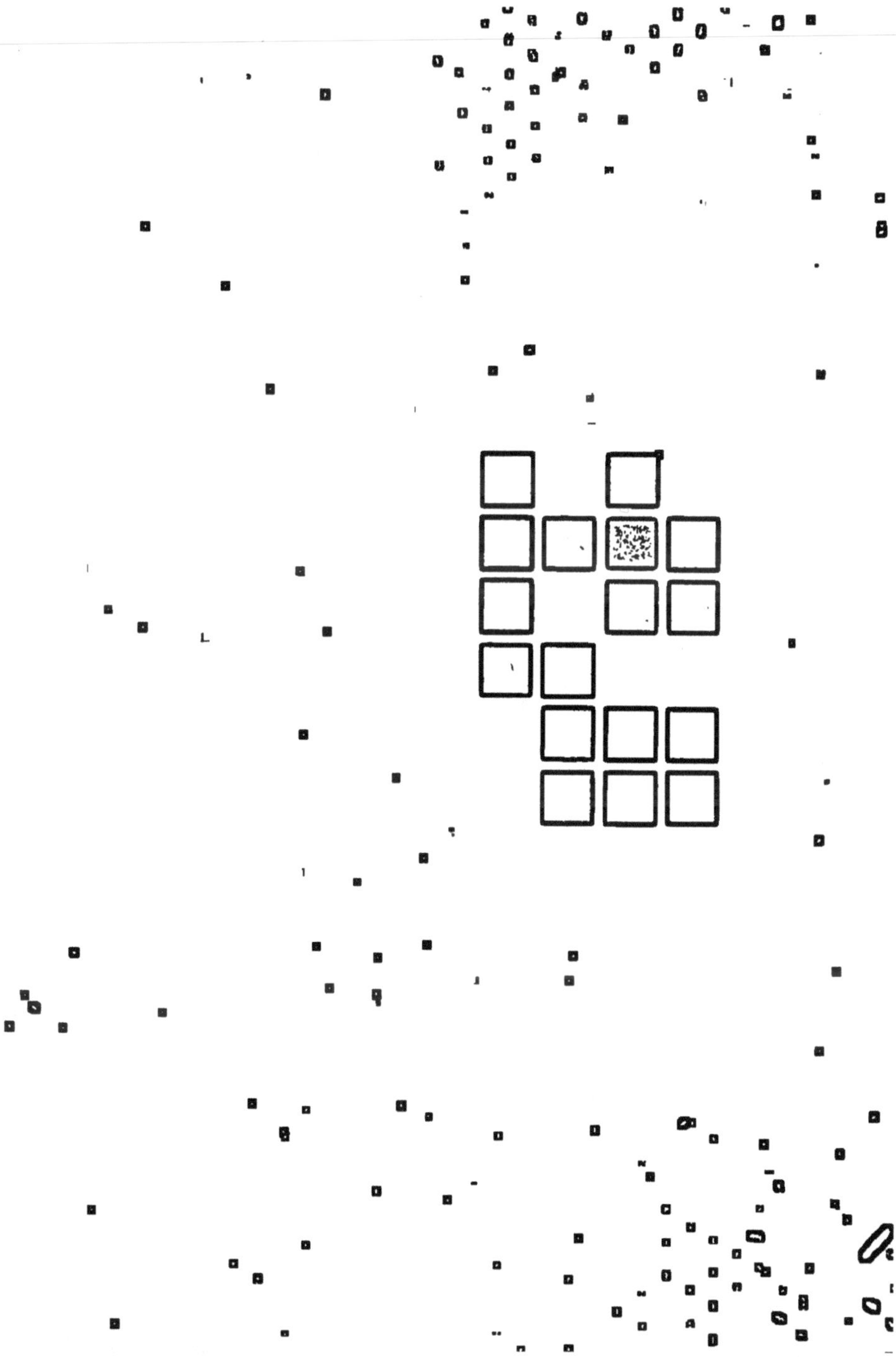

CPSIA information can be obtained
at www.ICGtesting.com
Printed in the USA
LVHW081524200922
728846LV00011B/368

9 781371 944612